About Island Press

Since 1984, the nonprofit organization Island Press has been stimulating, shaping, and communicating ideas that are essential for solving environmental problems worldwide. With more than 1,000 titles in print and some 30 new releases each year, we are the nation's leading publisher on environmental issues. We identify innovative thinkers and emerging trends in the environmental field. We work with world-renowned experts and authors to develop cross-disciplinary solutions to environmental challenges.

Island Press designs and executes educational campaigns, in conjunction with our authors, to communicate their critical messages in print, in person, and online using the latest technologies, innovative programs, and the media. Our goal is to reach targeted audiences—scientists, policy makers, environmental advocates, urban planners, the media, and concerned citizens—with information that can be used to create the framework for long-term ecological health and human well-being.

Island Press gratefully acknowledges major support from The Bobolink Foundation, Caldera Foundation, The Curtis and Edith Munson Foundation, The Forrest C. and Frances H. Lattner Foundation, The JPB Foundation, The Kresge Foundation, The Summit Charitable Foundation, Inc., and many other generous organizations and individuals.

The opinions expressed in this book are those of the author(s) and do not necessarily reflect the views of our supporters.

Right of Way

Right of Way

RACE, CLASS, AND THE SILENT EPIDEMIC
OF PEDESTRIAN DEATHS IN AMERICA

Angie Schmitt

 ISLANDPRESS | Washington | Covelo

Library of Congress Control Number: 2020933352

All Island Press books are printed on environmentally responsible materials.

Manufactured in the United States of America
10 9 8 7 6 5 4 3 2 1

Keywords: autonomous vehicle, criminalization, crosswalk, Families
for Safe Streets, infrastructure, jaywalking, *Manual on Uniform Traffic
Control Devices*, pedestrian, racism, speed, speed cameras, self-driving
cars, SUV, the Sun Belt, traffic safety, traffic violence, Vision Zero

Our complacency is killing us.
—*Deborah Hersman, CEO, National Safety Council*

Contents

Author's Note   xi

Foreword by Charles T. Brown   xiii

Introduction: Outline of an Epidemic   1

Chapter 1:   The Geography of Risk   17

Chapter 2:   The Profile of a Victim   33

Chapter 3:   Blaming the Victim   47

Chapter 4:   The Criminalization of Walking   63

Chapter 5:   Killer Cars   77

Chapter 6:   The Ideology of Flow   99

Chapter 7:   A Hard Right Turn   115

Chapter 8:   Pedestrian Safety on the Technological Frontier   125

Chapter 9:   The International Context   141

Chapter 10:   Families for Safe Streets   157

Conclusion   173

Acknowledgments   181

Notes   183

About the Author   229

Author's Note

The writing portion of this book was completed in early February 2019, before the COVID-19 pandemic took hold in the United States. In other words, it was written in what people have already started referring to as *the Before*. The publishing process is such that there is about a six-month lag between the completion of writing and the first sale, so I want to briefly address this consciousness-altering event that took place in between.

Though the pandemic will likely impact the problem of pedestrian deaths in many ways, at least at the onset of the crisis, it is difficult to predict the full extent. As a result of the reduction in commuting trips and leisure car trips, I would expect the number of pedestrian deaths will almost certainly decline dramatically this year. If we have a recession, which seems assured, that may be true for a longer period. However, mass quarantine has reduced congestion and increased speeding in many crowded metro areas, just as more people are out walking and biking, producing potentially dangerous conditions.

One thing that is all but assured right now is that this pandemic will bring Americans much closer to death and force us to consider some of the ethical trade-offs we make when it comes to the protection of human life. Early in the crisis, many right-wing figures, including President Trump, used traffic deaths—some 37,000 annually—to make the case that some amount of loss of life is an acceptable price to pay for a strong economy. (In the case of the pandemic, we're talking truly staggering figures.) It was a bad analogy in a lot of ways, but it helped emphasize the strange tolerance we have in our culture for traffic deaths and how they can desensitize us to other forms of cruelty and injustice.

It is also worth noting that while a bad economy may hide them, it won't fix the problems addressed in the book. Before the global pandemic, we had settled into a "new normal" where pedestrian deaths were consistently about 50% higher than they had been a generation before. So without a change in some of the contributing factors (vehicle styles and weights, engineering conventions, demographic trends), when the economy rebounds, I would expect to see the same pattern emerge. Without addressing them we will see perhaps tens of thousands of unnecessary deaths over the next decade or two.

At this point we can only hope that the devastation from this illness will be limited and we will emerge with a renewed sense of care for our fellow citizens and their health and well-being. This book, I hope can help planners and overlapping disciplines put the values of care, empathy, and caution over habit and convenience to save lives in the same way that we are taking on this terrible global crisis.

—March 2020

Foreword

As one of the nation's leading voices and thought leaders in transportation equity, I have devoted my entire career to creating equitable, healthy, and sustainable communities. In doing so, I have been methodical and intentional in the use of my power, my pen, and my privilege to highlight and humanize the disparities and injustices faced by historically disadvantaged population groups in the United States.

As a racialized black planner and street-level researcher, I am often called upon by many in the industry to offer ways to improve pedestrian and bicycle safety in North America. Although most of the brainstorming focuses on the normative experiences of the general population, I am deliberate in encouraging additional analyzes across varying and intersecting social identities such as income, race, ethnicity, ability, sex, gender, sexual orientation, and religious affiliation.

At the nexus of this unwavering fight for justice and truth-telling is the genesis of my appreciation and admiration for my dear sister Angie Schmitt. I have always known my sister Angie, racialized as white, to commit herself to speaking courageously and unapologetically through multiple platforms about the inequities and injustices facing pedestrians, bicyclists, and transit users along America's roadways. In this dynamic new book, *Right of Way*, she uses her vigor and thirst for justice to challenge the status quo and traditional norms and narratives. From spatial inequality and inequities to systemic and institutional racism to thematic and episodic news framing to climate change and autonomous vehicles, she sheds LED lights on the epidemic of traffic violence in the United States and across the globe. In doing so, she eloquently balances the "fierce urgency of now" with the supreme importance of humanizing every victim in every story in the book. She also graciously and unselfishly uses her purpose, power, and privilege to do as the great Dr. Cornel West once said: "You must let suffering speak, if you want to hear the truth."

I am most often asked by well-meaning persons, usually racialized white persons, "What can I/we do as allies to aid in the eradication of pedestrian injuries and fatalities in low-income and minority communities across America?" My short answer usually stresses the importance of intentionality, empathy, and the courage to act expeditiously. Henceforth, I will add to my list, "Follow Angie."

—Charles T. Brown, MPA, CPD, Senior Researcher and Adjunct Professor, Voorhees Transportation Center, Rutgers University

Introduction: Outline of an Epidemic

IGNACIO DUARTE-RODRIGUEZ HAD JUST been trying to grab some cigarettes. That Friday night in March 2018, the seventy-seven-year-old grandfather set off from his son's house on Phoenix's northwest side. It was a short walk to the market, across North 43rd Avenue.

Two other pedestrians had been killed on that stretch of 43rd Avenue in the three previous years, Rodriguez's grieving son and grandson would later tell a local news outlet.[1] There were, after all, no crosswalks and no traffic light. There were just six lanes of roaring, indifferent traffic.

Nobody knows much about the last moments of Rodriguez's life. The key witness, the driver of the 2008 or 2009 sedan (a Chevy Malibu?) who struck Rodriguez, fled the scene, leaving him to die in the road.

It was, in conventional respects, just another sad incident. In a city where about one hundred people lose their lives trying to cross the street every year, deaths like Rodriguez's are treated as a private tragedy at best or a traffic inconvenience at worst.

But they are part of a mounting epidemic. Ten other pedestrians would lose their lives on roads in the greater Phoenix area over the seven-day period in which Rodriguez was killed—people like Denise-Marye Sileci-Caruso, age sixty-six, another hit-and-run victim, who was killed the same day as Rodriguez while walking to her job at a local gym, or Patti and Ronald Doornbos, both sixty, a married

1

couple from Calgary who were killed in the suburb of Fountain Hills a few days later in a horrific quadruple fatality involving a distracted driver and a Ford Explorer.

Had eleven people been shot by a mass shooter in Phoenix, it would have made national news. By contrast, routine pedestrian deaths do not inspire furious press conferences or congressional hearings. Three of that week's victims were never even identified by name in the press. Nevertheless, their deaths represent an alarming—and until very recently, largely unexplained—trend.

In 2018, more pedestrians were killed in the United States than at any point in a generation. That year—the most recent for which we have official data—6,283 pedestrians died, a number not seen since the mid-1990s.[2] (An additional 1,500 were killed in driveways or parking lots and other locations that are considered private property and so are not counted as "traffic fatalities."[3])

In the United States, about 50 percent more people die while walking or using a mobility device today than a decade ago.[4] In all but the most unusual circumstances, these kinds of deaths never attract any sustained attention. But the sharp, sustained rise in pedestrian deaths has not been seen in the United States since the 1980s. It represents a reversal of the pattern of gradually improving outcomes seen in traffic safety for more than a generation.

The mounting crisis is so unexpected and unusual that for a long time, experts dismissed it as perhaps an aberration. But year after year now, as the death count has risen, the reality has become harder and harder to ignore.

There is something exceptional and new happening to the most vulnerable travelers in the United States, and the escalation is distinct from what we have seen for other groups. Over the same decade, from 2009 to 2018, by contrast, drivers and passengers have seen their fatality rates mostly unchanged—rising less than 2 percent.[5]

What has changed? What is killing pedestrians? What can we do about it—and why haven't we done it already?

We know that pedestrian deaths are not just random occurrences. There is a clear pattern in where they occur: along streets like 43rd Avenue—wide, fast arterial roads, especially in lower-income areas.

There are patterns in who is killed: older people, men, and people of color are disproportionately at risk. We know what kinds of vehicles are most likely to kill: large trucks and SUVs. We know what kinds of neighborhoods (low-income, black, and Latino) and what areas of the country (the Sun Belt) where people are mostly likely to be struck down. Finally, we know what times to day (night) pedestrians are most likely to be struck.

If we analyze these patterns, they tell us very clearly that pedestrian deaths are not just random acts of God or bad luck, nor are they the result of individual decision-making or laziness (although both bad luck and bad decisions often play a role). Pedestrian deaths are part of a systemic problem with systemic causes.

Like gun deaths, pedestrian deaths are influenced a great deal by policy, such as the speeds limits we impose on local roads, local zoning rules, and public budgets. Culture and vehicle design and technology play roles too.

But culprit number one is the way we have designed commercial streets like North 43rd Avenue, where Rodriguez was killed. Six lanes wide, 43rd Avenue separates a residential neighborhood from a modest shopping center across the street. Stores like the ones at 43rd Avenue and West Rose Lane—a Mexican carnicería, a pawnshop—generate a lot of trips.

Most of these trips, especially in a place like Phoenix, are made by car. But in this part of Phoenix and neighboring Glendale (43rd Avenue is the boundary between the two cities) is a moderate-income Latino neighborhood where many people rely on walking and transit. The public right-of-way—the avenue and the narrow sidewalk that borders it—does not reflect it, however. The marked speed limit on 43rd Avenue is 40 miles per hour—a speed at which being struck by a car is, statistically speaking, a death sentence for a majority of pedestrians and especially so for an older person like Rodriguez.

Even though there were no painted stripes on the roadway, the intersection where Rodriguez was struck is, legally speaking, a crosswalk. Pedestrian right-of-way laws are commonly misunderstood. But in most states, almost *every* intersection is considered an *unmarked* crosswalk, meaning that pedestrians have the legal right to cross there, even if there are no stripes on the road.

If Rodriguez had wanted to avoid dodging speeding cars, he would have had to travel about five blocks in either direction to the nearest marked crosswalk. In other words, for the option of maybe twelve seconds of "Walk" signal, the seventy-seven-year-old would have had to make a two-thirds of a mile detour—twice. Almost every pedestrian put in this position will make the decision to chance it rather than make the hike, which may itself be dangerous.

This kind of scenario is not unusual in the sprawling Sun Belt city of Phoenix. For Rodriguez, the cigarettes were across six lanes of high-speed traffic, each more than fourteen feet wide. It is a perilous journey of roughly eighty-six total feet—about the same length as the distance from home plate to first base.

People without cars in cities like Phoenix, in situations like Rodriguez's, are playing a high-stakes game in which they bet their life that they can make it to first base before the ball is caught, before the wall of traffic closes in. And a small but growing number of them are losing that bet.

About every ninety minutes, one person is being killed walking on a street somewhere in the United States. The circumstances are always different, and many factors are at work in almost every fatality. But Rodriguez's case is typical in many ways, from the demographic profile of the victim to the setting. He was a person with vulnerabilities in a high-risk setting who was failed by the infrastructure.

Confronting this pedestrian death crisis will require a commitment to protecting people like him. But that has not been the priority in the United States, especially in cities like Phoenix.

Following his father's death, Rodriguez's son, Felipe Duarte, pleaded with the city for something that could give meaning to his loss. "They have to do something with this intersection," he told Fox 10 Phoenix. "If his dad would be the last of this, I think that would be something that he would be proud of," said Constantino Escarcega, a family member.[6]

More than two years later, however, the intersection of Rose and 43rd was unchanged.

The lack of urgency around the problem may, in part, reflect the relatively low status of those being killed. Walking deaths fall disproportionately on those who are poor, black and brown, elderly, disabled, low-income, or some combination thereof—marginalized people with fewer political resources to demand reforms. Their experiences and viewpoints are often lost in a system in which few influential people from politics, media, or business are forced to, for example, rely on the bus in hostile environments like outer Phoenix. Among people privileged enough to avoid these kinds of situations—a category that includes most Americans—many view pedestrians as an annoyance or irritation, a potential obstacle on their journey.

That lack of sympathy frequently colors the way these deaths are portrayed. Pedestrians are almost always tacitly blamed for their deaths: for not wearing bright enough clothing, for texting, for wearing headphones, for not making eye contact, and most commonly, for "jaywalking." For example, even though the driver fled the scene and was still at large, original reporting on the Rodriguez case stated that Rodriguez "was not in the crosswalk when he was hit" but failed to mention two facts: that, legally speaking, he was in an *un*marked crosswalk and that there was no safe crossing anywhere nearby.[7]

Pedestrian victims also contend with an American culture of complacency around traffic deaths more generally. The general acceptance of these deaths as tragic but inevitable has headed off the necessary work of recognizing solutions and finding the will to implement them, even as the numbers have soared.

Understanding the systemic causes is the first step to saving lives. Given the right level of public commitment and resources, pedestrian deaths are preventable.

Some leading US cities have begun to demonstrate how these kinds of deaths can be gradually eliminated. New York City, for example, is one of more than forty US cities that is modeling its safety policies on a concept pioneered in Sweden, called Vision Zero, that seeks to entirely end traffic deaths over the long term. The city has retimed more than a thousand traffic signals and overhauled the design of hundreds of road elements in pursuit of that goal. Between 2013 and 2017 alone, for example, pedestrian deaths dropped 45 percent in New York City, reaching the lowest level since 1910. In New York City, for example, total traffic fatalities are about one-seventh of what they were in the 1990s, although the city's progress has reversed somewhat since 2017.

The goal of eliminating traffic deaths entirely might seem far-fetched, but some global leaders are already closing in on that goal. In 2019, Oslo, Norway, the capital city of the world's leader on traffic safety, nearly succeeded in doing so. That city of 673,000 had just one traffic death, and a total of zero pedestrians or children were killed on its roads.[8]

Meanwhile, many of the United States' international peers have seen their safety records continue to improve as the US pedestrian safety record has deteriorated over the last decade. (For comparison, over that same period, pedestrian death rates dropped 36 percent in Europe.)[9]

So why is the United States falling dangerously behind? What explains that 50 percent increase in pedestrian deaths in the United States since 2009?

American street design (as discussed), car culture, and sprawl all contribute. But a handful of recent trends have made the problem a lot worse.

Low Gas Prices, Strong Economy

An obvious explanation for skyrocketing pedestrian deaths is that Americans are simply driving more. In fact, they are driving about

280 billion more miles a year than they did in 2012 following the severe economic downturn.[10] Whenever the country emerges from a recession, the pattern has been more driving. And when more people drive, more people get killed in crashes.

But there has been only a 10 percent increase in total driving miles by Americans since the depths of the recession in 2009—not nearly enough to explain the 50 percent increase in pedestrian deaths.[11] Even when adjusted for miles driven, pedestrian deaths today are at their highest point since 1998.

In some ways, however, the economic recovery after the 2008 financial crisis may have been especially dangerous. For one, gas has been very cheap. In 2015, on an inflation-adjusted basis, US gas prices were lower than they were in 1947.[12] And when gas is cheap, more marginal drivers—like teenagers—get out on the roads and cause wrecks.

Auto lending has also been increasingly lax. Since 2009, auto debt held by Americans increased 75 percent, inspiring comparisons to the subprime mortgage crisis.[13] Although that trend has created concerns about predatory lending, it has allowed more lower-income people to purchase cars and has contributed to a decline in public transit use nationwide. (Public transit ridership in cities is very closely associated with lower traffic deaths[14] because transit eliminates car trips and helps provide an alternative for the riskiest drivers, such as drunk drivers and those with bad driving records.)

SUVs

Americans are driving more than they used to. But more importantly, they have been doing that driving in bigger vehicles. In a May 2018 study, the Insurance Institute for Highway Safety analyzed all the factors in crashes involving pedestrians, hoping to tease out what was causing the increase. The group found that between 2010 and 2016, the number of pedestrian fatalities involving SUVs increased 80 percent.[15]

The growing preference for SUVs among American car buyers is a long-running trend, with fits and starts dating to the 1990s. But it is still a relatively new phenomenon. In 1983, for example, SUVs were practically nonexistent, accounting for just 3 percent of the vehicles sold in the United States.[16] In the mid-2010s, however, SUVs began dominating car sales in ways never seen before, overtaking sedans as the most popular vehicle type. By 2018, SUVs were 48 percent of sales, with sedans (cars) accounting for just over 30 percent of sales and pickup trucks accounting for most of the remainder.[17]

Today, more pedestrians are getting hit by big heavy trucks than ever, and owing to the heft of these larger vehicles, pedestrian crashes are becoming more deadly when they do occur. Between 2010 and 2016, the odds of a pedestrian crash being fatal increased 29 percent.[18]

The news of the connection between SUVs' roaring sales and soaring pedestrian deaths came as a surprise to many traffic safety observers and people in the media, but it should not have. Studies dating to the late 1990s have shown that SUVs are much more dangerous

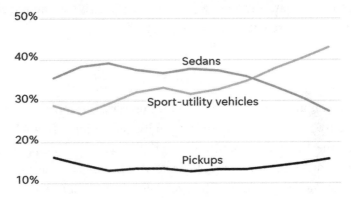

Americans are trading sedans for SUVs.
(Photo: Detroit Free Press *via Zuma Press)*

for pedestrians than regular cars. That information had simply been forgotten, ignored, or even intentionally buried.

The National Highway Traffic Safety Administration (NHTSA), for example, has known about the connection between rising pedestrian deaths and SUVs since at least 2015. That year, the agency quietly issued a report finding that SUVs are two to three times more likely to kill pedestrians when they strike them and four times more likely to kill child pedestrians.[19]

Demographic Change

Americans are driving more and are driving cars that are more deadly, and yet a third factor puts people in harm's way: because of certain demographic trends, more Americans are walking in the most dangerous places today than they did in 2009. In addition, more Americans today have physical vulnerabilities that make them more likely to be killed when they are hit.

The Sun Belt region of the United States is by far the most dangerous for pedestrians (for reasons, see chapter 2). On this issue, the region is a complete outlier. According to an analysis by Smart Growth America, nineteen out of twenty of the most dangerous metropolitan areas in the United States for pedestrians are in the Sun Belt.[20] Arizona, for example, has three times the pedestrian fatality rate of New York and Colorado and six times that of Minnesota.[21]

These Sun Belt metro areas—the most dangerous ones—are almost without exception the fastest-growing places in the United States. The twenty-two large metro areas in the Sun Belt have captured almost half the US population growth since 2010, according to the Kinder Institute for Urban Research at Rice University. And some of the most deadly metro areas—like Houston and Dallas, which each have added a million people since 2010—led the pack.[22]

Maricopa County, where Phoenix is located, for example, added almost six hundred thousand people between 2010 and 2018. In other words, it grew more than ten times as fast as the comparatively much safer Philadelphia County, Pennsylvania.[23]

Within metro areas, migration trends are also putting more people in harm's way. The geography of poverty has shifted considerably in this century. Between 2010 and 2015, about half the growth in poverty took place in US suburbs, according to the Institute for Research on Poverty at the University of Wisconsin–Madison. In the United States today, more than three million more people are living in poverty in suburbs than in cities.[24]

Suburbs are a dangerous place to be poor. Suburban areas like Cobb County, Georgia, and Oakland County, Michigan, that were once homogenous and wealthy have become progressively more racially and economically diverse since the early 1990s. These places and their streets, almost without exception, were not designed to accommodate people walking or relying on transit.

In addition, gentrification in major US cities may also be contributing to the problem. Demographic groups that are less likely to own cars—black and Hispanic people—are being pushed into more hostile environments on the suburban fringes, places that lack sidewalks and streetlights. This problem is especially pervasive in expensive coastal metros like Seattle that offer some of the best conditions for pedestrians—at least for those who can afford to live within urban neighborhoods.

Finally, as a nation, we are aging, and older adults are particularly vulnerable to pedestrian crashes. Those over age sixty-five account for about one in five pedestrian fatalities, and people over seventy-five, like Rodriguez, die at about twice the rate of the population at large.[25] As the US population ages, the demographic that is most at risk is swelling.

Driver Distraction

What about smartphones? Everyone's favorite theory about what is killing pedestrians is distraction. Unfortunately, it is difficult to say how big a problem distraction is because we do not have very good data about it.

The US Centers for Disease Control and Prevention, for example, estimated that 3,450 people were killed—out of some 40,000 total traffic deaths—by crashes involving distraction of any kind, not just cell phone distraction, in 2016.[26] The NHTSA estimated that just 562 of those deaths were either bicyclists or pedestrians. Perhaps more difficult to believe, however, is that the agency reported that the proportion of people dying as a result of distraction remained relatively unchanged from 2012 to 2015.[27]

That is almost certainly an undercounting. Traffic safety officials rely on police reports to identify and correctly report instances of distraction—and many police departments' crash reports still do not contain a standard reporting mechanism for cell phone distraction. In addition, correctly identifying cell phone distraction after a crash may require a level of investigation that police departments typically do not undertake following traffic crashes.

We do know, however, that people who have smartphones are distracted by them—a lot. Some of the best information we have comes from the tech company Zendrive, which was able to track actual cell phone use from three million drivers through censor technology embedded in their phones.

Zendrive found that practically everyone who owns a smartphone is distracted by it an alarming portion of the time while driving. Owners of smartphones use them on eighty-eight out of one hundred trips, the data showed, and average about 3.5 minutes of use on a one-hour trip. More worryingly, this study only counted physical manipulation of the phone with the hands, not voice commands.[28] Zendrive estimates that at any given moment, about three-quarters of a million drivers are using hand-held cell phones.[29]

We also know that this practice is extremely dangerous. Taking your eyes away from the road for as long as two seconds increases the chances of crashing as much as twenty-four times, studies have shown.[30] Using mobile technology—even the kind that is now standard in the dash-mounted entertainment systems of most new cars—is surprisingly mentally taxing and interferes with a driver's ability to perform more complex driving tasks, such as making left turns.

That being said, we know that the ubiquity of smartphones does not in itself guarantee escalating pedestrian carnage. Smartphones have penetrated European and Canadian markets at similar rates, and yet Europe and Canada have seen pedestrian fatalities decline over the same period (dramatically, in the case of Europe, although it has ticked up moderately in some wealthy countries like the United Kingdom).[31] So although we know that distracted driving is likely worsening the problem, it is difficult to say exactly how much.

What About Distracted Walking?

Smartphones are hugely distracting, and pedestrians are certainly not immune. For example, we know that people are falling a lot more when walking, even when inside their own houses, thanks to smartphone-related distraction. A 2013 study using Consumer Product Safety Commission information estimated that smartphones caused an additional fifteen hundred walking injuries in 2010 and that the number of injuries was rising at a rate of about two hundred a year—and the researchers believe that the figure was an undercounting.[32]

But even if the rate had been undercounted by a factor of two or three, it would still represent only a small share of the 137,000 pedestrian injuries treated in hospitals annually[33] (and that study includes non-traffic-related injuries—like a pedestrian who walked into a pole).

Although pedestrian distraction may be a minor factor, we can be confident that distraction is not what has increased deaths 50 percent in a decade. Here's why:

1. **Most pedestrian fatalities occur at night.** About 75 percent of pedestrian fatalities occur at night. It is not impossible that

people are staring at their phones while walking around at night, but it is somewhat less likely. Having a glowing phone lit at night might even improve visibility for pedestrians, which is a major factor in these crashes.

2. **Most pedestrian fatalities occur outside crosswalks.** About three-quarters of pedestrian fatalities (73 percent) occur outside of intersections—meaning that the pedestrian is not in a crosswalk, marked or unmarked, when struck.[34] People could still be distracted by cell phones when they are running across a road midblock or walking along a road with no sidewalks, but many of the situations in which pedestrians get killed are not the kind of relaxing crossings that would make checking one's phone tempting.

3. **Low-income and elderly people are killed disproportionately.** The kinds of people being killed while walking are not the stereotypical smartphone addicts. Rather, older people are overrepresented in the statistics. We also know that low-income people are disproportionately likely to be killed. Those living in neighborhoods where the median per capita income is less than $21,000 are killed while walking at twice the rate of those in neighborhoods where people earn more than $31,000 per capita.[35] Many older people and many lower-income people own smartphones. In general, however, the groups most likely to be killed while walking are some of those who we would expect to be the least wired.

Are Americans Simply Walking More?

What about the so-called return-to-cities movement? Are more pedestrians being killed simply because a lot more Americans have been inspired to ditch their cars?

Walking and cycling for transportation have become much more celebrated recently. And there is some good evidence—real estate demand, for example—that more and more people want access to neighborhoods that offer at least some destinations within reach of a stroll.

But some of the best data we have show not much change or even a decline in walking since 2009. We do not have great information about how many people are walking and how far they are walking. The most comprehensive study of American's travel habits, however, showed a 9 percent reduction in walking trips of all kinds between 2009 and 2017.[36]

The Response

As these factors have culminated to produce a crisis that is killing thousands of Americans, the public response has been muted. State and federal transportation programs have simply not been oriented around prioritizing pedestrian safety and, in many cases, make things worse. That is especially true in the areas where safety reforms are most desperately needed.

To begin, the scale of resources dedicated to solving the problem is wildly out of scale with the costs. Twenty-two US states have amended their constitutions to forbid any gasoline tax revenues at all from being spent on sidewalks.[37] Many of these laws were passed in the 1960s with the financial backing of highway construction lobbyists.[38]

At the federal level, bicyclists and pedestrians now represent about one in five traffic deaths, but they receive less than 1.5 percent of all federal infrastructure funding.[39] Increasing political polarization may also play a role. Just as the pedestrian death crisis was beginning to present itself in 2012, and in an era of loud and renewed interest in active transportation, the Republican-led US Congress substantially reduced federal funding support for walking and biking programs. In addition, following the election of Donald Trump in 2016, the newly regulation-averse US Department of Transportation slow-walked reforms that could have, for the first time, made automakers more accountable for their design impacts on pedestrian safety.

Cities Take the Lead

There is hopeful work taking place, however, at the city level, where sensibilities about traffic safety have been undergoing a sea change. Seattle is one of a growing number of US cities that has made a commitment to try to end traffic deaths altogether. Seattle is using a variety of policy and design approaches—lower speed limits, bicycle lanes, retimed traffic signals, to name a few—to save lives.

In December 2019, as she announced a series of reforms—including funding for intersection upgrades—Seattle Mayor Jenny Durkan made a statement that helped affirm this new vision: "We must make our sidewalks and roads safe for everyone—too many of our residents have lost their lives in traffic incidents, often the most vulnerable," she said. "That is unacceptable."[40]

Chapter 1

The Geography of Risk

S AA'MIR WILLIAMS WAS JUST SEVEN MONTHS OLD when his mother pushed him in a stroller to the corner of Roosevelt Boulevard in Philadelphia the night of July 9, 2013, and paused to look for an opening in traffic.

Saa'mir was a doted-on baby brother, the youngest of four sons to Samara Banks, a twenty-seven-year-old daycare teacher. That night, the whole family was together, waiting at the curb, bound for their apartment across the street in the Feltonville neighborhood. The oldest boy, Saa'yon Griffin, was just five years old.

They were headed home from a party at a relative's house nearby that Saturday night at the height of summer. It was close to 10 p.m. There had been a water fight at the party, and everyone was tired and happy as they approached the road.

To live near Roosevelt Boulevard, Philadelphia's most notorious street, is to live in the shadow of a serial killer, however. Every year, an average of twelve people die along Roosevelt's fifteen-mile-long passage through the city.

Standing on the side of its roaring twelve lanes, it is easy to see why. The boulevard is a jumble of access roads and turn lanes. It stretches about three hundred feet across, about the length of a football field. Roosevelt would take well over one minute for a fit, younger man

17

walking at an average speed to cross. That is a long time to be exposed to traffic traveling near the posted speed limit: 45.[1]

For Philadelphians living nearby, a high-stakes game of Frogger stands between them and their work or the things they need every day. Roosevelt has every kind of risk factor that makes a street deadly for pedestrians.

As the Banks family made their way home that July 2013 night, two men—Khusen Akhmedov, age twenty-three, and Ahmen Holloman, thirty[2]—were speeding down Roosevelt, one man driving an Audi and the other a souped-up Honda. The pair had been drag racing for miles, weaving in and out of lanes as fast as 79 miles per hour.

Witnesses would later testify that they heard a loud boom. "They saw stuff in the air," said Latanya Byrd, Samara Banks's aunt. "They thought it was debris. They had no idea."[3]

When Banks and her sons were struck, the cars were going as fast as 70 miles per hour. The force of the blow was catastrophic. The bodies of Banks, baby Saa'mir, almost-two-year-old Saa'sean, and four-year-old Saa'deem were thrown as far as 210 feet, according to reports.[4]

Shortly after the crash, Byrd remembers getting a call from a cousin. "I got to the scene and I just seen cars blocking off the road," she said. "My husband and I couldn't get through. Me and my daughter just ran toward wherever it was. They would not let us get to her. They covered her up."[5]

The boys lived long enough to be transported to the hospital. After that, the family was never allowed to see Samara or her three youngest boys again. Their faces and bodies were too badly disfigured. "To identify them, they just took a picture, maybe a partial of their face," said Byrd.[6]

Saa'yon, five years old at the time, was the only survivor. Akhmedov, an ambulance driver, was charged and convicted of third-degree murder and sentenced to seventeen to thirty-four years in prison.[7] The sentence—but not the conviction—was overturned on appeal in 2017, however.[8]

This notorious crash—the near annihilation of a whole family, three of them children under age five—was a galvanizing case in Philadelphia, but it was just the tip of the iceberg in many ways. Roosevelt Boulevard sees about seven hundred total crashes annually. In 2018, it was the site of an astronomical twenty-one deaths—about one in five of the traffic fatalities that occurred within the city of Philadelphia.[9]

Pedestrian deaths are not random. They happen in geographic clusters, at intersections, and they happen along radiant lines—on thoroughfares like Roosevelt Boulevard.

In the planning industry, these kinds of roads are called suburban arterials: wide, high-speed roads that have a lot of commercial and residential destinations that people want to access on foot or wheelchair. In the United States, a majority of pedestrian fatalities—52 percent—occur on these kinds of roads, according to Smart Growth America.[10]

In Denver, For another example, 50 percent of all traffic fatalities occur on twenty-seven corridors, or 5 percent of the street network.[11] In Albuquerque, the story is much the same, with 64 percent of traffic fatalities occurring on 7 percent of the city's roads.[12] Planners call this kind of cluster a high-crash network. Almost every city has at least one road like Roosevelt.

For example, in Rockford, Illinois, just three roads account for 40 percent of all pedestrian crashes, and one road accounts for almost one-fourth of them.[13]

Pedestrian deaths, in other words, are a design problem. Certain streets are designed to kill.

"If you map out where those deaths are happening, they're not for the most part in downtowns or neighborhoods," said Emiko Atherton, director of the National Complete Streets Coalition. "They're on these roads that were never intended for people to walk on."[14]

After her niece's death, Latanya Byrd became an advocate for safer streets in Philadelphia. She joined with other Philadelphians who lost family members to car crashes and helped found a group called Families for Safe Streets Greater Philadelphia (FSSGP) to advocate for safety improvements. Together they lobbied for three years in Harrisburg, the state capital, and at home in Philadelphia to add automated speed cameras on Roosevelt. Speed cameras have been shown to reduce fatalities as much as 55 percent in cities like New York[15] and might have prevented the racing incident that killed most of Banks's young family.

After the years-long campaign, including testimony from Byrd in Harrisburg, Families for Safe Streets finally prevailed, winning special permission to install a limited number of speed cameras on Roosevelt Boulevard only. The first ones went live in late 2019.[16]

Philadelphia has long-term plans for more dramatic changes to Roosevelt, but that street will be tricky and expensive to change because it has so many driveways and lanes. In the meantime, a traffic light with bright lighting was added where Banks and her boys were killed. Philadelphia even renamed the passage "Banks Way."

"Gaps" in the Infrastructure

The Roosevelt Boulevard of Rockford, Illinois, is called State Street. In 2018, Michael Smith, a graduate student at the University of Illinois, conducted a study to find out why this five-lane federal highway was so deadly. Smith installed cameras along key intersections and recorded pedestrian behavior. He found that many pedestrians were "breaking the rules," but it turned out that in a lot of locations, that behavior had a rational explanation: the infrastructure was hostile.

State Street serves as an important commercial corridor for the region, but its land use is suburban. Pedestrians have to navigate a collision course of commercial driveways and parking lots to report for their shift, grab a burger, or buy a bag of diapers. Sidewalks are intermittent, beginning and ending at random points. The traffic signals on State Street in the area Smith examined do not even have walk signals. And bus stops were mostly just a pole in the ground.[17]

Pedestrians have worn a path in the sidewalk beside State Street, the most dangerous road in Rockford, Illinois. (Photo: Michael Smith)

Smith's video footage showed that pedestrians were adapting their behavior to the environment. In one video, a man in a wheelchair is seen rolling out to the intersection of Longwood and State. He reaches the curb and then turns around, rolls off into a gas station driveway, and then rolls into the street. For a few moments he rolls right along the curb in the street, mixing with car traffic, before turning the corner and rolling up to the intersection again.

Smith saw wheelchair users perform this same maneuver over and over again. He noted that there is an affordable senior housing complex near the intersection, but there is no curb ramp at the intersection that could accommodate wheelchairs.

Again and again on State Street, Smith found that the infrastructure was failing people who were vulnerable. The situation was similar at bus stops, where pedestrians were put in a dangerous position by the lack of amenities. Rather than stand on the side of the road next to a pole in the grass in the rain or the hot sun without a place to sit, for example, bus riders would wait under an awning of a nearby business. "And then the moment a bus would come, you'd see a mid-block crossing, running across the street," Smith said in 2018.[18] Many bus riders in Rockford rely on buses that come just once an hour, which adds to the pressure to dash across the busy street to avoid missing their connection.

Thanks in part to these conditions, State Street sees only about one hundred pedestrians a day, and the people who walk along the street are not powerful politically. Rather, they are struggling to survive on the margins of a transportation system not designed with them in mind. Some engineers might even argue that such a small number is not worth the trouble of accommodating.

But ignoring the needs of these pedestrians turns out to be very dangerous. "When you take 100 persons a day, 365 days a year you get some statistical likelihood that there's going to be an accident," Smith said.[19]

There is a lot that can be done to repair roads like Roosevelt and State, however.

New York City's "Boulevard of Death"

Not too long ago, New York City's Roosevelt Boulevard equivalent—Queens Boulevard—was known locally as the Boulevard of Death. Between 1990 and 2014, 189 people—predominately pedestrians—were killed on this ten-lane raceway through some of the most densely populated, most transit-dependent neighborhoods in the United States.

But in 2014, city officials overhauled the road. They painted the outside lane green and added plastic bollards—a series of evenly spaced posts—creating a protected bike lane. On the curbside, they added a red-painted lane reserved for city buses. The redesign was cheap—according to the *New York Times*, the cost was just $4 million[20]—but it was remarkably effective. There was not a single traffic fatality on the road following the redesign until 2018.[21]

To reduce pedestrian deaths, roads like Queens Boulevard—and State Street and Roosevelt Boulevard—need to be fixed. The kinds of issues Smith documented—the dangerous gaps in the pedestrian infrastructure—need to be resolved, and vehicle speeds in areas where pedestrians are present need to be slowed down.

The urgency of repairing the nation's roads is only increasing as poverty in the United States increasingly shifts to where suburban arterials get their name.

A Suburban Problem

Tara Boulevard in Clayton County, Georgia, was named for the fictional Tara Plantation in the movie *Gone with the Wind*. The 1939 classic was filmed in part in Clayton County, south of Atlanta. At the time, it was rural farmlands, a picturesque setting for a period piece about the antebellum South.

This part of Georgia remained mostly rural farmland until the 1970s. Since then, however, wave after wave of suburban growth has overwhelmed its 143 square miles.

Before it was overhauled in 2014, Queens Boulevard was referred to as the Boulevard of Death. Between 1998 and 2014, 189 people were killed there. (Photo: New York City DOT)

Since New York City added a bike lane and a bus lane on Queens Boulevard, pedestrian deaths and injuries there have plummeted dramatically. (Photo: New York City DOT)

Only eleven thousand people lived in Clayton County in 1940.[22] Today's population is more than two hundred times as large. Atlanta's notorious urban sprawl has long since leap-frogged past Clayton County altogether, toward Henry and Fayette Counties to the south. Clayton County is now a suburban county. But the face of the suburbs is changing, and in many ways, the old infrastructure is ill-suited to this new era.

Clayton County saw its first big boom in the mid-1970s, as blue-collar white workers flooded into the county, fleeing desegregation orders in the Atlanta public schools. Growing bedroom communities like Clayton, Cobb, and Gwinnett Counties made little to no accommodation for pedestrians. This period of suburban growth coincided with the height of the highway era in the United States. The Interstate Highway System, started under President Dwight D. Eisenhower in 1956, was well under way, and it had opened vast swaths of formerly rural lands to suburban development.

During this era, Clayton, like Atlanta's other suburban counties, was resistant to joining Atlanta's transit system, MARTA (the Metropolitan Atlanta Rapid Transit Authority). In 1965 and 1971, Cobb, Gwinnett, and Clayton Counties, led in some cases by openly segregationist political leaders, all voted against joining MARTA. *Atlanta* magazine later called those decisions "referendums on race" and the point where "it all went wrong" for Atlanta.[23] As a result, Atlanta's suburban "collar counties" that surround Atlanta's urban counties were designed almost exclusively for drivers.

Despite their early efforts at segregation, counties like Clayton have experienced dramatic racial change. The first waves of migration began when the Atlanta Housing Authority began shuttering high-rise public housing projects in the 1990s. Spurred on by the federal HOPE VI housing program, which encouraged the creation of mixed-income housing, public housing in Atlanta was decimated, and only a small portion of those units were replaced by mixed-income housing.

"The lack of affordable housing in more walkable areas pushed a lot of people to more suburban areas along streets that were designed for just cars," said Sally Flocks, founder of PEDS (Pedestrians Educating Drivers on Safety), an Atlanta-based pedestrian advocacy group.[24]

In addition to migrants from Atlanta, these collar counties have seen successive waves of highly diverse migration from other parts of the United States, including the Rust Belt, since the 1970s. By 2010, the notion of white suburbs and a black inner city was completely outdated. That year, 87 percent of Atlanta's black population lived in the suburbs (compared with just 47 percent in 1980).[25]

Perhaps no suburban county typified that change better than Clayton County. By 2018, Clayton County was 69 percent black.[26] It had been 75 percent white just a generation before in 1990.

"During the '90s, Clayton County goes from a suburb that's white and becomes a place where many black people move to for the ideal suburban life," said King Williams, an Atlanta-based writer and documentary filmmaker whose work explores gentrification in Atlanta, "but also many who are poor as well."

Those who moved to Clayton County in later waves of growth were less likely than their predecessors to have a car. Today, about 22 percent of the population lives below the federal poverty line.[27]

Now it is suburban counties like Clayton, Gwinnett, and Cobb where pedestrians are increasingly getting killed, said Flocks.[28] The county has been held up by national news outlets as an example of the difficulties presented by the suburbanization of poverty.

"This place isn't meant for poor people," said Lauren Scott, a twenty-eight-year-old single mother and Clayton County resident who was featured in a 2015 *Washington Post* article.[29] (The *Post* followed her transit and walking commute to a job interview; It took four hours round trip.)

Tara Boulevard is now one of the most dangerous roads in Georgia. The posted speed limit is 55 miles per hour. The street serves three bus routes, yet it lacks very basic safety infrastructure such as streetlights and sidewalks. Clayton County pedestrians have worn dirt paths in the grass up and down Tara Boulevard.

Tara Boulevard was never designed to accommodate large numbers of pedestrians; it was designed to be a rural highway, and the mismatch is deadly. Seven people were killed on Tara Boulevard between 2011 and 2015. Another seventeen were seriously injured.

In 2018, the Georgia Department of Transportation named Tara Boulevard one of its "focus corridors," which makes it eligible to receive modest additional resources to address safety problems.[30] Meanwhile, the Clayton County Police Department's solution has been to ticket pedestrians.[31]

Suburban commercial development norms—drive-throughs, large street-facing parking lots with no pedestrian walkways—add to the problem. A 2017 study by the Center for Transportation Research at the University of South Florida found that the presence of a Walmart store, Family Dollar, or fast-food restaurant significantly increased the odds of a pedestrian crash. A low-income census tract with fifteen hundred residents could expect to have 1.8 more pedestrian crashes over a four-year period if it contained a Walmart and an additional 0.68 crash if it contained a fast-food restaurant like McDonald's or Taco Bell.[32]

Suburban governments, especially lower-income ones, are building infrastructure to accommodate these kinds of businesses or are permitting the businesses to build it themselves, without providing any safe access for people on foot—and that gets people killed.

Charles T. Brown, a research specialist at Rutgers University whose work focuses on bicycle and pedestrian issues (and author of the foreword of this book), said that historic displacement (shuttering of public housing) and contemporary displacement (gentrification) have produced a dangerous situation. "You take a population that was wholly reliant on transit and you take them to a suburban location that lacks transit," said Brown. "Then they're walking on streets that don't have the infrastructure to support them, and that's high-speed roads with SUVs.

"If you wanna find out where death happens," he continued, "look at where the speed is."[33]

Speed

Chief among the risk factors for pedestrians, according to Leah Shahum, director of the Vision Zero Network, a group that supports cities trying to improve traffic safety, are design features that promote speed. Wide travel lanes, shoulders free of obstacles, and generous turning radii all promote speed. And speed and pedestrians are a dangerous combination.[34]

"There's a level of physical impact that our bodies can survive and there's a level that we cannot," Shahum said in a 2018 press briefing.[35] "We know that when crashes happen . . . if the speeds are lower and manageable that folks are going to be able to walk away from that."

Speed is perhaps the most crucial factor that will determine whether a pedestrian will walk away from a crash unscathed or will be killed. And critically, the force of the blow rises exponentially as speeds increase. For a pedestrian struck at less than 20 miles per hour, risk of death is less than 5 percent, according to a 2011 study by the AAA Foundation, but the risk rises fast; 65 percent of pedestrians struck at 40 miles per hour or more will be killed.[36] At 60 miles per hour, the force of the blow is like falling off a twelve-story building.[37]

"Small differences in speed produce huge differences in the amount of raw force unleashed in a crash," said Neil Arason, a Canadian traffic expert, in his 2015 book, *No Accident*. "Doubling the speed leads to four times the kinetic energy."[38]

The Sun Belt

Speed and geography in the United States are linked. You find it at the epicenter of the pedestrian safety crisis in the United States: the Sun Belt, from the Carolinas to Southern California. Of the top twenty most dangerous metropolitan areas for pedestrians ranked by Smart Growth America in 2019, all but one—Detroit—were in the South or Southwest.[39] Florida in particular is a horror show for pedestrians, with nine of the top twenty most dangerous metropolitan areas, including all six of the worst-rated ones.

Since the 1940s, cars have been the dominant organizing principle in neighborhood and city planning in the United States. Huge portions of every US metro area have been designed to prioritize driving speed over pedestrian safety.

But in the Northeast and some parts of the Midwest, cities like Cleveland, Philadelphia, and Boston came of age during the streetcar era or earlier. These precar neighborhoods have narrower streets than newer cities and buildings that are oriented toward them. As a result, they are inherently safer for pedestrians.

That is not the case for cities like Fort Myers, Florida, and many of the other cities topping Smart Growth America's list. A good rule of thumb is that if a city or state developed after the invention of air conditioning, it is likely to be a dangerous place to walk. Texas and Georgia, for example, have more than twice as many per capita pedestrian fatalities as Massachusetts, even though people walk at much higher rates in Boston than in Houston.[40]

"In most of these states, their built environments were constructed with Eisenhower's Interstate Highways System as the model," said Atherton of the National Complete Streets Coalition.[41]

Geoff Boeing, professor of urban planning at the University of Southern California, analyzed the street networks across the United States and found different patterns based on the "era" an area was developed.[42] Boeing found that places that developed prior to 1940—central Philadelphia, Pittsburgh, Brooklyn, and the central cores of small towns and big cities alike across the country—have a high level of what Boeing calls "griddedness." In other words, those places had a tight network of streets that were highly connected to one another, forming a rough grid with lots of right angles and four-way intersections. A walkable, fine-grained street network—the traditional street grid—is very important for making walking useful and comfortable for pedestrians. Portland, Oregon, is famous for having a very "griddy" network of blocks. Boeing also found that griddedness helps predict lower car ownership, even when controlling for income, geographic terrain, and commute length.

Between 1940 and 2000, however, street grids fell out of style. Communities that were built during this period were also more likely to have streets that wound like outstretched fingers into cul-de-sacs and fed into megablocks of dangerous suburban arterials. (Since 2000, Boeing reported, in a bit of hopeful news, the trend away from grids has reversed to a large extent.)[43]

This pattern—griddy versus winding streets and the time frames at which they were dominant—illustrates why Florida is so dangerous for pedestrians. The overwhelming majority of Florida's growth took place during the era where roads were extremely hostile to pedestrians. In 1940, Florida had just 1.9 million residents; today, it has 21.6 million people. By comparison, Pennsylvania (population 13 million today) has added just 3 million people since 1940.[44]

Regional Culture

The transportation culture in many Sun Belt cities compounds an already difficult situation. When there are few people walking in the first place and those who walk are very marginalized, building political support for changes that might benefit people who walk, wheel, or take transit is a tough political battle.

In Phoenix, for example, almost one hundred people are killed while walking every year. In May 2018, however, almost every member of the city's Complete Streets Advisory Board, a group of volunteers appointed to make recommendations to address the problem, resigned en masse, saying that their work was "maligned by developer lobbyists, disrespected by City staff, and dismissed by ill-prepared political bodies."[45] The following year, a Vision Zero plan developed by city staff that would have recommended actions shown to reduce the bloodshed—such as adding bike lanes on major thoroughfares—was rejected by the Phoenix City Council.[46]

The opposition to the plan was led by city councilman Sal DiCiccio, who told his nineteen thousand Facebook followers, in all caps, that Vision Zero would "DOUBLE YOUR TRIP TIMES AROUND TOWN—AND LIKELY YOUR TAXES."[47]

Meanwhile, Atherton said that classism and racism help explain the lack of concern. "We have the solutions. We actually have the funding; we're just not spending it well," Atherton said. "We just don't have the political will."[48]

That lack of political will, especially in cities like Phoenix, has a lot to do with who is being killed.

Chapter 2

The Profile of a Victim

E veryone knows Portland, Oregon, as a bike-friendly city. And in many ways, the city lives up to its reputation.

Portland city government takes traffic safety seriously and is working to eliminate traffic deaths altogether. To that end, it has installed almost four hundred miles of bikeways.[1] In 2018, for example, the city lowered residential speed limits to 20 miles per hour. In general, these types of interventions are very beneficial for pedestrians.

Yet one factor that best predicts whether you will get killed while walking in Portland is whether you live east or west of 82nd Avenue. This avenue is the boundary where East Portland—or, as the local news site *Willamette Week* once called it, "the other Portland"—begins.[2]

Portland is a predominately white city, but more than half—57 percent—of East Portland residents identify as being Hispanic, black, Asian, Native American, or multiracial.[3] East Portland is poorer, less educated, and less white than the rest of the city, and these demographic factors all increase the risk of dying in a pedestrian crash.

Although just over one-fourth of Portlanders reside in East Portland, about half of all pedestrian deaths occur there. And of the total traffic deaths in Portland in 2018, about 70 percent were in East Portland, according to city data.[4]

The physical condition of East Portland's infrastructure helps explain the disparity. Portland may be known for its sleek, modern streetcars and well-landscaped bike lanes, but there is wide inequality in where those sought-after urban amenities are installed. In East Portland, even the most basic elements of safe pedestrian infrastructure are often lacking.

Willamette Week reporter Corey Pein took a close look at the problem in 2011. At the time, he reported that East Portland's crosswalks were, on average, a quarter of a mile apart. "It's not uncommon to see people in wheelchairs using roadways because the sidewalks are inadequate or missing," he wrote.[5]

East Portland—all fifty square miles of it—contained only three city-maintained bike racks, Pein wrote, and it was served by just one frequent-running bus route.[6] In addition, East Portland has the worst street lighting in the city, according to reporting by *Willamette Week*, an issue that was listed as *the* top concern of black pedestrians in the city in 2019.[7]

That year, Portland Bureau of Transportation officials pledged to invest more resources in East Portland to remedy the problem. High death rates on the east side of the city have been thwarting the city's progress toward its goal of achieving Vision Zero. Of Portland's thirty "high-crash intersections," twenty-eight are in East Portland, the city reported.[8]

These kinds of disparities are found in black and brown neighborhoods across the United States, and they help explain why people of color are so much more likely to be killed in a pedestrian crash than white people.

Statistically, black men are about twice as likely to be killed while walking (or wheeling) as white men and four times more likely to be killed than the general population. The same is true for Hispanic men.[9]

Tamika Butler, a transportation consultant with Toole Design Group, told NPR's *Marketplace* in 2019 that racism is clearly a factor in where infrastructure resources are deployed. "When you take data of race and socio-economic status and you overlay it with where there are the most traffic incidents, and the most traffic deaths and serious injuries, communities of color and low-income communities light up those maps," Butler said.[10]

Usually, this infrastructure disparity is not the result of overt racism, where individuals are making conscious decisions to deny people certain amenities based on race or ethnicity. Rather, this type of inequality reflects a systemic racism that is a legacy of segregation, housing segregation, and implicit bias.

Why are people from certain racial and ethnic groups at heightened risk? The best information we have shows that black, Hispanic, and Native American people *do* walk more than non-Hispanic white people.

According to federal travel data, about 15 percent of Hispanic people rely on walking as their primary form of transportation. That is almost 50 percent higher than the percentage of non-Hispanic white people. Black people, meanwhile, are about 30 percent more likely than white people to rely primarily on walking.[11]

In addition, both black and Hispanic people are also much more likely to take transit—a mode that requires a fair amount of walking—than white people. Black people use transit, for example, at about triple the rate of white people.[12] Latinos are twice as likely to lack access to a car as white people.[13]

In his 2019 book *Barrio America*, Penn State history professor A. K. Sandoval-Strausz wrote that many Hispanic people brought a different transportation culture with them when they began immigrating to the United States in large numbers in the 1960s. They were coming from countries that were much more dependent on walking. In Mexico in 1960, for example, there was only one car for every forty-five people. At the time, the ratio in the United States was about one to three. "In a very real sense," Sandoval-Strausz wrote, "Latin American immigrants were importing a different understanding of the urban landscape, one that arose from the simple fact that they had not grown up in a U.S.-style car culture."

As the rest of the United States was in the middle of a sprawl extravaganza, Latinx immigrants established flourishing walkable commercial districts in neighborhoods like Oak Cliff in Dallas and Little Village in Chicago.

In addition to culture, economics plays a role. People who live in poverty take about 50 percent more walking trips than those who have higher incomes. And black and Hispanic Americans are twice as likely as non-Hispanic white people to live in poverty.[14]

But even though additional exposure plays a role in the disparities, it does not fully explain why black and brown people are much more likely to be killed, according to Robert Schneider, an associate professor at the University of Wisconsin–Milwaukee who specializes in pedestrian safety. "It's likely that they're walking in environments where the conditions are riskier, where the streets are designed with higher speeds and more lanes to cross," he said.[15]

Black and brown neighborhoods—like in East Portland—are being passed over for needed safety improvements. People living in neighborhoods of color receive different treatment than white neighborhoods, said Rutgers' Charles T. Brown. "We live in racially segregated areas," he said. "These neighborhoods have been disinvested, and highways have been plowed through them."[16]

Detroit

Detroit is the blackest major city—overall 82 percent black—in the United States. For many reasons related to its history and culture, the Motor City is also a dangerous place to walk. A 2018 *Detroit Free Press* investigation ranked it the most dangerous US city for pedestrians based on fatalities per capita.[17] Other analyses have shown that it is an outlier among Midwest cities for pedestrian trauma.

The kind of institutional neglect of basic safety infrastructure often seen in black or brown neighborhoods is apparent across Detroit. The city's well-documented financial troubles play an important role. As recently as 2014, a shocking 40 percent of the streetlights in Detroit were broken or missing.[18] Missing safety features like streetlights can be a life-or-death matter for pedestrians, 75 percent of whom are killed at night.[19]

Street lighting is hardly a matter most people would consider racially sensitive, but it has been linked to segregation and inequality before. After five black men were shot by police in Southeast Seattle in 2008, then-mayor Greg Nickels decided to tour the neighborhood. He noticed that a high number of streetlights were burned out or broken. In this neighborhood, the majority of residents were people of color, nearly half were refugees, and about the same number earned poverty wages.

Nickels instructed city staff to investigate the problem. It turns out that Seattle's streetlight replacement system relied on residents to report outages. In Southeast Seattle, however, residents were less trusting of City Hall and were not communicating the outages like white neighborhoods did. To remedy the problem, the city changed the way it handled streetlight repairs, making the replacement process automatic around the time the equipment was set to expire. That reform not only helped eliminate the racial disparity, but it also resulted in better service for everyone. White neighborhoods preferred the new system as well because residents did not have to go through the trouble of calling the city to complain.[20]

Detroit's experience shows how much investment in street lighting—especially for at-risk communities—can improve safety. Thanks to a major initiative, including a partnership with the state, the city issued bonds for $185 million in 2014 to replace and repair fifty-five thousand lights with LED lighting over a two-year period.[21] The initiative was intended to reduce crime, but it also had a dramatic impact on pedestrian safety.

Following the replacement of the nonfunctioning streetlights, the city's pedestrian death rate fell 40 percent in just two years. More impressive is that the decline occurred amid a backdrop of soaring deaths nationwide. By comparison, for example, pedestrian deaths in Michigan rose 47 percent between 2009 and 2018.[22]

The improvement was most dramatic for pedestrians killed in dark or low-light conditions. In 2013 and 2014, before the project began, an average of twenty-four people were killed every year walking in low-light conditions in Detroit. In 2017, after the project's completion, the figure had dropped to just one.[23]

Too often, the agencies responsible for infrastructure decisions are not in tune with the needs of communities of color. One of the most dramatic examples of infrastructure inequality is the situation faced by Native Americans. Native people suffer the worst pedestrian safety outcomes of any racial group in the United States. Indigenous men are almost five times as likely as the general US population to be killed while walking.[24] A 2018 study by University of Minnesota researchers Kathryn Quick and Guillermo Narváez helps shed light on the causes. Indian reservations and tribal lands are typically located in rural areas where roads lack elements that make them safe for walking such as sidewalks and crosswalks. Reservations, though, function a lot more like cities or small villages where many people rely on walking to get around, which means that tribal citizens and visitors are often forced to cross and walk along the shoulders of rural highways, right next to high-speed traffic from heavy trucks.

Near the tribal service center of the Leech Lake Band of Ojibwe, in central Minnesota, for example, people have worn footpaths toward US Route 2, a high-speed rural highway with no sidewalks or walk signals.

For their 2018 study, researchers Quick and Narváez surveyed twenty-two people at four reservations in Minnesota. Among tribal elders and residents, pedestrian safety was listed as one of the top concerns. Tribal residents identified infrastructure conditions, like lack of streetlights, as the key issue. "As soon as I get on the rez I know I need to start looking out for pedestrians," one interviewee told the researchers.[25]

Pedestrians have worn paths in the grass near US Route 2, between residential areas and a grocery store as well as tribal service center for the Leech Lake Band of Ojibwe in central Minnesota. There is no crosswalk or pedestrian refuge. (Credit: Guillermo E. Narváez, University of Minnesota)

But Quick and Narváez found that tribal concerns were not registering with the transportation officials. In interviews with officials from the Minnesota Department of Transportation, pedestrian safety never came up. Even when Quick and Narváez pressed the issue, they reported that the officials downplayed the problem or emphasized individualized strategies, like seat belts and drunk-driving campaigns, rather than structural fixes.[26]

Institutionalized racism and lack of diversity in planning and engineering are likely factors. One of Quick and Narváez's conclusions was that traffic safety officials need to do a better job of listening to tribal residents. "The solution . . . involves paying more attention and respect to the expert, local knowledge and informed judgment of people with intimate familiarity of the conditions on the ground," they wrote.[27]

Less than one-fourth of Native Americans live on reservations, however, so other factors are also likely at work. Native people who live in cities face many of the same types of discrimination as black and Hispanic residents. Increasingly, gentrification may be contributing to the disparity as well.

Gentrification

Research has shown, for example, a connection between bike infrastructure and displacement. According to a 2019 University of Colorado study, cities that had aggressively added protected bike lanes from 2000 to 2012 saw dramatic reductions in traffic fatalities of all types, but a large portion of the safety improvements could be explained simply by changing demographics.[28] In other words, the cities that were adding a lot of bike lanes were getting whiter—an average of 10 percent whiter—and white people are simply less likely to be killed in traffic than people of color. It is unclear whether the effect was simply white people outbidding people of color for homes near the safety infrastructure or if newly white neighborhoods were simply better able to secure those kinds of safety amenities, the study's authors said.[29] It may have been a bit of both.

Older Adults

It is not just people of color that face special risks while walking or wheeling. Older adults are another, often intersecting, group that is not being well served by the current paradigm. According to the National Highway Traffic Safety Administration, people over age sixty-five are about 35 percent more likely to be killed while walking than people in their twenties.[30]

Research suggests that older people may, in fact, walk less than the general population. And when older people walk (or wheel), they engage in less risky behavior than other groups. For example, they are more likely to be struck while in crosswalks, and they are less likely to walk at night.[31]

Older people face some obvious challenges moving about dangerous environments on foot or by wheelchair or walker, however. In many cases, they have more difficulty seeing, and they may move more slowly. When they are struck, it is more difficult for them to recover. In addition, they move about in an environment that is subtly biased against them. Perhaps the best example is traffic signals.

Guidance used by traffic engineers around the United States calls for the walk phase at a traffic light to be timed for a walking speed of 3.5 feet per second. This timing is based on how long it takes a relatively fit middle-aged adult man to walk. But as writer Graham Beck pointed out in a 2009 article for AARP, "Many older people walk closer to three feet per second, and those with mobility aids might move as slowly as 2.5 feet per second."[32]

In crossing a sixty-foot-wide street, for example, older people—or anyone who moves more slowly than the presumed average walking speed—will "require closer to 24 seconds to cross," Beck wrote. "If they're given only 15 seconds, they're left stranded in the middle of the road."[33]

When the light turned green on October 4, 2017, ninety-year-old David Grinberg was two-thirds of the way across Fell Street in San Francisco. For him, it was a fatal shortfall—Grinberg was struck by a woman driving an SUV who accelerated blindly through the intersection. Paramedics were on the scene minutes later, but it was not enough to save him.

The incident was predictable. The location where Grinberg was struck was between a public housing facility for low-income seniors and a park.

"The proximity of the senior home to the Panhandle [park] is obvious to residents who live nearby," wrote *SFWeekly*'s Nuala Sawyer at the time. "On any sunny afternoon, benches along the northern end of the park are filled with elderly Russian and Ukrainian women gossiping, and Asian seniors doing exercises under the trees. But in order to get there, the dozens of seniors who live at Mercy [Family Plaza]—many of whom are in wheelchairs or use walkers—must cross four lanes of Fell Street, which has a speed limit of 30 mph."[34]

Traditionally, traffic engineers have designed signal timings to minimize delay for drivers and have timed crossings with nondisabled, physically fit men around middle age in mind. A 1990 excerpt from a design manual produced by the Institute for Transportation Engineers makes the priorities clear. It begins by stating that the key engineering manual that sets signal timing standards for the nation's engineers called for timing signals to a pace of 4 feet walked per second (reduced to 3.5 in 2009). It continued,

> There are, however, various categories in the general population that walk at a slower rate. For example, some female pedestrians walk slower than some male pedestrians; very young children, the elderly, and the handicapped also walk at a slower rate. Research on pedestrian characteristics verify that over 60 percent of pedestrians move slower than 4 feet per second and 15 percent move slower than 3.5 feet per second.
>
> Although this may imply that the lower walking speed (3.5ft/s) should be used when calculating pedestrian signal timing, many engineers argue that the slower rate creates longer cycle lengths, ultimately resulting in longer vehicle delays.[35]

Some engineering guidance to this day still recommends against giving pedestrians less than 3.5 feet per second to cross the road. For example, Utah still uses the 4-feet-per-second standard for timing traffic lights.[36]

The emphasis on speed over the safety of older pedestrians will only become more costly as the population ages. People over sixty-five are the fastest growing demographic in the United States and will account for one in five US residents by 2030, according to the US Census Bureau.[37]

In fact, the aging of the US population may partly explain why pedestrian deaths have been soaring. As early as 1993, researchers were predicting that the growing elderly population would lead to an increase in pedestrian fatalities.[38] Again in 2013, right before pedestrian deaths started skyrocketing, the US Centers for Disease Control and Prevention warned of the possibility that pedestrian deaths would grow as the population became older and more diverse.[39]

City leaders and engineers can rise to the challenge by working to make cities and suburbs safer for older Americans. New York and Portland, Oregon, for example, have created a "Safe Routes for Seniors" program that offers special accommodations—such as longer crossing times—in areas where there are senior centers or other popular destinations for older people.

Even cities that do not adjust crossing times can make it easier to cross safely by installing pedestrian islands in intersections that give walkers a safe, protected place to wait if they do not make it across in a single cycle.

Other At-Risk Groups

Looking broadly at who is being killed while walking, a variety of other at-risk groups are also worth mentioning. One of the most remarkable disparities in pedestrian deaths is by gender—in 2017, men accounted for 70 percent of those killed while walking or using a wheelchair[40]—but the reasons are not fully understood. Men and women walk at about the same rates.

There is evidence that men take more risks, however. Men are much more likely to be killed in overall car crashes than women. Women might also be protected, ironically, by their fears of other dangers, like crime. Women are slightly less likely to be killed while walking at night, which may reflect social norms against women walking at night and rational fears about assault.

People with lower incomes are also more likely to be killed while walking, a host of evidence shows. According to a 2014 *Governing* magazine analysis, census tracts with high poverty rates have about twice as many pedestrian deaths as those with low poverty.[41] Other studies have also found increased risk for people with less than a high school education and for people whose primary language is not English.[42]

Another factor that puts people at risk is lacking a home. A disproportionate number of people killed while walking appear to be homeless. There is not much research on this subject, but some data suggest that a very large proportion of pedestrian deaths are from this population. A 2014 study by the US Centers for Disease Control and Prevention, for example, found that homeless people in Nevada were more than twenty times more likely than the general population to be killed while walking.[43]

In addition, Austin police officials report that a shocking 40 percent of pedestrians killed in that city in 2016 were homeless.[44] One of those victims was Sarah Jane Villegas, a twenty-five-year-old woman who struggled for years with addiction. What led Villegas to try to cross Loop 360—a high-speed state highway—on a rainy night two days before Christmas in 2016 is unknown, but she did not make it across. She was struck by multiple vehicles and killed.

It is easy to imagine why homeless people would face increased risk: they are likely to have higher exposure to traffic overall, spending much more time on sidewalks and streets than sheltered people. "People are often displaced and forced to live in places not meant for human habitation, such as underpasses and along roadways," Karen Dorrier, a manager with Austin's homelessness outreach team, told the local news station KUT in 2018.[45]

Compounding the problem, some homeless people may, like Villegas, have alcohol, drug, or mental health issues that complicate their judgment when interacting with fast-moving traffic. Drawing on the homelessness data, the Austin Transportation Department recently suggested that more affordable or emergency housing for homeless people should be explored as a solution to traffic deaths.[46]

The issue of alcohol use is a risk factor on its own. According to the Governor's Highway Safety Association, 36 percent of pedestrians killed in 2013 had a blood-alcohol concentration above 0.08, which surpasses the legal limit for driving. This finding sparked a rash of victim-blaming headlines about the danger of "drunk walking." The percentage of alcohol-involved pedestrian crashes, however, is very similar to the percentage of drivers in fatal crashes who are intoxicated: in about 28 percent of overall traffic fatalities, one person is intoxicated.[47] The intoxicated pedestrian percentage may not be directly comparable, however, because it excludes those younger than sixteen.

Nevertheless, it is clear that walking around intoxicated affects judgment, increasing the risk of getting killed by a car or truck. The question is, what is the appropriate response? Many media and institutional actors have defaulted to treating drunk walking like drunk driving—basically finger wagging.

In truth, intoxicated people who resort to walking may lack good alternatives. They can call an Uber or Lyft—if they can afford it. They can also avoid traveling, but that might not always be safe or practical. People might simply be encouraged to moderate their drinking overall. In some countries with much better safety records, like Sweden, alcohol sales are much more tightly controlled, and drinking is more socially discouraged.

Short of that kind of wider cultural change in attitudes and policies around alcohol consumption, it is probably necessary for cities—and for drivers—to assume that some number of impaired pedestrians will be using the roadways and therefore build in some protections. About one in eight American adults is an alcoholic, according to a 2017 study.[48] Extra care should be made to design college campuses, bar and entertainment districts, and areas near homeless shelters with features that promote slow driving speeds.

Finally, it is important to remember that the groups mostly likely to be killed while walking in the United States are not distinct. People who have overlapping marginalized identities—an older black man who lives in a low-income neighborhood, for example—will be the most vulnerable. As we think about how to solve this problem, we have to think about who has been denied the kind of support they need to make it home safely.

Chapter 3

Blaming the Victim

In April 2011, Raquel Nelson stood in a courtroom in Cobb County, Georgia. The twenty-nine-year-old single mother was on trial for the death of her four-year-old son, who had been the victim of a hit-and-run crash.

Nelson, a black woman, was facing up to three years in prison before an all-white jury. She was charged with vehicular homicide. The astonishing thing was, she did not even own a car.

The night that her son, AJ Newman, was killed—April 10, 2010—Nelson had taken her three children out for pizza.[1] They had been celebrating; it was her birthday the following day.

The trouble had started when the family missed their bus home. Transit in Cobb County, where the family lived in Atlanta's northern suburbs, is miserable, offering minimum service. Nelson and her children had to wait more than an hour for the next bus.

By the time they arrived back at their apartment complex in Marietta, it was 9:15 p.m. and dark. The children were tired. Nelson was juggling grocery bags. Home was just across Austell Road—a dimly lit, four-lane high-speed road with an additional turn lane. The speed limit was 45 miles per hour. Traffic was rolling past at close to highway speeds.

The family made it safely to the skinny concrete median at the center of the road. But as they stepped off the tiny refuge for the perilous final leg of their long journey, AJ broke free from his mother's grasp to follow his sister, who had already crossed safely. Nelson ran to chase him.

Meanwhile, Jerry Guy, a partially blind driver with two previous hit-and-run convictions, was speeding directly toward them in a van. Guy struck the mother and her two children and did not stop. Nelson and her younger daughter suffered only minor injuries in the crash, but little AJ was killed.

Later Guy would tell prosecutors that he had been drinking earlier in the day and thought he had hit a basket in the road.[2] He was sentenced to six months in prison on a plea deal for fleeing the scene.

As tragic as it was, the whole incident might have been just another forgotten pedestrian death. None of the circumstances were especially unusual. In metro Atlanta alone, 839 pedestrians were killed in the decade leading up to Newman's death.[3] But Nelson's story would become national news after Cobb County solicitor general Barry Morgan made the decision to try the grieving mother for her son's death. Nelson, not Guy, was responsible for AJ's death, Morgan argued, because she was jaywalking at the time of the crash.[4]

On those grounds, Nelson was tried and eventually convicted of vehicular homicide, jaywalking, and reckless conduct. Her case is one of the most stunning examples of a common phenomenon surrounding pedestrian deaths: blaming the victim.

Who is responsible when a pedestrian is killed? Every case is different, of course, but the way we view these incidents in a general sense reflects certain cultural assumptions and wider power dynamics.

In some Nordic countries where biking and walking are the dominant modes of transport, drivers are automatically assigned a greater share of legal responsibility when they strike vulnerable road users like pedestrians or cyclists. Drivers in the Netherlands, for example, are automatically considered fully responsible if the victim is a child.

The United States is a driving culture, however, and that affects the way we perceive blame and responsibility in these cases, usually in ways that are not beneficial to pedestrians. Police, juries, the media, and even traffic safety officials are all susceptible to what pedestrian advocates call windshield bias. This bias is apparent in the language used by traffic safety officials charged with protecting the public, who emphasize pedestrians' safety responsibilities to an extreme degree while minimizing the responsibilities of drivers. It is seen in the legal system, in police accounts, and in courtrooms—like the one that holds a woman whose son was struck by a car, who herself was injured trying to rescue him, as equally culpable as the stranger who struck, killed him, and fled. And it is seen repeated in subtle and explicit ways in the language and framing choices in media accounts of pedestrian deaths.

Traffic Safety Officials

In traffic safety, maybe nobody embodies windshield bias quite as proudly as Alberto Gutier, director of the Arizona Governor's Office of Highway Safety. In 2018, Arizona was named the deadliest state for pedestrians.[5] For Gutier, though, the problem can be boiled down to one thing: laziness on the part of people who were killed and injured. In an interview with a *Phoenix New Times* reporter in 2018, Gutier held up a sign saying, "Use xwalks stupid," lamenting that his concept for pedestrian safety signage had been "vetoed."[6]

In Gutier's defense, this mindset is deeply embedded in the social psychology of American traffic culture. The idea that any minor infraction by pedestrians—such as jaywalking—ought to be tantamount to a death sentence is rarely questioned. It is, in fact, the unspoken subtext of much of the official messaging around pedestrian deaths.

Although there is a lot of tough talk about jaywalking in Phoenix, we also know that there are simply not enough crosswalks there. Only about one-third of pedestrian deaths in Phoenix, including those that took place in crosswalks, were within five hundred feet of a crosswalk, the *Arizona Republic* found when it investigated the causes of the crisis in an April 2019 expose.[7]

But Gutier accepted no responsibility for the state's role in the crisis. A 2018 story by ABC 15 in Phoenix paraphrased him as saying, "In an overwhelming majority of crashes involving pedestrians, the pedestrian is at fault. Too many people are jaywalking."[8]

It is interesting to contrast the emphasis on the relatively minor infraction of jaywalking with much more serious misconduct by drivers. Phoenix city data show, for example, that in nearly one-third of pedestrian fatalities, the driver does not stop. These crashes are hit-and-runs. This kind of behavior, although a felony, does not arouse the same kind of anger and finger wagging from top officials, however.[9] It is certainly never used to frame drivers as a group as "heartless," "reckless," "lawless" or whatever would be the countercharge to "lazy" or "stupid" pedestrians.

Consider how the Pennsylvania Department of Transportation responded when there was a rash of pedestrian crashes in Harrisburg in December 2018, including a pair of siblings—a seven-year-old girl and an eight-year-old boy—who were struck and injured by a truck near their elementary school.[10]

At the time, Pennsylvania Department of Transportation spokesman Fritzi Schreffler told the local ABC affiliate, "Being a distracted pedestrian is as dangerous as being a distracted driver. I always tell pedestrians it's incumbent upon them to make sure they're making eye contact with [a] driver. Just because a traffic signal is red and they have got the pedestrian light to go does not actually mean that that person is going to stop."[11]

In other words, Schreffler said that pedestrians' responsibility goes well beyond what is legally required. Even in the legal right-of-way, they are not safe. Drivers, she reminds them, cannot be trusted to hold up their side of the bargain.

But even while Schreffler assumes that drivers will fail to yield to pedestrians, she accepts that dangerous behavior. She does not go on to impress upon drivers their legal duty to yield. Nor does she take aim at hit-and-run drivers, even though the perpetrator in one of the cases she was responding to was literally still at large when the ABC news story was published.

Why do traffic safety officials often feel the need to emphasize pedestrian responsibilities to such a degree while driver misbehavior is taken for granted? It may partly reflect the relatively low status of pedestrians compared to that of drivers. The superior political power of drivers, being such a dominant majority, is also likely a factor.

Regardless of the reason, one of the repeated mantras of traffic safety officials is the notion of shared responsibility. When the subject of pedestrian safety comes up, traffic safety officials start sprinkling the words "shared responsibility" around almost at random.

In the National Highway Traffic Safety Administration (NHTSA) recommendations to drivers and pedestrians, the agency leads with ten rules for pedestrians, imploring pedestrians to, among other things, make eye contact, wear bright clothing, avoid texting, and carry a flashlight. The NHTSA then follows with nine rules for drivers. But even in its rules for drivers—which, again, follow the list of ten different rules for pedestrians—the NHTSA sees the need to emphasize pedestrian responsibilities. The first rule for drivers reads: "Look out for pedestrians everywhere, at all times. Safety is a shared responsibility."[12]

AAA, meanwhile, tops its list of "Tips for Pedestrian Safety" with the following admonishment: "Drivers and pedestrians alike share the responsibility of keeping themselves and others on the road safe."[13]

None of that is bad advice in and of itself, but the emphasis on pedestrian behavior seems odd given the enormous power imbalance in play. A Toyota Sequoia, for example, weighs six thousand pounds (vehicle weights and their impact on pedestrian safety are discussed in chapter 5). Official sources, however, say that the driver of this vehicle has more or less *equal* responsibility for pedestrian safety as a 111-pound woman trying to cross the road. The subject of relative vulnerability of either party is almost never broached, even though it is intuitively understood that if there is a conflict between the driver of a Toyota Sequoia and an elderly woman, the consequences to the two parties will, in fact, be very different.

Alissa Walker, a writer for the real estate news site Curbed, calls this kind of admonishment "pedestrian shaming."[14] The most common complaint is jaywalking, but pedestrians frequently get shamed for wearing dark clothing, wearing headphones, not making eye contact with drivers, drinking, and even assuming that drivers will stop for them when they have the right-of-way.

Media Treatment

We see the same sort of tropes—victim blaming—frequently from the news media and law enforcement. A classic of this genre comes from Doug MacEachern, a former *Arizona Republic* columnist. His August 2014 column was titled, "You Can't Protect Stupid Pedestrians from Themselves." In that column, MacEachern devotes several paragraphs to outlining Arizona's efforts to address its nation-leading pedestrian fatality problem. He concludes, however, that those very limited efforts will never end pedestrian-car crashes "in large part because you can never make pedestrian stupidity go away entirely."[15] The basis for his column is an anecdote of his drive to work.

The same sorts of assumptions are often implicit in hard news reporting as well. After seven pedestrians were killed in June 2018 in Montgomery County, Maryland, for example, WJLA, the local ABC affiliate, ran a headline that blamed "lazy" pedestrians. The description was borrowed from Captain Tom Didone, who heads Montgomery County's Traffic Division. Didone told the news station, "They're being lazy, not getting to the crosswalk."[16]

One reason news and police reporting about pedestrian crashes can be one-sided is structural. Perfect information about what causes pedestrian crashes is often not available—and often many factors are at play—but the information that is available is, in many cases, lopsided. Because a dead or incapacitated pedestrian is not around to tell his or her side of the story, the driver's account may be the sole basis for the police report.

"The victim is usually at the very least in shock and hyped up on endorphins and not able to communicate as well as the driver, who did not have a traumatic experience," said Steve Vaccaro, an attorney who specializes in bicycle crashes in New York City. In that city, as in many other places, pedestrian victims are also more likely not to be native English speakers, which can be an additional barrier to making their case with authorities.

In addition, traffic collisions, even fatal ones, are rarely the subject of in-depth investigations by reporters or police, which means that there is almost never a follow-up story with any real reporting. Media accounts often rely exclusively on a single police report.

It is clear that local news reporters often view pedestrian deaths as routine and unsexy. Even so, it can still be remarkable how rote and uncritical media coverage on the subject is. The May 2018 death of eighty-year-old Arnulfo Salazar is a good example. Salazar was killed while walking near his home in Charlotte, North Carolina, when an off-duty police officer driving a marked police car struck him. Salazar's family told the local news station, WSOC, that he was an "avid walker" and in great shape. They were devastated by his death and distrusted the police explanation.[17]

Because Salazar was killed by a police officer, his death was bigger news in Charlotte than the average pedestrian crash. Even so, it was not enough to prompt much in the way of investigation. Three different news outlets—WSOC, Charlotte's *Patch*, and the *Charlotte Observer*—all reported, based on police reports, that Salazar "ran into the path" of Officer Jeffrey Page's car.[18]

None of these journalists asked, why? Why would Salazar "run into the path" of a speeding car? Was he suicidal? Was he not of sound mind? (That would conflict with the family's account of his overall health and mental state.) Did he simply misjudge the speed of the car? None of the media accounts offered any further explanation at all.

Was a reader supposed to take it for granted that an eighty-year-old man was running around Charlotte at a speed that would make him impossible for attentive drivers to avoid?

Pedestrians do not have perfect judgment. Sometimes it is hard for them to make accurate split-second assessments about the speed of cars. But in this case and most others, pedestrians are not even given the assumption of a rational self-preservation instinct. The police officer's assignment of fault to the dead octogenarian in Charlotte goes almost completely unquestioned.

News accounts of the death used other information, again obtained directly from police reports, to place blame on Salazar. For example, police told a WSOC reporter that Salazar was not wearing reflective clothing. Salazar's daughter, Jimena, took issue: "It was six o'clock—plain daylight. Why would he be wearing reflective gear before that time?"[19] Pedestrians are under no legal obligation to wear special reflective gear anyway. Nevertheless, the inclusion of that statement—which likely would never have been challenged had not Salazar's daughter had the opportunity to comment—shifts blame to the victim, who is not here to tell his side of the story.

Finally, the media reports all said that Salazar "was not in a crosswalk" when he was struck. You see this phrase incessantly in accounts of pedestrian deaths. The implication is clear: the pedestrian was jay-walking and so is at fault in the crash.

But reporters generally never dig any deeper. For example, not being in a marked crosswalk does not necessarily mean that someone is, in fact—legally speaking—jaywalking. Almost every intersection, under most state laws, is an unmarked crosswalk where pedestrians have the right-of-way, and many journalists—and even police—are not aware of that.

More important is that reporters rarely ask if there was even a crosswalk anywhere nearby. In Salazar's case, it is not clear from media accounts exactly where he was struck, but on State Highway 49, or Tyrone Street, where he was killed, crosswalks are about one-third of a mile apart. By repeating the "not in the crosswalk" statement without studying the context, the reporter sidesteps the question of whether the road itself offered sufficient pedestrian infrastructure and misses an opportunity to tie Salazar's death to wider systemic failures.

Researchers who have studied media treatment of pedestrian deaths call the inclusion of these kinds of details "counterfactuals." Tara Goddard, professor of urban planning at Texas A&M University and coauthor of a 2019 study exploring this phenomenon, wrote that these counterfactuals "imply that a victim could have avoided death or injury if they had behaved differently."[20] Goddard and her colleagues were able to demonstrate empirically that the inclusion of counterfactuals in reporting made readers more likely to place blame on pedestrians.

Dangerous Conventions

When news reports of pedestrian deaths are analyzed with a critical eye, many problematic conventions emerge. MacEwan University researcher Heather Magusin analyzed seventy-one headlines from media accounts of ten pedestrian fatalities that took place in Edmonton, Alberta, in 2016. The study used critical discourse analysis to look at the way subtle language choices reinforce larger power dynamics.

Magusin found almost all the media accounts of pedestrian deaths used a few different syntactic and grammatical cues that subtly placed blame on the victims. For example, almost every account—all but three—used the passive voice to describe the events—"A pedestrian was hit by a car" rather than "Driver hits pedestrian." In this way, almost every account "distanced the driver from the act," she wrote.[21]

In addition, in nearly every case, reporters avoided constructing the events so that the driver was the agent of violence, Magusin found. Thirty-three accounts named the vehicle, rather than the driver, as the source of injuries: for example, "pedestrian hit by a car." Even in the case of drunk driving, the driver "was never directly associated with active verbs of death or violence," she wrote, "suggesting that, regardless of culpability, there is resistance to associating drivers with the violence of traffic incidents."[22]

In most cases, the coverage treated the victims in a strikingly impersonal way as well. In a majority of the cases—forty-two—there were no biographical details about the victim whatsoever. In an additional eighteen cases, the only additional information provided was the person's age. Only eight accounts used a humanizing description—for example, "beautiful young girl" or "always happy"—to describe the victim. Sympathetic coverage was more likely, Magusin found, when the victim fit the profile of a "perfect victim," such as a young girl.[23]

A 2018 study identified a similar pattern when media accounts of cycling deaths in Hillsborough County, Florida, were analyzed. University of South Florida researchers Julie Bond and Erin Sheffels analyzed 189 media accounts of 84 cycling deaths between 2009 and 2018. Among other things, they concluded that media accounts were more likely to blame the victim if there was evidence that the victim was from a lower socioeconomic class. For example, one account noted that the victim was a landscaper and then, in the same sentence, noted that he was improperly riding against traffic when he was struck.[24]

These kinds of reporting conventions influence the way readers perceive the problem. Goddard and her colleagues' 2019 study used thirty-five thousand randomly selected adults to test the way different framing and linguistic choices in news stories influenced the way readers assigned blame in pedestrian fatalities. The research team found that when the pedestrian was centered in the description of events—"Pedestrian struck and killed on east side"—readers were 30 percent more likely to blame the pedestrian than when the driver was centered—"Driver hits, kills pedestrian on east side." In addition, readers who were exposed to articles that had a "thematic" framing, as opposed to centering on individual behavior, were 150 percent more likely to blame "other factors," such as road design.[25]

"The point of this wasn't to say we should just blame drivers outright," said Goddard. "The point was to just show that not only is this framing pervasive; [it] affect[s] people's perception. It's one complex piece of why people don't view this as a public health crisis in the way we do other things."[26]

Goddard said that further research is needed, but it is clear that the problem begins higher up the chain. Part of this is bias found in police reports or press releases upon which news reports are based. The lack of scrutiny from journalists is still a problem. "Don't just uncritically quote those and replicate the language," she said. "As a journalist that's not your job. It's your job to probe it."[27]

Thorough and compassionate reporting on pedestrian deaths is rare, but it can make a big difference. When a mother of seven, Terra Nolden, age thirty-six, was killed in December 2019 in East Cleveland, Ohio, Fox 8 News did not simply reprint the police report. The station sent reporters out to speak to the family and local officials, demanding answers.

Councilwoman-elect Juanita Gowdy is quoted as blaming the Ohio Department of Transportation, which had taken down a number of traffic signals on the street—including at the intersection where Nolden was struck—and was not planning to replace them for months. Other local news stations followed up. One reporter spoke with local organizer Art McKoy, who said of the transportation officials, "The life of this young lady is on their hands."[28]

That kind of reporting was remarkably effective. A week later, the Republican governor of Ohio, Mike DeWine, traveled more than one hundred miles to meet with Nolden's family and hold a press event with leadership in East Cleveland. DeWine promised to have the traffic light installed at the intersection that weekend.[29]

Tragic "Accidents"

Although much of the media coverage around the issue of pedestrian deaths has been harmful, a hopeful shift has begun. Activists for bicyclists and pedestrians in New York especially have campaigned for years to change the way traffic crashes are described.

Transportation Alternatives, an advocacy group, and Families for Safe Streets, a group founded by grieving NYC families who lost loved ones in traffic, have led the charge to drop the euphemistic term *accident* and replace it with the more neutral *crash* or *collision*.

People from the field of traffic safety have been complaining about the term *accident* in the United States since the 1940s. William Haddon, the first head of the then-called National Highway Safety Agency, formed in 1970, "deplored" the term, according to Barron Lerner, a professor of public health at New York University. "He believed [it] made automobile crashes sound inevitable and, by implication, not preventable," Lerner wrote in his 2011 book, *One for the Road*.[30]

Today, however, thanks to efforts like those from Transportation Alternatives, we are seeing a framing shift. In 2013, the New York Police Department changed the name of its Accident Investigation Squad to the more neutral Collision Investigation Squad. "In the past, the term 'accident' has sometimes given the inaccurate impression or connotation that there is no fault or liability associated with a specific event," said Ray Kelly, the city's police commissioner, in announcing the changes.[31]

The shift has permeated the field more widely. More than two dozen state departments of transportation have also moved away from using the term *accident*. A 2016 *New York Times* article quoted Mark Rosekind, head of the National Highway Traffic Safety Administration at the time, as saying, "When you use the word 'accident,' it's like, 'God made it happen.'"[32] And in 2016, the Associated Press updated its industry-standard style guide to advise reporters against using the term *accident* "when negligence is claimed or proven," in which case, the AP wrote, it could be read as "exonerating the person responsible."[33]

Trial by Commenter

Victim blaming is something that all families who lose someone who was walking or biking have to deal with at some point, often on the worst day of their lives, said Kristi Finney, whose twenty-eight-year-old son was killed by a drunk driver while biking in Portland, Oregon, in 2011.[34]

Even though Dustin Finney was killed by an inebriated driver who would eventually be sentenced to five years in prison (the driver's blood alcohol concentration was twice the legal limit when he was tested three hours after the crash occurred), there were still people—a police officer, newspaper commenters—who blamed Dustin, his mother remembers.[35] For example, Dustin was not wearing a helmet, but if he had been, he would have survived, one officer said. But there was not any truth to the officer's statement, said Finney. "I also wondered about the bike helmet thing," she said. "I found out later it wouldn't have made a difference."[36]

After her son's death, she, along with a few other grieving families in the greater Portland region, founded a group called Oregon and Southwest Washington Families for Safe Streets, which helps advocate for changes that can prevent deaths like her son's. Finney reaches out to families who have lost loved ones in traffic crashes and tries to help them get involved with pressing for safety improvements. Parents like her will often testify, using first-person stories, in favor of safety improvement projects.

Finney said that everyone in the group—at least when the death was a pedestrian or a cyclist—has had a similar experience of being blamed for their injuries or death. "It is almost universal I would say if you are not in a car," she said. "They're blamed just for being on the road." She continued, "Someone who's walking on a crosswalk, has the right of way—people will still go online and say, 'My parents taught me how to look before I cross.'"[37]

Raquel Nelson's Stand

Generally, the kinds of assumptions Finney described are never formally challenged. They add to the pain and trauma and stigma the physical crash causes. They may also stand in the way of justice and remuneration for those that were killed and harmed and their families.

But Raquel Nelson's case in Georgia was one of the rare ones that broke through and made people question the standard narrative around pedestrian deaths. In July 2011—just three months after the death of her son AJ—she was sentenced to a year of probation by a Cobb County judge. But the judge also offered her the choice of a retrial.

She chose to fight. That was the beginning of a three-year legal battle to clear her name. A Georgia appeals court upheld her conviction in 2012, but with help from a lawyer who took her case pro bono, Nelson appealed to the Georgia Supreme Court. In 2013, however, the state's highest court refused to hear the case, upholding her conviction.[38]

Throughout Nelson's ordeal, however her case generated an outpouring of sympathetic media coverage—and outrage. In the summer of 2011, Nelson's story was featured on the *Today Show*, National Public Radio, and CNN.[39] A petition calling for her conviction to be overturned had been signed by 135,000 people.[40]

The Nelson case helped highlight the injustice of strict penalties for pedestrian infractions in absence of adequate pedestrian infrastructure. The closest crosswalk in Nelson's case would have required the family to walk two-thirds of a mile out of their way in the dark.[41]

In addition, Nelson's conviction on the charge of vehicular homicide for the crime of jaywalking was widely seen as racist. The NAACP called it "a grave miscarriage of justice when the mother who is still grieving is forced to fight harder for her freedom than the man who killed her son" and said that the case was part of a wider pattern of overzealous prosecution of black defendants.[42]

Yolanda Pierce wrote in the *Guardian* that the Nelson case was an example of criminalizing the poor: "I believe the jury convicted Nelson for the crime of being poor in this country—the crime of not being able to afford a vehicle; the crime of needing to take two buses to buy groceries; the crime of living in an apartment complex located on a busy highway; the crime of being reminded that while many of us live in relative luxury, others are risking their lives for basic necessities."[43]

In June 2013, more than two years after her conviction, Nelson's long ordeal finally came to an end when Cobb County prosecutors agreed to drop the reckless conduct and vehicular homicide charges in exchange for a guilty plea on the jaywalking charge. It was too late to save her son, but Nelson's fight helped shed light on an injustice affecting countless people across the United States. In return, she was ordered to pay $200 and was free to return to her life.[44]

Chapter 4

The Criminalization of Walking

In June 2017, Devonte Shipman, a twenty-one-year-old Jacksonville, Florida, resident, posted a video to his Facebook page that went viral. The footage—shot shakily from a cell phone—showed Shipman and a friend after a Jacksonville sheriff's deputy had stopped them for crossing the street against the light.

It was a relatively routine enforcement for Jacksonville police, and it was not—like so many videos of this genre—a violent confrontation. But the episode—something about the officer's demeanor combined with the pettiness of the offense—still outraged the thousands of people who saw Shipman's post.

When initially approached by Deputy J. S. Bolen, Shipman and his friend seemed genuinely confused.

"What was it we did wrong?" Shipman asked.

Bolen quickly explained that they crossed against the light. He continued, "Get to my car. You are being legally detained. If you disobey . . . I will put you in jail."

Shipman and his friend protested. "For crossing the street, officer?"

"Walk to my car. I'm about to put you in jail," said Bolen.

Shipman—Bolen warned—could be jailed "for seven hours" for a litany of offenses he accumulates while standing there "calmly"—as the *Florida Times-Union* described it—asking questions.[1]

Finally, Shipman gave up and walked to the cruiser, where he was ticketed for jaywalking and for not carrying an ID.

Later that night, Shipman posted the video on his personal Facebook page, and from there it began making its way across the internet. It was shared thirty-seven hundred times before being picked up by all the local news stations and eventually the *Washington Post.* The case prompted an internal investigation by the Jacksonville Sheriff's Office.

Among the more than a half million people who viewed the video was Topher Sanders, a reporter at the nonprofit investigative news organization ProPublica. Sanders, like many others, saw the incident as racial profiling. It made him wonder how often young black men were being stopped by Jacksonville police for jaywalking and how they were being treated. The local newspaper noted that Shipman had been improperly cited for failing to carry an ID, but there is no law in Florida requiring pedestrians to carry a photo ID. (Only drivers are required to do so.)

ProPublica teamed up with the *Florida Times-Union* in Jacksonville and conducted perhaps the most comprehensive investigation of jaywalking enforcement ever. Reporters at the two news organizations combed through twenty-two hundred Jacksonville jaywalking cases between 2012 and 2016.

Their findings confirmed Sanders's suspicions and worse. The review found that a disproportionate number of tickets were issued to black residents, particularly those living in the city's poorest areas. Black people were three times as likely as white people to be ticketed for a pedestrian infraction in Jacksonville, and black people who lived in the poorest zip codes were six times as likely.[2]

The tickets, starting at sixty-five dollars, were more than just a headache for the people stopped. The review found after five years, about half the cases had not been resolved, meaning that they had been neither paid nor dismissed. For very low-income people, they were often life-altering, resulting in crushing collections cases or a potential cascade of legal penalties, such as suspended driver's licenses.

Jacksonville police defended the enforcement on safety grounds, but Sanders and his team found that there was essentially no relationship between high-risk locations for pedestrians and where the tickets were issued.[3] Despite the frequent ticketing, pedestrian safety in Jacksonville eroded during the five-year study period. In fact, the city was ranked the fourth most dangerous metro area in the United States for pedestrians by a national group the same year that Shipman was stopped.[4]

The investigation also raised more fundamental questions about the fairness of Florida's jaywalking laws themselves. There are twenty-eight different infractions on the books in Florida that regulate pedestrian behavior. In addition to what we generally think of as jaywalking, pedestrians in Florida could be stopped and cited for not crossing at a right angle, for walking on the wrong side of the road, for not crossing using the shortest route, or for not walking on the sidewalk, among other things.

The rules were so profuse that practically anyone walking any length would run afoul of one of them, the reporters determined. In fact, Jacksonville sheriff's deputies themselves were caught on video on multiple occasions violating one of Florida's dozens of walking statutes.

Even the police officers charged with enforcing these laws did not seem to understand them. As in Shipman's case, the investigation found that officers often cited people incorrectly. In about half of the 353 cases in which someone was ticketed for not crossing in a crosswalk, the ticket was issued erroneously.[5]

The review also found that Jacksonville police fell victim to a common misunderstanding about jaywalking laws: they assumed that everyone crossing outside a crosswalk was jaywalking.[6] But under Florida law, *every* intersection is treated like a crosswalk, whether or not it is striped—*except* when it is located on the block between two marked crosswalks with traffic signals.

A Pattern of Unequal Enforcement

As alarming as the results of the Jacksonville investigation turned out to be, it is not that exceptional as far as jaywalking enforcement goes. Because the offense is so petty, giving police broad discretion over their response, jaywalking lends itself to biased enforcement. The same pattern seen in Jacksonville has been observed almost everywhere it has been analyzed.

In Sacramento in April 2017, for example, a twenty-four-year-old black man, Nandi Cain Jr., was stopped by police for jaywalking. The stop ended with an arrest, but not before a bystander had filmed police punching Cain eighteen times.[7] The beating made national headlines. To make matters worse, it turned out that Cain was not even jaywalking; dash cam footage later showed that he was crossing legally in an *un*marked crosswalk at an intersection.

A follow-up investigation by the *Sacramento Bee* found that in the year prior to this incident, black residents had received 50 percent of the city's jaywalking tickets, despite making up just 15 percent of the population.[8]

The situation is remarkably similar in Seattle. Black residents received 26 percent of the city's jaywalking tickets in 2016, according to a *Seattle Times'* investigation,[9] despite making up just 7 percent of the city's population.

The bias persisted even as Seattle's police department was under scrutiny for racist enforcement. In 2010, a Seattle police officer was captured punching a teenage girl who had been stopped for jaywalking, and the video went viral. As a result, Seattle police dramatically reduced the number of jaywalking tickets they were issuing, but six years later, the racial disparity had actually gotten worse. In 2017, vexed by the intractableness of the problem, one Seattle City Council member, Lorena Gonzalez, said that she would explore potentially eliminating the city's jaywalking statute altogether, but the issue was never brought before the full council for vote.[10]

The data make a compelling case that jaywalking enforcement is usually racially biased, and it is hard to say whether it actually provides any safety benefit either.

In the United Kingdom, for example, there is no equivalent violation to jaywalking, but the pedestrian safety record there puts the US data to shame. The UK has about half the pedestrian deaths per capita as the United States.[11] The same is true for most of the countries that have the best traffic safety records. In Norway, for example, pedestrians are encouraged to cross at certain locations, but there is no rule against jaywalking, and it is certainly not a crime that police go around punching people for violating. (Cultural differences in traffic safety are discussed in chapter 9.)

The level of risk involved in jaywalking is more complex than many people realize. According to the Governors Highway Safety Association, 72 percent of pedestrians who were killed in 2016 were struck outside an intersection.[12] This figure is often used to imply that most pedestrians who are struck are "jaywalking" and hence at fault, but that notion does not hold up to close scrutiny.

Federally sponsored research in the 1990s looked more closely at the types of situations in which "serious pedestrian crashes" occurred. It found that in serious crashes, pedestrians are stuck in crosswalks almost as often (25 percent of the time) as they are struck "midblock" (26 percent). In the additional almost 50 percent of crashes, pedestrians are struck outside of what are seen as typical pedestrian crossing scenarios. Pedestrians are struck surprisingly often when they are not even on the roadway (8.6 percent of the time). (In most of these cases, pedestrians were struck in parking lots or driveways or when they were standing on the sidewalk where it overlapped with a driveway.) In almost 8 percent of cases, pedestrians are hit by a vehicle traveling in reverse. In 9 percent of cases, the pedestrian was "walking along the roadway," often on a road that did not have sidewalks or where sidewalks were obstructed. And in almost 5 percent of cases, the victim was working on a road construction project, responding to a disabled vehicle, or a child playing in the road.[13] If you look critically at the origins of jaywalking laws, however, it becomes clear that they were initially more about power than safety.

The Origins of the "Jay" Walker

Just over one hundred years ago, around the time automobiles first began appearing in US cities, the concept of jaywalking did not exist at all. On the contrary, prior to the 1920s, pedestrians had unrestricted and unquestioned freedom to roam the streets.

All that changed in the mid-1920s with the introduction of the concept of jaywalking, according to University of Virginia historian Peter Norton. Jaywalking laws amounted to a radical redefinition of what streets were for—and who their rightful users were. And contrary to public perception, Norton said that it did not just happen naturally.[14]

If you look at a historic photo from the early 1900s—of Boston or Cleveland, for example—you will notice that there were no crosswalks at all. Pedestrians amble casually across the streets: women wearing long flowing dresses, men in top hats, and children in knee socks.

At that time, streets, which occupy as much as 30 percent or more of the land area in many cities, functioned as a broad public space. Children used them for play. Merchants sold goods from carts. Neighbors would pause to have a conversation while making their way to alight a streetcar. But even then, that era was fading fast. As soon as cars began appearing on the streets, they started killing people—a lot of people.

The first person ever killed by an automobile in the United States was real estate agent Henry Bliss. In 1899, while exiting a New York City streetcar, Bliss was struck by an electric taxi, or horseless carriage, as they were called then.[15]

It would be more than a decade after that before cars were widely available to the public, but car ownership grew dramatically between the mid-1910s and the early 1920s. Henry Ford's famous innovation—assembly-line production—helped reduce the price of a

Model T from $950 to $290 between 1910 and 1924. And practically overnight, cars started flooding into cities. In St. Louis, for example, there were sixteen thousand registered vehicles in 1916; by 1923, the number had ballooned to one hundred thousand.[16]

By then, traffic deaths had become a widely recognized urban crisis. During the 1920s, about two hundred thousand people were killed. Disproportionately, they were children. In 1925 alone, cars killed about seven thousand children across the United States. City dwellers, and especially parents, were furious, and their fury was overwhelmingly aimed at drivers. On a particularly violent day in 1927 in New York City, eight children were killed in separate crashes. In one case, a mob of onlookers attacked the driver of the truck that struck a child.[17]

In contrast to modern media accounts, the news at the time was unflinching about where to lay the blame: on drivers. The *St. Louis Star*, for example, referred to drivers involved with pedestrian fatalities as "killers." In 1923, an editorial in the *St. Louis Post-Dispatch* said that even in the case of "a child darting into the street" in "the excitement of play," the "plea of unavoidable accident in such cases is the perjury of a murderer."[18]

The notion of Americans' love affair with the automobile—of an eager, frictionless adoption—is a carefully manufactured notion, according to Norton. In the 1910s and 1920s, there was an intense political struggle over the role of the car in American city life. That struggle came down to a fight over who would control the streets: drivers or pedestrians.

On the pedestrian side, the battle was waged in large part by mothers, many of them grieving children lost in car crashes. They formed chapters of the National Safety Council in St. Louis, Philadelphia, and Cleveland, for example, and fought for traffic safety reforms. A major flashpoint came in 1923 when forty-two thousand Cincinnati residents signed a petition for a referendum that would have required cars to have speed governors that limited them to 25 miles per hour within city limits.

On the drivers' side, an aligned group of auto interests (auto dealers, auto clubs, oil companies—what Norton calls "motordom"[19]) was also getting organized to defend their interests. Their goal was towering: to reshape cities for the benefit of drivers. In 1921, for example, at the behest of automotive clubs, boy scouts handed out flyers to pedestrians in Hartford, Connecticut, instructing them how to cross the street and explaining "jay walking."

By the 1930s, the issue had mostly been settled, and streets were redefined as a space for drivers. Pedestrians' movement was tightly restricted to crosswalks, and even then only at the convenience of drivers. One of motordom's most critical victories was the introduction and eventual acceptance of the concept of jaywalking. Around the time of the Cincinnati ballot measure, auto interests began producing propaganda that advanced the notion of the "jay walker." In the 1920s, "jay" was a derogatory term, and branding people who crossed the street midblock as jays was a powerful rhetorical slight. "A jay was a dumb hayseed, a hick, a rube," Norton wrote. "Someone stuck in the nineteenth century."[20]

A turning point came in 1924 when US commerce secretary Herbert Hoover, just five years prior to his election as US president, helped convene a National Conference on Street and Highway Safety. The conference was dominated by auto industry groups, and participants were asked to write a set of model traffic regulations to be used in cities across the United States. In the end, they recommended that pedestrian access be limited to crosswalks—a new concept—and, even then, that pedestrians should only be able to cross essentially when there was no traffic.

This recommendation was a dramatic reordering of the transportation hierarchy. When it was released in 1927 with the backing of the US Department of Commerce, many cities adopted it wholesale. By the 1930s, jaywalking laws were ubiquitous.

It is difficult to overstate just how successful the concept of jaywalking was in shifting blame. Like in the case of Raquel Nelson, when a pedestrian is struck by the driver of a car or truck today, the justice system is often shockingly punitive.

Pedestrian advocates like Atlanta's Sally Flocks, however, are emphatic that jaywalking enforcement does not help keep pedestrians safe—and sometimes it is actively harmful. In 2014, metro Atlanta was ranked the eighth most-dangerous for walkers.[21] The big problem for pedestrians in Atlanta is not inattention or misbehavior, said Flocks, but the roads themselves. "The places where pedestrian fatalities are rising is in the mid suburbs," she said. "Crosswalks are sometimes over a mile and a half apart."[22]

What is really needed in Atlanta are safer crossings, better speed management, and continuous sidewalks, Flocks said, but the messaging that federal agencies use for pedestrian safety contributes to their marginalization by blaming them for the problem. "The education for pedestrians is, 'Cross at crosswalks and wear bright clothing,'" she said. "If you're saying it was their fault they weren't in a crosswalk, it takes the burden off the Department of Transportation."[23]

Although there is not much evidence that jaywalking enforcement improves safety, some approaches do help pedestrians. For example, evidence shows that environmental factors influence how likely pedestrians are to jaywalk in the first place. In the early 1980s, researchers Jason Leonard and Richard Liotta conducted a series of experiments and found that pedestrians were less likely to jaywalk at intersections that presented the walk signal quickly.[24] Other studies have shown that crowded sidewalks, the presence of bus stops, the width of the road, and importantly, the distance to the nearest crosswalk all influence whether a pedestrian will cross mid-block.[25]

A 2014 study conducted by the Federal Highway Administration was able to use environmental factors—like the presence of a right turn lane or the distance between crosswalks—to predict with 90 percent accuracy whether or not a pedestrian would cross mid-block. The study suggests that adding crosswalks, especially at streets where there are bus stops, is an important way to combat jaywalking.[26]

Second, there is good evidence that enforcing yielding rules for drivers helps pedestrian safety, as discussed later in the chapter. There is no a snappy term, no "jaywalking" equivalent for drivers who fail to yield to pedestrians when they are required, and perhaps that is why it is not widely recognized as a problem. Nevertheless, failing to yield—jay driving, if you will—is extremely common, and it is dangerous.

Failing to Yield

A 2018 study in Milwaukee found that at noncontrolled crosswalks—crosswalks with no traffic lights or stop signs—drivers were only yielding to pedestrians 16 percent of the time.[27] A 2014 Chicago study observed the exact same proportion: 16 percent.[28]

As bad as baseline yielding rates are for pedestrians, there is evidence that they are worse for people of color. A 2014 study by researchers from the University of Portland and University of Arizona tested racial bias in yielding behavior in Portland, Oregon. Compared with the three white research subjects attempting crossings, black pedestrians waited 32 percent longer to cross and were passed by twice as many cars.[29]

Nichole Morris, a research psychologist at the University of Minnesota, experienced the high-stakes guessing game facing pedestrians firsthand while conducting an experiment measuring yielding at crosswalks in St. Paul.[30] Morris and a team of researchers spent months crossing sixteen crosswalks in St. Paul, Minnesota, in 2017 and 2016. The experiment was designed to test drivers' adherence with Minnesota law, which requires them to yield to any pedestrian who has lifted at least one foot off the curb to step into the crosswalk, provided that the driver has been given enough distance to stop safely. Dressed in plain clothing, the researchers attempted twenty crossings at each crosswalk twice a week.

When the experiment began, St. Paul had already been making efforts to improve driver yielding to pedestrians. Through a campaign called "Stop for Me," St. Paul police had been conducting "targeted enforcement" whereby plainclothes officers had posed as pedestrians, pulled over drivers who failed to yield, and issued them warnings.

Despite the police effort, when Morris began her research, the yielding rate was terrible: only about 32 percent of drivers were complying with the law. What was worse is that in about 11 percent of cases, drivers were doing something even more threatening: passing cars that *did* yield. Passing a driver who has stopped for a crossing pedestrian can be fatal because the stopped car blocks the view of the pedestrian who is moving right into the path of the oncoming passing car.

Conducting this kind of research was frightening, especially at the beginning, said Morris. "I would have these panicky moments where I would say to myself, 'Is this too dangerous?'" Morris said. "I have to be very honest with anyone working on this study that we are risking our lives to do this work."[31]

The goal of Morris's experiment was to see if driver yielding could be improved by using tricks from the field of human factors psychology. The experiment showed that with the right attention and strategy, it could.

One thing that helped tremendously was a pair of signs. The signs, which looked like regular traffic signs, displayed the yielding rate from the previous week. Each week, Morris and her team updated the signs with the numbers they had recorded. The signs drew on the principles of social norming and implied surveillance to encourage people to yield.

Social norming is meant to apply social pressure to engage in a behavior by suggesting that the majority of people are doing it. The first week Morris and her team posted the sign it read: "Percent of drivers stopping for pedestrians—Last Week: 44%, Record: 44%."

Over time, however, the strategy worked. The signs got people's attention and got them talking about the issue, including a huge

This sign was posted in St. Paul, Minnesota, during an experiment that tested using methods from behavioral psychology to improve yielding. (Photo: Nichole Morris, University of Minnesota)

round of media attention in August 2018. All of a sudden, people all over St. Paul were debating whether 44 percent was a good or a bad yielding rate.

Over the next few weeks, with more enforcement, with social norming, and—finally—with some small changes to the infrastructure, Morris and her team were able to raise the yielding rate dramatically. For the final phase of the experiment, they installed small yellow vertical "Stop for Pedestrians" signs in the middle of the street, within the center line. At the end of the experiment, after months of enforcement, media attention, and various rounds of street-design changes, the pedestrian yielding rate rose to 72 percent, and the number of drivers who were passing yielding drivers—an extremely dangerous maneuver—fell to just 1 percent.[32]

Chapter 5

Killer Cars

ON A SUNNY DAY IN OCTOBER 2017, twenty-two-month-old Neallie Junior Saxon III, still in diapers, was playing in front of his grandmother's house in Deerfield Beach, Florida. The street where he toddled with some neighbor children, NW Fourth Place, is a quiet, narrow residential one with speed humps—the kind of street that tens of thousands of people live on across Broward County. That day, it was full of children playing, as they often did, with parents and neighbors watching from their front porches.

Neallie's mother, Jasmine Smith, was inside the house, when "they just said my baby got hit by a car. . . . I ran outside and he was laying there in so much blood, lifeless," she told a local news station. She cradled the little boy in her arms and started begging him, "Come back to me please, come back to me."[1]

Mirlande Mardice told investigators that she was distracted by watching other children near the street as she drove and that she never saw the one-year-old child. She struck little Neallie with her 2007 Hyundai Santa Fe and did not stop until she reached a stop sign a few hundred feet away. At that point, neighbors, who had witnessed the little boy being crushed, dragged Mardice out of her car and started beating her.

"People were hysterical," the local newspaper reported. "The child's aunt passed out in the street."[2]

Mardice suffered broken facial and skull bones and was treated at a nearby hospital. "They beat her unmercifully," a neighbor told the local news station WPLG. Mardice reportedly fought back, screaming, "No, I didn't mean to! I wouldn't do that to a child!"[3]

Neallie was airlifted to the hospital, where he died the following day.

Witnesses had mixed opinions about whether Mardice was trying to flee or simply unaware. His mother told the local news that she was certain the driver had seen the boy. The police investigating the case, however, were willing to give Mardice a pass.

"He was shorter than the bumper, and the driver—possibly distracted by the other children—probably couldn't see him," a spokeswoman for the Broward County Sheriff's Office is paraphrased as telling the local newspaper.[4]

A teddy bear and a truck were placed at the spot of the crash as a memorial. More than two years later, Mardice has not been charged or cited in the case.

Could a standing, nearly two-year-old really be rendered invisible by the bumper of a midsized SUV, as police assumed in this case? If so, how did vehicles that have that kind of vulnerability end up on the roads?

The car Mardice was driving, a 2007 Santa Fe, is not a huge SUV by US standards. It weighs thirty-eight hundred pounds—about fifteen hundred pounds less than a 2007 Cadillac Escalade—but it is still about one thousand pounds heavier than a Honda Civic.

The Santa Fe belongs to a class of cars—crossover vehicles—that have experienced huge growth since the introduction of the first model, the Toyota RAV4, to the United States in 1996. In 2018, crossover SUVs topped cars (sedans) as the top-selling US vehicle type.[5] It is hard to overemphasize just how suddenly and completely crossovers have come to dominate the auto market in recent years. When the economy was still recovering from a recession, in 2012, the vehicle mix was almost the opposite: 83 percent of vehicles sold in the United States were sedans.[6]

"The sedan segment is dying," Tom McParland wrote on the auto news site Jalopnik in 2018. That year, for example, Ford was selling about half as many Fusions as it did just a few years earlier, in 2014, he noted. "Honda is struggling to sell the Accord. Think about that for a second—the Honda Accord is pretty much the car to beat for the mid-size sedan segment, and always has been, even when it constantly battled with the Toyota Camry to be number one. Now it's sitting on the lot while the CR-Vs gobble up the sales."[7]

Responding to the changing market, Fiat Chrysler announced that it would stop making sedans for US sales altogether in 2016. By 2018, the others of the Detroit-based "Big Three" automakers—Ford and GM—had also all shifted focus away from sedans to trucks and SUVs, laying off workers across the Rust Belt as they ended production of the Cruise, Focus, Taurus, Fiesta, and hybrid vehicles like the C-Max and Volt.[8]

Hyundai marketed the Santa Fe specifically to families with children as a carpool car and had great success, at times struggling to keep up with supply.[9] Among crossovers, the vehicle is considered a safe one. In fact, U.S. News and World Report ranked it the cheapest car to insure in 2009.[10]

Riding High

For buyers of crossover SUVs, being higher off the ground is a big selling point. In a 2014 article for the Atlantic, Alexis Madrigal wrote that in the 2010s, buyers "settled into the idea that they might not actually go off-roading with their vehicles. They would not climb mountains. But they liked riding high."[11]

But with riding higher—as well as added weight—come some drawbacks in terms of visibility in addition to other risks to pedestrians, especially children. The top of a Hyundai Santa Fe's bumper is two-and-a-half feet high.[12] Compared to the Honda Civic, the top bumper height is nearly a foot higher, producing a bigger blind spot.

Is that height potentially enough to obscure a two-year-old child? It turns out that the answer is yes—easily.

Just how big are the blind spots around big vehicles? It varies a lot, depending on the type and the model, but they can be scandalously large.

In a special report in 2019, WTHR News in Indianapolis used a traffic cone approximating the height of a toddler to measure the blind zone in front of twenty-two vehicles. For the car that rated worst, a Cadillac Escalade, the cone was not visible to a five-foot, four-inch-tall woman sitting at a normal posture in the driver's seat until the cone was ten feet two inches away. In a Dodge Ram, it was nine feet ten inches. In a Ford Explorer, it was eight feet five inches. The best performer, a Toyota Camry, on the other hand, was three feet three inches.[13]

Rear blind spots can also be massive. In 2011, the consumer safety group KidsandCars.org did an experiment to test out the blind spot behind an SUV. The organization found that it could place sixty-two children in a group behind the rear of the car and all sixty-two would be totally invisible in both the rear window and rearview mirrors.[14]

Children between ages one and two, like Neallie Saxon, are particularly vulnerable to what are known as frontovers and backovers, slow-speed collisions in which the driver slowly strikes or rolls over a child who is standing or sitting in the car's blind spot. According to KidsandCars.org, an astounding fifty children *per week* are injured or killed in backover collisions—most in their own driveways. In 70 percent of the cases, the driver is a parent or close relative.[15] These collisions are called "bye-bye crashes" because often a child will run to wave good-bye to a mom or dad, unaware that the driver cannot see them, before being crushed under the wheels.

Neallie's case is more similar to a frontover. These collisions are rarer, but they have been rising as the number of Americans driving SUVs and pickup trucks has risen in recent years.

In 2019, the consumer safety group KidsandCars.org and news station WTHR in Indianapolis conducted an experiment to see how many children could sit in front of a 2011 Chevy Tahoe before they would be visible to the driver. Seventeen children were completely obscured by the forward blind zone. More would have fit, but the organization was limited by how many children they could find whose parents agreed to participate. (Photo: KidsandCars.org)

Between 2006 and 2010 in the United States, 358 children were killed in frontover collisions. By comparison, between 1996 and 2000, the number was just 24.[16]

"We can't see over the hood like we used to be able to," Amber Rollins, director of KidsandCars.org told the ABC news affiliate in Arizona. "And with the increase in popularity with big trucks and SUVs and we see a lot of people raising them and putting big tires on them, all of that stuff increases the blind zones."[17]

These kinds of deaths—if they take place in driveways, as many do—are not included in official government traffic fatality reporting. Moreover, they are just the tip of the iceberg when it comes to pedestrian deaths involving SUVs in the United States.

In 2018, a team of investigative reporters at the *Detroit Free Press* and *USA Today* started investigating what was causing the rise in pedestrian deaths.[18] "I think, like a lot of people, we started out with the assumption that maybe this is a crisis of distraction, especially distracted walking," *USA Today* reporter Nathan Bomey, who was part of the investigative team, said.[19]

Instead, quite quickly their focus shifted to SUVs. Between 2009 and 2016, there was an 81 percent increase in the number of pedestrians killed in crashes with SUVs, according to a report by the Insurance Institute for Highway Safety in 2018.[20] As vehicles get larger and heavier, pedestrian crashes, when they do occur, are becoming more deadly. In just five years, from 2010 to 2015, holding the number of pedestrian crashes equal, the odds of dying in a pedestrian crash increased 29 percent.

It is not just that SUVs are heavier—although they are heavier—and that exerts greater force. Being taller, they also, critically, strike pedestrians higher on the body.

The heights of the front ends of cars and SUVs vary quite a bit, but this information is not publicly collected and made available anywhere by automakers or safety regulators. So, for research purposes, I went out and measured.

For sedans—a Volkswagen Jetta and a Ford Fiesta—the top of the front end was about two and a half feet high. A minivan, meanwhile—a Chrysler Town and Country—was a little bit higher: closer to three feet. Some crossover SUVs—a Ford Escape and a Buick Encore—are just a bit higher than that: slightly more than three feet. But there is a wide range. A Jeep Wrangler and a Jeep Grand Cherokee, for example, are about three-and-a-half-feet tall—a full foot higher than a sedan.

The Ford Expedition and the GMC Sierra—a full-size SUV and a pickup, respectively—are both nearly four feet high where the hood meets the front end.[21] In addition, the shapes are important. The front end of a large pickup or SUVs is very boxy and flat compared to the sloping front end of the Ford Focus.

The author standing in front of a sedan. Sedans strike pedestrians low on the body, causing injuries to the legs and throwing them up on the hood. (Photo: Angie Schmitt)

The author in front of an SUV. SUVs strike pedestrians higher on the body and can push them under the wheels. (Photo: Angie Schmitt)

That high front end is very bad news for pedestrians because higher bumpers hit pedestrians higher on the body, where our vital organs live. To put it in perspective, the top of the front end of a Ford Focus would hit me, at five foot six, in the upper thigh. A crossover SUV, meanwhile, would strike me just above the waist. The top of the front end of the Sierra and Expedition would strike me right in the middle of the chest.

Getting struck by a car in the abdomen is much worse for survival odds than getting hit in the legs. A 2006 study comparing 526 pedestrian crashes involving SUVs and cars found that those struck by SUVs were at substantially higher risk for injuries to the abdomen.[22]

That is one reason the National Highway Traffic Safety Administration (NHTSA) estimates that pedestrians struck by an SUV are two to three times more likely to be killed than those struck by a car.

And for child pedestrians, who are more likely to be hit in the head, the risk is about quadrupled.[23]

Pedestrians who are hit low in the body—by a Ford Focus, for example—tend to fall forward and hit the front of a car, with their head hitting the windshield, which often cracks and warps. Often the motion of the car pins them to the windshield, where they remain until the car comes to a stop.

Meanwhile, not only might a child like Neallie Saxon be rendered invisible by the high profile of an SUV; he might then be struck in the head—the kind of injury most likely to be fatal—and then pushed under the tires and run over.

Auto safety researchers have been warning about this problem since the early 2000s. But the catastrophic impacts of SUVs for pedestrian

The author's four-year-old son in front of a lifted Ford F250.
(Photo: Angie Schmitt)

safety had been forgotten—or ignored—at least until pedestrian deaths started their recent upward march.

One of the first to name the problem was university researcher Clay Gabler, who studies injury biomechanics. In the early 2000s, he conducted a study that found that large SUVs were causing about 110 deaths for every 1,000 collisions with pedestrians compared to about 45 deaths for sedans. When Gabler was interviewed for the science news site *New Scientist* in 2003, he said that there needed to be attention paid to the increased risk that SUVs presented to "the forgotten crash victims:" pedestrians. "Despite over 4000 pedestrian deaths a year, there are no pedestrian impact safety regulations under serious consideration in the US," he said at the time, calling for "radical design changes" to SUVs, especially changes that would make the front ends more sloping and "car-like."[24] But those calls were obviously ignored.

High hoods may also present special risks to wheelchair users. In 2018, Neil Kelly was the subject of an article in the *Cincinnati Enquirer* with the headline "Dear Drivers: This Man Would Like You to Stop Hitting Him."[25] The twenty-eight-year-old Cincinnati resident, who has been partially paralyzed since birth, was struck by vehicles on three separate occasions during a ten-month period while trying to commute by bus to his downtown job as a social services worker.

Not every crash was serious, fortunately for Kelly. But even though he said in interviews, ironically, "I've been really lucky," getting constantly hit by cars was nearly debilitating. The first time he was hit, in October 2017, he was trying to cross a downtown Cincinnati street on the way to his office. There were two right-turn lanes at the intersection where he crossed. The driver in the outside turn lane yielded, but the driver of an SUV in the inside lane did not see him and continued her turn.

Kelly missed three days of work after that first crash. But worse, he said, was the damage to his wheelchair. The special wheelchair he uses cost $50,000, and it was totaled. Nonetheless, Kelly was forced to continue using it for an additional ten months while he haggled with the insurance companies.

Visibility was likely a factor, he said. In each case, the vehicle was a large vehicle—two SUVs and one church van. "I think part of the problem was that I'm lower than most adults," he said. "Not so low that I'm shorter than a kid. I measured it. I think I'm like four-foot-seven from the top of my head to the ground."[26]

That is fifty-five inches, which is taller than any of the full-size SUVs and pickup trucks I measured, but not by a lot. It is only about eleven inches taller than the front end of a Ford Expedition and only ten inches higher than a GMC Sierra.

Wheelchair users like Kelly are already at increased risk for being hit by cars trying to cross the street. A 2015 study found that the pedestrian mortality rate for wheelchair users was 36 percent higher than that of the general population.[27] These visibility issues are compounded by a range of other issues wheelchair users face in the pedestrian environment, from sidewalk obstructions to inaccessible curbs.

Trying to adapt, Kelly has since gotten an orange flag to make himself more visible. "I take a lot of time to cross the crosswalk now," he said. "I really only have the use of one hand, so I really pay attention to my right side. Because I'd really be in trouble if something happened to my right arm."[28]

Runaway Horsepower

Another vehicle trend may also be aggravating the pedestrian safety crisis. Research has shown that "overpowered cars"—cars with a high horsepower-to-weight ratio—promote speeding. A 2016 study found that drivers of vehicles in the top 10 percent in horsepower-compared-to-weight were 38 percent more likely to speed by more than 10 miles per hour than drivers of those in the bottom 10 percent.[29]

Unfortunately for pedestrians, vehicles have gotten much more powerful in recent years. According to the Insurance Institute for Highway Safety (IIHS), the average vehicle power (horsepower per one hundred pounds) increased by 60 percent for cars, 65 percent for pickup trucks, and 66 percent for SUVs between model years 1985 and 2015.[30]

The IIHS reports that among 1981 model year vehicles, for example, 98 percent of vehicles had less than two hundred horsepower and 45 percent had less than one hundred by model year 2019, a majority had horsepower above two hundred. And fully 24 percent had horsepower above three hundred.

Officials at the US Environmental Protection Agency (EPA) sounded the alarm about this horsepower arms race in 2008 and called for an end to six-hundred-horsepower sports cars and four-hundred-horsepower pickup trucks,[31] but that call has been unheeded. Since the mid-1980s, increases in horsepower have eaten away almost all the increases in fuel economy, EPA data show. "In the two decades before model year 2004, technology innovation was generally used to increase vehicle power, and weight increased due

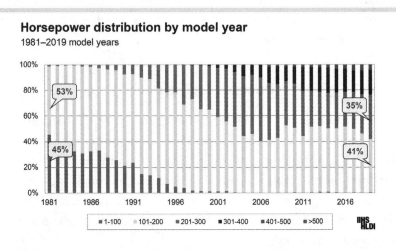

Cars have become much more powerful over the last few decades, which may play a role in the pedestrian safety crisis. (Graph: Insurance Institute for Highway Safety)

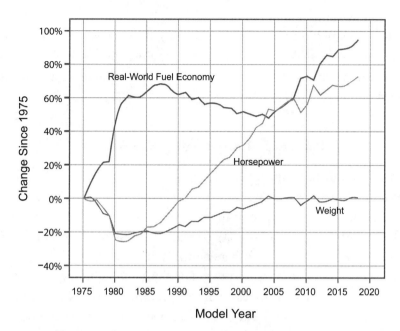

*(Source: US Environmental Protection Agency, 2019,
Automotive Trends)*

to changing vehicle design, increased vehicle size, and increased content," the agency wrote in a summary of industry trends. "During this period, average new vehicle fuel economy steadily decreased and CO_2 emissions correspondingly increased."[32]

Eric D. Lawrence, an auto writer for the *Detroit Free Press*, said that the motivation for carmakers is much the same as with SUVs: sales and hype. "Fiat Chrysler, for instance, got tremendous mileage, pardon the pun, by going all-in on horsepower," he said. "A beast like the Dodge Demon"—840 horsepower—"was only a limited-run production, but the publicity helped move other high-horsepower Dodge offerings."[33]

Dodge's marketing for these vehicles also shamelessly targets the most dangerous group of drivers: young men. A 2010 Super Bowl ad aired to 106 million people for the Charger (horsepower 707) was called "Man's Last Stand" and, according to one analysis, presented the car "as a last defense of manhood against the symbolic castration betokened by the encroaching forces of bureaucratization and empowered femininity."[34]

Pedestrian Impact Safety Regulations

Even though the concept has been occasionally debated since the 1970s, US vehicle safety regulations have never imposed any standards on automakers specifically to protect people outside the vehicles: pedestrians or cyclists. The United Nations has recommended such regulations for all member countries since 2004,[35] and the European Union imposed rules to protect pedestrians beginning in 2010.[36]

Europe's New Car Assessment Programme (Euro NCAP) tests and scores vehicles on head impacts to pedestrians at 40 kilometers per hour (about 25 miles per hour) for both adults and children. To improve their scores, automakers have introduced safety features such as "active hood systems," which raise the hood automatically during a collision with a pedestrian so as to soften the blow (Tesla uses these systems in Europe, and Buick uses them in China).[37] Automakers have also adjusted by making their hoods slighter higher and more deformable so to soften the impact and have added such features as automatic emergency braking.

Passive safety features on the front ends of large vehicles have been shown effective. A study from Germany found that pedestrians struck by cars with some of the highest Euro-NCAP pedestrian safety ratings were 35 percent more likely to survive a collision than those hit with cars with some of the lowest.[38]

In 2015, the Obama administration made a move that would have been a major advancement. Citing SUV dangers specifically,[39] the US Department of Transportation introduced a plan to add pedestrian safety scores to crash ratings that the NHTSA gives to cars. In its proposed rule-making, the NHTSA noted that efforts to regulate vehicles for pedestrian safety in Europe and Japan "have likely contributed to a downward trend in pedestrian fatalities."[40]

This overdue step forward would not have specifically imposed any requirements on automakers in the name of pedestrian safety; it is just a rating system. Strong ratings in the new car assessment program are nevertheless very sought after by automakers, who use them for marketing, and the ratings would act as a strong enticement to challenge them to design safer vehicles.

Not all automakers were happy about the proposed new safety ratings, however. In its comments to regulators, General Motors, which is heavily invested in SUVs and pickups, objected to the creation of a separate category for pedestrian safety.[41]

Some foreign automakers appeared to be more receptive. In its comments, Toyota said that the pedestrian safety score would help promote "global harmonization" with standards in Europe and other countries.[42] (Japan, where Toyota is headquartered, has regulated vehicle design for pedestrian safety since 2003.)

When Donald Trump was elected president in 2016 on an antiregulation platform, the pedestrian safety ratings measure in the United States stalled. The NHTSA would not tell the *Detroit Free Press*, for example, during the newspaper's investigation when the rule would move forward.

Finally, late in 2019, the NHTSA announced that it would be updating its five-star rating system to "consider new technologies tied to the safety of pedestrians and other vulnerable road users such as cyclists."[43] Exactly what is in the new rule will not be known until it is released, but according to the NHTSA news release, it seems that the agency will limit its ratings to whether or not cars include partially automated features like automatic emergency braking or automatic pedestrian detection. The NHTSA will likely stop short of evaluating how different body designs and different vehicle styles affect pedestrian safety.

Back in the 1960s and 1970s, after Ralph Nader published *Unsafe at Any Speed*, these kinds of improvements—passive safety features,

features that protect someone from devastating injury even in the event of a crash—were added to the interior of cars. Additions like airbags, seat belts, and padded dashboards all help absorb the impact of the blow when someone seated inside a car is in a crash. (All were initially opposed as standard equipment by auto companies. Airbags, for example, did not become standard until thirty years after they were invented, a decision that was litigated all the way to the US Supreme Court.)[44]

To help save pedestrians, the front ends of cars need to be soft and collapsible. Hard internal parts, like engines, need to be moved away from the bumper. Hoods can be designed to pop up slightly and then give slightly like a cushion when they strike a person, experts say. "All these [are] things you see on the interior of the car—let's get airbags to soften it up, remove sharp edges," said Shaun Kildare, research director for the consumer safety group Advocates for Highway and Auto Safety. "So now we have to apply that to the outside of the vehicle."[45]

Consumer advocate Clarence Ditlow told *Automotive News* before his death in 2016 that "pedestrian protection is one of the last frontiers of vehicle safety." He added, "NHTSA has been reluctant to regulate it because it so closely relates to styling."[46]

In part due to the soaring popularity of SUVs, even nongovernmental safety groups seem hesitant to impose any restraint on their sales or marketing. Lacking action by the federal government, the Insurance Institute for Highway Safety, an independent, industry-funded safety group, moved in 2019 to add its own category to its influential safety rankings to incorporate pedestrian safety, but the ratings will only evaluate tech additions like pedestrian detection systems and automatic braking (discussed in chapter 8), not differences in vehicle shape or size and its impacts on pedestrian safety. In fact, the organization gave three of the four top safety ratings in its first round to SUVs.[47] A spokesperson for the organization said that "SUVs and pickups are not going away. Forcing design changes to the front ends of vehicles is more of a challenge."[48]

Big Cars, Big Profits

The unfortunate reality is that the big, blunt noses of SUVs that kill pedestrians also sell cars—and at a big markup for automakers. In 2017, the average selling price for a midsized crossover SUV was $37,800, according to a Kelley Blue Book analysis—or about $13,000 more than the average midsized sedan. The selling price for small crossovers averaged $28,350, almost $9,000 more than a compact car.[49]

That extra sales price becomes "margin builders for automakers," a market analyst for Kelley Blue Book told *Automotive News*.[50] "They cost more or less the same to build."

But although consumers have clearly embraced SUVs, it has not been without encouragement from the auto industry. The auto industry spends a staggering amount of money trying to influence consumers. In 2018, the industry spent $34.5 billion on advertising. Outside of retail in general, no US industry spends more on advertising than the auto industry. These ads work, and they overwhelmingly pushed Americans toward SUVs and large trucks.

Nine of the ten top-advertised vehicles in late 2017 were SUVs or pickups, according to an analysis by CNBC.[51] Ford, for example, spent $180 million in 2017 advertising its F-150 pickup, but only $10 million advertising its Fusion and C-Max (a hybrid sedan) combined. Chevy, meanwhile, spent a little over $100 million advertising its Silverado, compared to just over $10 million advertising the Volt, its hybrid vehicle, and practically nothing advertising the Bolt, its electric vehicle.[52]

As the market moves toward SUVs, even the cars that remain on the market have been growing in size. For its 2019 model, Kia added 3.2 inches in length to its Forte compact car. Volkswagen added 1.3 inches to its 2019 Jetta, and Toyota added 2 inches to its Avalon. A 2011 Fiesta, for example, before Ford killed it, was 14 percent wider, 10 percent longer, and 37 percent heavier than the Fiesta of the 1970s.[53] "Passenger cars are attempting to compete with SUVs," Cars.com editor Joe Wiesenfelder said, by getting bigger.[54]

The same bigger, wider, heavier trend is apparent in some of the oldest SUV models as well. The 2019 Toyota RAV4—one of the best-selling cars in the United States—weighs about one thousand pounds more than its 1999 version. The 2018 Jeep Cherokee weighs about eight hundred pounds more than its 1999 version.

The Dark Appeal of the SUV

One of the early critics of SUVs, former *New York Times* Detroit bureau chief Keith Bradsher, has said that the same features that kill pedestrians help automakers sell cars. Bradsher, author of the 2002 book *High and Mighty*, wrote that with SUVs, automakers tapped into primitive subconscious human impulses.[55] Those were not always so magnanimous.

One of the pioneering minds of the SUV industry, Bradsher wrote, was marketing savant named Clotaire Rapaille. His ideas about Americans' base desires helped shape marketing and vehicle design at Chrysler in the 1990s. Rapaille's theory was that Americans are terrified of crime. He blamed this fear not on a rational assessment of crime risks but on exposure to violent television and video games and the aging of the US population in general.

"The archetype of a sport utility vehicle reflects the reptilian desire for survival," Bradsher wrote.[56] In other words, Americans liked the idea of being able to potentially crush whatever or whoever stood in their way. "I usually say, 'If you put a machine gun on top of them, you will sell them better,'" Rapaille is quoted as saying. "Even going to the supermarket, you have to be ready to fight."[57]

Although *High and Mighty* was published in 2002, in hindsight much of it looks prophetic. In 2014, for example, BMW unveiled a bulletproof version of its X5 sport utility vehicle, which it described

The 1997 RAV4 weighed as little as twenty-six hundred pounds.
(Photo: Wikimedia Commons)

The 2019 RAV4 Hybrid is much larger and heavier than its original de-
sign. It weighs about eleven hundred additional pounds and has a much
more aggressive—meaner-looking—front end. Those kinds of features
help sell SUVs, but they kill pedestrians. Excluding pickup trucks, the
RAV4 was the best-selling car in the United States in 2018.
(Photo: Wikimedia Commons)

as "AK-47 proof."[58] By late 2019, one newspaper reported that "the market for bulletproof vehicles is exploding."[59]

Safety researchers call these kinds of features on a car or truck—how likely a particular model is to kill or injury occupants of *other* vehicles when there is a crash—aggressivity. In addition to killing pedestrians, some of the popular features in SUVs—such as high-riding front ends—also have horrifying impacts for drivers of sedans. An IIHS study analyzing crash statistics from 1989 to 2016 found that SUVs were 32 percent more likely to kill occupants of *other* cars in a crash,[60] even though a great deal of energy has been invested by automakers to reduce "overlap" crash problems in recent years.

Without any pushback, there is no sign that SUV sales are slowing down. A more disturbing recent development, from a safety perspective, is the embrace of SUVs by police forces. About one hundred thousand police vehicles are sold in the United States annually, MotorTrend estimates,[61] and the SUV is now the vehicle of choice.

The Police Interceptor Utility, a modified Ford Explorer, has been the highest-selling police vehicle since 2014.[62] "The 2020 Ford Police Interceptor Utility is a beast," Chris Terry, a Ford product communications spokesman, told the *Detroit Free Press* in 2018, bragging that it could go up to 150 miles per hour. "When a car blows past you at 120 miles an hour, you need to get that person off the road as quickly as possible in the interest of public safety."[63] (Police chases kill about 355 Americans annually, according to the Bureau of Justice Statistics. About one-third of those killed are innocent bystanders.[64])

To make matters worse, police SUVs are often outfitted with so-called bull or push bars—steel or aluminum bars affixed to the grille. These add-on features add to the aggressivity of the front end of SUVs. The bars give these trucks a macho, intimidating look and can be seen as an example of the creeping militarization of police equipment.

Push bars or bull bars should probably not be allowed at all on vehicles that are used for city driving. Researchers reviewed nine studies in 2012 and found that these bars increase risks to pedestrians, especially child pedestrians, by concentrating the force of the blow as much as ten times. The international team of researchers urged regulators to take action.[65] Bull bars have been banned in the United Kingdom for their deadly effects on pedestrians since 2010, but in the United States, the NHTSA has never been involved with regulating aftermarket vehicle modifications.

Unfortunately, under the Trump administration, that seems unlikely to change. "Under President Trump, the bureaucracy in Washington is being hollowed out," *USA Today*'s Bomey said. "Career bureaucrats are leaving. When you have that lack of manpower in addition to the lack of resources to actually run NHTSA, there may not be enough people to handle it."[66]

Even the antiregulation Trump administration might be forced to act if public pressure were really intense, he added. But there has not been much outcry on the public's behalf. "People aren't rising up and demanding this," he said.

Meanwhile, as SUVs have gotten more fuel efficient in the last decade, "the liberal critique of the SUV has faded," he added. "Americans are sort of culpable from a cultural perspective," he said. "We don't really think about this as a health crisis."[67]

Chapter 6

The Ideology of Flow

In 2008, Whitney Stump got fed up with watching drivers run the stop sign in front of his house in Muncie, Indiana. Stump, a twenty-seven-year-old father and graduate student, reached out to city officials and requested a crosswalk. But Muncie City Hall refused his request, saying that a crosswalk was not needed because the intersection—the corner of Dicks and North Streets—was not by a school.

So Stump took matters into his own hands. He went out to the quiet residential corner and carefully painted a crosswalk himself.

To Stump's credit, the paint job looked professional. Local police and city hall were not pleased, however. His act of resistance made the national news after he was arrested not once but twice; the second time, police caught him touching up his work. Stump eventually served ten hours in jail on charges of criminal mischief but was unapologetic to the end. "If they're not going to provide a safe environment for me and my community, then I believe I have a moral obligation," he told a local news station.[1]

This character—the crosswalk vigilante—pops up in the news every so often. In 2013, Anthony Cardenas of Vallejo, California, "got tired of seeing people get run over here all the time" and painted a crosswalk on a four-lane street near his home. He was arrested but "received a hero's welcome" in his neighborhood upon posting bail, CBS Sacramento reported.[2]

More recently, in 2019, two local men painted a crosswalk on 16th Street Southeast in Washington, DC, following the death of a thirty-one-year-old pedestrian. The District Department of Transportation said that it had planned to install a crosswalk at the location, where it had been requested more than 250 days prior to the death of Abdul Seck, but city officials told radio station WTOP that they were waiting for the right weather.[3]

These kinds of stories—local man with a paint can versus traffic safety authorities—can be a little amusing. But they are symptomatic of the real sense of anger people feel when being refused a basic, low-cost safety amenity like a crosswalk.

These stories also raise a good question: Who dictates where and when crosswalks are needed? In the traffic engineering profession, that responsibility belongs not to nearby residents, elected officials, or even the engineering staff in the town, but to an obscure technical book called the *Manual on Uniform Traffic Control Devices*.

The *Manual on Uniform Traffic Control Devices*

The *Manual on Uniform Traffic Control Devices* (*MUTCD*) is one of the key federal guidebooks for US road design, mandating the rules for signals and signs that run through every city and hamlet in the United States. The purpose of this eight-hundred-page document is to provide uniformity in the look of highways across the nation, from the northern territories of Alaska to the tropics of Key West.

The *MUTCD* not only tells engineers where and when to install crosswalks, it also tells them how they should look, which road signs are allowable and what they should say, what color they should be, and what font they should use. And the *MUTCD*—quite clearly—discourages traffic engineers from installing crosswalks. To understand why, a little background on the ideology in the transportation engineering profession is needed.

"When considering how to make an intersection safe, engineers begin with a bias toward flow," wrote Dan Albert in *Are We There Yet*, a history of the American automobile. "The technocratic language of highway and traffic engineering obscures an ideology. Traffic engineering trades safety for mobility."[4]

Crosswalk Warrants

This same kind of ideology—rules that privilege the speed of cars and trucks over the safety of pedestrians—is seen throughout the *MUTCD*. One of the most striking examples of this "bias toward flow" is the manual's instruction about where and when to add a marked crosswalk with a traffic signal.

The *MUTCD* instructs engineers that a crosswalk with a traffic signal is only "warranted" if ninety-three pedestrians *per hour* are crossing at the location in question. Failing that, the *MUTCD* states that a crosswalk with a traffic signal can be warranted if *five* pedestrians are struck by cars at the location *in a single year*. In other words, five people have to be maimed or killed in a single year at a single location for it to warrant delaying drivers with a traffic light.

The reason is that traffic engineers do not want to inconvenience drivers. The rule, said Christopher Monsere, professor and chair of civil and environmental engineering at Portland State University, is "purely delay based. We know from the research that giving vehicles a red signal is the best way to get pedestrians across," Monsere said. "The warrant to get that . . . is very high."[5]

In recent years, more progressive engineers have begun speaking out about the bias toward flow. One of them is Peter Furth, a professor of civil engineering at Northeastern University. In 2016, Furth testified to the Boston City Council that standard engineering practices were putting pedestrians in the city at risk.

For example, the Landmark Interchange by Fenway Park in Boston required pedestrians to wait almost two minutes to cross the street. The signals, Furth testified, were programmed by a standard engineering program called Synchro, which "is based on minimizing auto delay, and it doesn't even calculate pedestrian delay." But two minutes is just too long to ask pedestrians to wait for a walk signal. Faced with that long of a wait, many will jaywalk, and some may get hit and killed, Furth testified.[6]

Throughout the *MUTCD*, pedestrians' safety is traded for time savings for drivers. Furth pointed out, for example, that to reduce vehicle delay, the *MUTCD* allows engineers to program traffic lights so that pedestrians have just enough time to get to the median, in the center of the street. Then they must wait—with traffic whizzing by—for a second walk signal to complete the crossing.

Defenders of the *MUTCD* will point out that engineers are allowed to use their so-called engineering judgment about many of these rules. In other words, there is a certain degree of flexibility to make decisions that deviate from the *MUTCD*'s guidelines, if local circumstances call for it.

Engineers nevertheless feel a lot of pressure to abide by *MUTCD* guidance. There is a common perception that engineers who abide by the manual's standards—and the municipalities and states they represent—are mostly shielded from liability, but that is not strictly correct; engineers simply have to document their engineering judgment if they deviate from the rules. The guidelines in this book are still powerful motivators, however, and the *MUTCD* carries with it the force of law.

The Most Powerful Engineers No One Has Ever Heard Of

The people who have the power to make changes to the *MUTCD* call themselves the National Committee on Uniform Traffic Control Devices (NCUTCD). They meet biannually in places like Columbus, Ohio, and Virginia Beach.

This group of men—the group is overwhelmingly male—are, generally speaking, from the old school of traffic engineering. Many received their training during the Eisenhower era, when completing the Interstate Highway System was the industry's primary focus.

Today, a new school of thought is threatening to disrupt the status quo at the NCUTCD, as seen by the culture clash flare-up at the committee's January 2019 meeting. That day, a progressive younger professional engineer named Bill Schultheiss proposed a change that would have advanced pedestrian safety across the United States. He proposed that every traffic signal in the country be required to have a pedestrian signal head that displays "Walk," "Don't Walk," and a countdown timer. Currently, there is wide variation. As the NCUTCD wrote in its minutes,

> Some States install pedestrian signals at nearly every traffic signal where other States have far fewer installations. There are many signalized intersections across the Country where there is regular pedestrian activity without any provision of pedestrian signal heads.[7]

Schultheiss—a twenty-year industry veteran who works for the Washington, DC–based Toole Design Group—proposed making these signals mandatory at every traffic signal. The change was especially critical, he argued, given the dramatic increase in pedestrian deaths currently under way.

The NCUTCD brought the mandatory pedestrian signal heads up for a vote. The change was supported by more than half the members, but it failed to get the supermajority two-thirds needed for passage because a minority of voting engineers chose to prioritize cost savings over pedestrian safety. The proposed change was shelved.

Signal heads only cost about $5,000 each—a rounding error compared to the cost of road projects—but some engineers were apparently concerned it would require additional investment, such as utility work or the construction of crosswalks. Those investments could theoretically cost as much as $50,000, some opponents reasoned.[8]

Schultheiss wrote on Twitter that the decision was a moral failure. "When we discuss [the] cost of infrastructure we are making policy decisions and value judgments regarding who is important and whose life has value," he said.[9]

In many ways, though, the NCUTCD was working as it was designed. Its bylaws—requiring a two-thirds majority vote for changes—are designed to be conservative and to make change difficult. Those rules are necessary, backers will say, to ensure that changes are not approved without sufficient data to support them. But it also means that the engineering profession is, by design, slow to respond to new problems—like a decade-long escalation in pedestrian deaths.

Group Bias

The NCUTCD is a publicly sponsored organization, with voting members appointed by some of the most important traffic engineering institutions in the United States. But in some ways it is an insular group. The committee does no real public outreach. It does not seek input from experts in adjacent fields—like public health and urban planning. The culture of the committee itself is part of the problem, Schultheiss said. "These committees can . . . like any committee, be influenced by the bias of the people on it," he said.[10]

Civil engineers as a group are not representative of the populations who suffer the most from poor walking conditions. Traffic engineers are by definition professionals who can afford cars and thus at a minimum may lack direct experience with waiting for buses along suburban arterial roads marked for speeds of 45 miles per hour. They are also unrepresentative in other ways. According to census data compiled by the government transparency group Data USA, 85 percent of civil engineers are male, and 80 percent are white.[11]

The industry has not been willing to confront these kinds of biases in a direct way, said Schultheiss. "There's no recognition of the history of discrimination and institutional racism within our system," he said. "We don't talk about it. We're afraid to talk about ethics, equity, and we hide behind these formulas. I think that's where our business has failed."[12]

Part of the problem, said Veronica Davis, a black civil engineer and principal at the Washington, DC–based planning firm Nspiregreen, is lack of representation in the industry. Davis said that she was one of just seven women in her class of one hundred civil engineers at University of Maryland. Maybe five total were people of color, she said.[13]

Today, traffic engineering's biases might be more subtle than previously, but in the past, many US infrastructure policies were explicitly racist. For example, in the 1960s, Davis's grandparents in Baton Rouge, Louisiana, were displaced when their whole neighborhood was leveled for the construction of Interstate 10. During that era, nearly one million people[14]—mostly low-income people or people of color—were displaced by highway projects. Neighborhoods of color were specifically targeted in a campaign of so-called slum clearance. "It was racism," Davis said, that made her grandparent's home a target, "because they weren't poor. They had master's degrees."[15]

Davis said that engineers have not been trained to think about the wider social consequences of their work. "Engineers aren't taught about public involvement," she said. "They're taught where the road needs to go. They're not taught about the people part."[16]

In a 2018 article in *PE Magazine*, an industry publication for traffic engineers, Schultheiss questioned whether the profession was living up to its code of ethics, which requires engineers to "hold paramount the safety, health, and welfare of the public." In practice, he wrote, many dangerous designs that would predictably produce deaths have become part of the "standard practice" in the field because they help promote speed for drivers.

"Is it ethical to seal engineering drawings for a project with deficiencies we know will likely result in people getting injured or killed because this was standard past practice?" he wrote. "When I discuss this question within my profession, it creates significant discomfort because nobody wants to feel complicit in the deaths of thousands of people every year and the related degradation of air quality and the environment. However, I and others believe we are undeniably complicit and ethically bound to change the system."[17]

These more progressive ideas have yet to be codified in some of the most important manuals, but that too is changing. In response in part to the slow evolution of guides like the *MUTCD*, more progressive engineering associations are increasingly releasing their own street design guides.

Perhaps the most notable are those issued by the National Association of City Transportation Officials (NACTO), an industry group representing transportation officials in twenty-five major US cities.[18] In 2011, NACTO released its bicycle design guide, which instructed engineers in how to create substantive, safe, and protected infrastructure for urban bicyclists. And in 2017, it followed up with a guide to designing public transit–oriented streets.

These guidebooks still do not have the clout of the *MUTCD*, yet they have been important in providing additional tools for engineers focused on more vulnerable road users. In 2014, the Federal Highway Administration gave its unqualified support to NACTO's *Urban Street Design Guide*, instructing engineers to use it "in conjunction with" other guidebooks like the *MUTCD*.[19]

Forward Cities

Instead of waiting for permission, some engineers and some cities are forging ahead to make safer conditions for pedestrians. Seattle, for example, is not waiting for the arbitrary ninety-three pedestrians per hour minimum to add a crosswalk. The city is piloting a program in which crosswalks are first installed and then pedestrians are counted afterward to see if they meet the ninety-three-per-hour threshold mandated by the *MUTCD*.[20] In the city's first experiment with this approach, on a six-lane arterial (15th Avenue NW at NW 53rd Street) in the Ballard neighborhood, early observations were that no pedestrians were crossing at the location.

A funny thing happened after the city provided a safe crossing, however: people started using it. After the crosswalk's installation, Seattle again measured the number of pedestrians crossing at the location, and it met the ninety-three per hour threshold.

Portland, Oregon, is also using a policy for installing crosswalks that does not conform to the conventional engineering wisdom. There, city rules call for a crosswalk at any place where twenty pedestrians are crossing per hour. In addition, Portland city guidelines call for a controlled crosswalk—with a traffic signal—every 530 feet within zones of the city that are considered "pedestrian districts." Outside of those areas, the standard is 800 feet. Portland's "spacing guidelines for marked pedestrian crossings" call for a crossing at every bus stop as well.[21]

Another leader is Montreal. In late 2019, Montreal mayor Valérie Plante proposed a "paradigm change" in the city's policy toward pedestrians. She announced that all twenty-three hundred traffic lights in the city would be updated with walk signals and countdown timers. In addition, the city planned to add four to six seconds of crossing time to every one to accommodate "the most vulnerable road users," such as older people and children.

Plante articulated the counterargument to the "ideology of flow" used in the *MUTCD* perfectly. "What is more important: the lives of people or [for traffic] to be more fluid, in a way that it goes faster?" Plante was quoted as saying. "For me, as mayor, the choice is obvious. It will always be security."[22]

Vision Zero

Against the ideology of flow has risen a countermovement with the radical premise that no amount of traffic deaths should be considered acceptable. The concept—known internationally now as Vision Zero—originated in 1995 in Stockholm. There, newly appointed Swedish road administration director Claes Tingvall had become fixated on a crash that had killed five young people. Their car had hydroplaned and struck a concrete lamppost. When Tingvall inquired about removing the post, he was told that doing so would be an admission of guilt on the part of the agency. "I was shocked over the mentality that prevailed," he told the engineering firm AF Consult in 2017. "That crashes were subject to moralization and the cause was always sought in the actions of the victims."[23]

At the time, Swedish transport policies called for balancing safety concerns with other priorities like cost savings and "accessibility." In other words, the government was willing to accept some number of deaths so as to facilitate fast travel—in a very similar way to how traffic safety is currently thought of in the United States.

Tingvall proposed a radical new way of approaching the issue. He argued that safety, not speed, should be the clear, countervailing priority. He called it an "ethical mandate"[24] and sought to design the nation's roadways to make the inevitable human mistakes less deadly.

Today, Sweden's traffic death rate is about one-third that of the United States' on a per capita basis. In Sweden in 2017, there were 254 traffic deaths, about half the number from 1997.[25] Between 2000 and 2017, traffic safety on a per capita basis improved almost four times faster in Sweden than in the United States[26] and Sweden has all but eliminated child traffic deaths. In 2012, for example, just one child under age seven was killed in a car crash in that country of ten million.[27] If the United States could match Sweden's per capita traffic safety record, nearly thirty thousand lives would be saved in the United States annually.

In the United States, people blame road users—pedestrians, drivers—when someone is killed. The National Highway Traffic Safety Association, for example, states that "94 percent of accidents are caused by human error."[28]

But as Tingvall noted, that is not the way it works in other fields, such as nuclear power or aviation. "In every situation a person might fail," Tingvall said. "The road system should not."[29]

He put forth a different conception of traffic risk. System designers— like traffic engineers—Vision Zero posits, share responsibility with road users for deaths or serious injuries that occur within the system. The Swedish policy is not to rely on education and trying to control the way pedestrians behave, and it does not do much enforcement. In rural areas, cameras are used, but not much in cities.

"There's not a lot of evidence that finger wagging about certain behavior produces differences in how people are behaving," explained Daniel Firth, who was Stockholm's chief strategy officer for transportation until 2017. There is a huge, overarching effort in Sweden to control drivers' speed, however. That is primarily achieved by engineering—by redesigning roads. "It should be really clear as a road user what the appropriate speed is, and in a lot of places, it should be almost impossible to go over it," said Firth.[30]

In Sweden, an approach called the "right speed in the city" method is used. Each street in Sweden is categorized based on uses and characteristics. It is a major arterial? It is an important busway? Is it a shopping area, with lots of foot traffic? Is it a street used by emergency services? Does it serve an industrial area?

"Based on these dimensions you put in this Excel file . . . it spits out the appropriate speed," said Firth.[31]

Then the street is redesigned to "self enforce." Speed bumps and speed tables—raised crosswalks—are used to slow down drivers in areas where pedestrians are present. In some places, streets may actually be physically narrowed with "bump outs" at intersections that shorten the crossing distance for pedestrians and force drivers to turn more slowly.

In addition, Swedish transport planners might plant trees near a road to narrow the road's look and feel. Visual cues can be used to tell drivers to slow down. If money is tight, paint can be used to visually narrow the roadway. Concrete bollards might also be placed in the middle of a street to force drivers to take tight, controlled left turns or give pedestrians a midblock refuge while walking to complete a crossing.

The guiding principle in Swedish traffic safety is to ensure that the human body is not exposed to impacts that will cause death and serious injury. So in areas where pedestrians are present—residential areas or shopping districts, for example—the speed limit is mostly limited to 30 kilometers per hour (about 18.5 miles per hour). At that speed, even when a pedestrian is struck by a car, the odds of survival are very high: only about 6 percent of pedestrians struck at that speed die.[32] On highways, Sweden uses barriers to prevent head-on collisions. In higher-speed areas where two cars might collide but pedestrians are not present, the country imposes speed limits of 50 kilometers per hour (about 31 miles per hour)—approximately the speed at which a right-angle T-bone-style crash will be survivable for drivers or passengers.[33]

Vision Zero in the United States

Sweden's transport safety policy has been praised by international experts and has been exported all over the world, including to the United States. More than forty US cities—including New York, Boston, Los Angeles, Chicago, Denver, San Antonio, Fort Lauderdale, and Macon, Georgia—have adopted Vision Zero policies aimed at entirely ending traffic deaths over time,[34] and many have had Vision Zero programs since the early 2010s. Perhaps the most substantive effort has been from New York.

In 2018, five years after New York City committed to Vision Zero, its traffic deaths fell to a record low of two hundred.[35] That was down almost a third from 2013 and the lowest number since 1910.

"Vision Zero efforts started in 2014, and we saw annual declines yearly through 2018," said Marco Conner, co–deputy director of New York City's nonprofit Transportation Alternatives, which advocates for better conditions for local transit riders, cyclists, and pedestrians. "I think that has been remarkable in the face of rising traffic fatalities nationwide during that period."[36]

Like in Sweden, street redesigns have been a core part of New York City's Vision Zero efforts. The city reports that it conducted hundreds of street safety interventions between 2013 and 2018, including adding bike lanes at a rate of about fifty miles per year. There are now more than 1,200 miles of bike lanes in the city—a 30 percent increase since the start of Vision Zero.

Protected bike lanes with some kind of physical delineation from traffic, like bollards or curbs, have been shown in particular to reduce collisions—not just for cyclists, but for motorists and pedestrians as well. A 2014 New York City Department of Transportation (NYC-DOT) report found that on six Manhattan corridors that have added protected bike lanes—on streets like Broadway, Columbus Avenue, and 8th Avenue—overall crashes were reduced 17 percent, and pedestrian injuries fell by 22 percent. Meanwhile, the bike lanes in general did not have any negative effect on vehicle traffic; the department reported that travel times on those streets stayed the same or in some cases even improved as much as 35 percent.[37]

New York City also made other efforts to slow speed, following Sweden's model. For example, NYCDOT added 363 speed humps in 2018.[38]

In pursuit of Vision Zero, NYCDOT has also given special attention to its intersections. One of the city's most effective measures was simply giving pedestrians a bit of a head start at traffic lights. Since 2013, the city has retimed almost four thousand traffic signals to add "leading pedestrian intervals," which give pedestrians a five- to seven-second head start crossing the street before vehicles get a green light. That few extra seconds is important because it gives pedestrians a chance to get into the center of the intersection—where they will be visible—before cars start making left turns. Left turns are very dangerous for pedestrians and difficult for drivers in part because a car's side pillar between the windshield and door obscures a driver's view.

Leading pedestrian intervals are inexpensive, costing around $1,200 each to install, but studies have shown that they can make a big difference. In 2016, NYCDOT found that fatalities and serious injuries declined 40 percent at the intersections where these timing devices were installed.[39]

The city has used other low-cost intersection treatments to ensure that drivers go slower when making left turns. It has also "hardened" more than two hundred intersections by installing bollards between the yellow lines at the center of an intersection.[40] The treatment is designed to force drivers making left turns to slow down and make the turn at a sharper angle.

Conner said that those two treatments—the introduction of leading pedestrian intervals and intersection hardening—seem to have had an enormous effect on pedestrian safety in particular. "From 2016 to '17, we saw the biggest drop in pedestrian fatalities that I've ever seen," Conner said. "It was a 38 percent reduction."[41]

New York City residents had called for the city to add leading pedestrian intervals as early as the 1990s. In 2007, Transportation Alternatives pressed Mayor Michael Bloomberg's office to add the treatments. "We know that failure to yield is the second-leading cause of fatalities in the city," said Conner. "The fact that it took almost twenty years since as far as we know they were first called upon to do it by advocates . . . It's mind-blowing to think of the lives that could have been saved if they would have done this earlier."[42]

New York City mayor Bill de Blasio deserves credit for what he has accomplished, said Conner, but in some ways, the effort has still been too limited. "He hasn't fully recognized the crisis, and that is a crisis we can actually do something about," he said. "I think we've kind of reached the limit of what can be done without a willingness to draw a line in the sand and say, 'We in the city are not going to prioritize the speedy movement or cars of the storage of cars over safety.' . . . People have gotten used to free parking and wide roads as a right. It's going to take political courage and a commitment to prioritizing life over the convenience of a few car owners."[43]

Mixed Results

Looking at US Vision Zero cities more broadly, the results are difficult to judge at this point. Through 2018, only New York City and, perhaps, San Francisco showed any clear, sustained decline in traffic deaths.

San Francisco's death rate also dropped to a one-hundred-year low in 2017, but in 2019, it had surpassed that number—twenty-three—by August.[44] Even in New York, 2019 was a bad year, with fatalities jumping 9 percent to 218 deaths.[45]

Portland, Oregon, is another city that has made a notable effort. After agreeing to Vision Zero in 2016, Portland lowered default speed limits in residential areas to 20 miles per hour.[46] More than $100 million has been spent on crosswalks as well as speed cameras and beacons that warn drivers that a pedestrian is crossing.[47] But in 2019, Portland was bracing to have its second bloodiest year since 2008.

Under fire in the local alternative weekly newspaper, *Willamette Week*, city commissioner Chloe Eudaly said, "It's deeply troubling. I've been asking myself, 'What are we doing wrong, and what can we do faster?'"[48]

Grassroots advocates say that there is simply a lack of political will for change. "The way that they're operating, in the same manner that they've been operating, they're going to get the same results," neighborhood activist Anjeanette Brown told the paper.[49]

Jonathan Maus, editor of the Portland-based transportation news site Bike Portland, said that city leaders still have not really broken the habit of prioritizing drivers' speed and convenience over safety. "For the first time in decades our city transportation department has lots of revenue and they're doing so many projects it's hard to keep track—but they still aren't taking the bull by the horns," he said.[50]

Even in Sweden, progress on Vision Zero has not been "linear," as New York City transportation officials would say. In 2018, traffic deaths in Sweden increased 28 percent over the previous year,[51] and Norway has recently surpassed Sweden as the world leader on traffic safety.[52]

"There's definitely a recognition in Sweden that it has . . . I wouldn't say stalled, but the early successes are going to be hard to replicate," said Firth. "There's a reason it's called Vision Zero and not plan zero, because we know this is going to be really, really hard."[53]

In some cities, Vision Zero efforts have also faced a painful back-lash. Los Angeles mayor Eric Garcetti introduced a Vision Zero plan in 2017. As part of the effort, the city conducted "road diets" on nine miles of roads on the west side of Los Angeles in 2017. In response, outraged neighborhood residents attempted to recall their city council representative, Mike Bonin, who was a supporter of Vision Zero.[54] And commuters who used local roads to avoid congested highways began fundraising for a lawsuit to overturn the city's decision. Eventually, the city capitulated and reversed a number of the projects.

Some experts say that it is simply too early to say whether Vision Zero is working in the United States. Most US cities are small enough that there is a fair amount of statistical noise in the data, especially when it comes to fatalities. "This will take time and leadership and the political courage to do what works," Vision Zero network director Leah Shahum said.[55]

Some international cities have made bigger commitments than any US city. London's mayor Sadiq Khan is having the front end of city buses redesigned and speed-limiting technology installed in his quest to reduce deaths and serious injuries by 50 percent by 2030 and eliminate them entirely by 2041.[56] Large portions of the city have speed zones dedicated as 20 miles per hour. City of London Police have an entire crash investigations unit that seeks to get to the bottom of every fatality and serious injury and make recommendations for systemic improvements that could help avoid the next one. London's traffic fatality rate is about half that of New York City's on a per capita basis.

But London also struggled with Vision Zero initially, said Firth. One of the city's first major moves was to paint bike lanes on the streets—"Cycle Superhighways," they were called. But many of them were low quality and put cyclists in a dangerous position.

"You almost have to kind of make a bunch of mistakes at the beginning before you get it right," said Firth. "That's what Vision Zero does. It puts this blow torch on you to do the right thing."[57]

Chapter 7

A Hard Right Turn

O N OCTOBER 3, 2015, FIVE HUNDRED elementary students convened in the parking lot of Biggs Park Mall in Lumberton, North Carolina. There, outside the JCPenney, Foot Locker, and GNC, in the county seat of Robeson County, a lower-income manufacturing region, they prepared to do something that is increasingly unusual in the United States: walk to school.

Of the 235 schools that took part in Walk to School Day across North Carolina, this October event—the fruit of successful collaboration between the state Department of Transportation and Division of Health—was the biggest ever.[1] There to cheer on Tanglewood Elementary students as they began their half-mile journey were many of Lumberton's notable people as well as "Rocky the Bear," the mascot of the local hospital district, which helped sponsor the event.

It was a lot of ceremony and preparation for a half-mile walk, but it reflects just how unusual walking to school has become in the United States. During the late 1960s, 48 percent of US schoolchildren got to school by foot or bicycle, but by 2009, the number had dropped to just 13 percent.[2]

The idea behind Safe Routes to School, a federally sponsored transportation program dating to 2000,[3] is that a little encouragement can make a difference. North Carolina's Safe Routes to School program had been offering support to schools like Tanglewood for years, providing not just pep rallies, but safety training for students and, on occasion, physical infrastructure upgrades, like crosswalks.

But in 2018, just as the pedestrian safety crisis in the United States was reaching its height, North Carolina officials slashed the program's budget by 90 percent. A state transportation official told a reporter, "We are committed to this program and the tenets of this program" but that the state's hands were tied, in part, by changes to federal regulations.[4]

State officials were referring to an obscure federal funding program passed in 2012. That year, just as pedestrian deaths were beginning their as-yet-uninterrupted climb, lawmakers in Washington, DC, signed a two-year, $105 billion national surface transportation spending package that weakened already meager federal support for biking and walking.

The spending bill, known by the shorthand acronym MAP-21, eliminated Safe Routes to School as a stand-alone program. It was folded into a larger program called "Transportation Alternatives," funded at just over $800 million a year. That dollar figure—amounting to a 33 percent cut from $1.2 billion—would become the total federal support for walking and biking.[5] States could still offer Safe Routes to School, if they chose, but they would have less federal support.

Keep in mind that 2012 was a time of intense national interest in walking and biking. Census estimates show that biking to work, for example, had increased 60 percent between 2008 and 2012.[6] Around this era, in 2014, the *New York Times* wrote an article about bike culture among young urban dwellers ("the bike-to-work generation") that was influencing mainstream fashion.[7]

But that kind of cultural zeitgeist did not seem to register in the US Senate. In September 2011, for example, Tom Coburn, then a Republican senator from Oklahoma, attempted to block a vote authorizing all highway spending unless his amendment, which called for zeroing out all federal support for biking and walking, was brought up for a vote.[8]

Even prior to this era, though, the safety of people on bicycle or foot was never really considered a core federal transportation concern. That, said Andy Clarke, who was head of the League of American Bicyclists from 2003 to 2013, was partly because of the two lobbying groups with the greatest power in Washington transportation discussions: highway builders and state transportation officials. "Highway guys would say, 'Why are we frittering away money on this stuff that isn't real?'" Clarke said.[9]

Meanwhile, state departments of transportation, like the Georgia Department of Transportation, and their professional associations for the most part offered only limited support. "Generally speaking, state DOTs and the people who work there just really don't feel like this is their responsibility, along with historic preservation and environmental protection and equity stuff," Clarke said. "It's a sense that it's just subverting their core mission of building highways for cars."[10]

Safe Routes to School—being a small, safety-related program aimed at children—had never been subject to attack before, however. It was first introduced in the late days of the Clinton administration and survived the George W. Bush presidency with little challenge. Up to this point, the partisan divide on biking and walking had not been very apparent. But 2012 was an antagonistic moment in the nation's capital. When MAP-21 passed, it was near the height of the Tea Party Obama backlash, shortly after Republicans took back the House of Representatives. "Bike-pedestrian issues were more the easy target," Clarke said. "The bike and ped stuff is 1 percent of the budget."[11]

The reasons for that are subject to debate. Overall, party polarization has been growing. In addition, urban-rural partisan division has become more entrenched, said Clayton Nall, associate professor of political science at the University of California, Santa Barbara. "Back in the day, the Republican Party was actually pushing urban policy," he said. "Corporate friendly urban policy, like opportunity zones."[12]

Since then, however, the Republican Party has become more overtly antiurban. Based on survey data of Americans' political attitudes, it is unclear when and why that happened, but there has been a shift, said Nall. "White flight has had this result of leaving very few white swing voters in urban areas who would benefit from this kind of spending," he said. "Because there are so few Republican voters in cities anymore . . . which is where a lot of these debates over bike and pedestrian infrastructure are happening . . . the Republican Party no longer sees who this would appeal to."[13]

Generational gaps may also play a role. Beginning in the early 2000s, there was a celebrated movement—by the media, anyway—away from driving and toward walking and biking, especially among younger generations. "Congestion and the high cost of car ownership may have cooled the romance between Americans and their cars, especially for younger adults," Mary Wisniewski at the *Chicago Tribune* wrote in 2018.[14]

Wisniewski was citing a survey sponsored by Allstate that showed that more than half of millennials thought that a car was not worth the cost of upkeep and that they would rather be doing something other than driving. But whatever young people's preferences—and rising housing costs in "walkable" transit-friendly areas do suggest a growing preference—younger people do not have the political clout, it seems, to put those values into practice. Despite millennials' stated preferences to drive less, Allstate's survey showed that they drive about as many miles as their parents: only 13 percent reported they could "live without access to a vehicle."[15]

Meanwhile, Congress was getting increasingly older. The average age of a member of the 116th US Congress was fifty-seven. For US Senators, the average age was just shy of sixty-three, according to Quorum Analytics.[16]

It is also possible that Republican opposition to biking, walking, and transit investment simply arose to some extent in response to growing interest in these modes in more progressive Democratic strongholds like New York City and Portland. Nall said that the survey data point to a sea change in partisan opinion around alternatives to driving around 2010. "This was around the time Republicans like [former Wisconsin Governor] Scott Walker were killing off High Speed Rail," which had been proposed and passed early in Obama's term as part of the stimulus bill, he said. "There's this message that cars are crucial to the American way of life and that Democrats are trying to engage in social engineering."[17]

Whatever the underlying cause, Republican-led assaults on transportation funding continued throughout the Obama administration and beyond. In 2015, for example, as Congress was gearing up to pass another transportation bill, Americans for Prosperity and a number of other right-wing groups associated with the infamous dark money political donors Charles and David Koch wrote a letter to Congress calling for total elimination of federal walking and biking funds.[18] They might have succeeded, given the new Republican majorities in the House and Senate, were it not for Rick Larsen, congressman from Washington state, who rallied minority Democrats on the House Transportation Committee to refuse to advance any bill that eliminated federal support for biking and walking.[19]

By 2015, when the bill was passed, pedestrian deaths were already 25 percent higher than they had been just five years prior, but the issue failed to register in federal negotiations. That year, Congress passed a mostly status-quo extension of the 2012 bill, leaving cuts to biking and walking mostly in place. That bill—the FAST Act, it was called—continues to fund US transportation programs today.

The lack of federal support for pedestrian safety is costly. In 2010, the National Highway Traffic Safety Administration (NHTSA) estimated the social and economic costs of traffic crashes to be about $836 billion.[20] The share that would be related to walking and biking injuries would be roughly $125 billion. In other words, bike and pedestrian crashes cost Americans the equivalent of about $400 per person per year in 2010. Since that time, pedestrian fatalities have increased dramatically.

Pedestrians and cyclists now account for about one in five traffic deaths in the United States. But these modes receive just about

1.5 percent of federal transportation funding, or about \$2.65 per American per year.

Austerity Meets Crisis

By 2018, the damage of some of these policies was apparent, even if no one in Washington was explicitly acknowledging the connection. That year was the most deadly year for pedestrians in a generation. But even as the crisis accelerated, states like North Carolina were scaling back their already anemic support.

In 2018, North Carolina officials slashed \$13.5 million from the state's \$15 million budget for Safe Routes to School. Part of the problem, they explained, was that MAP-21 required the state to provide a 20 percent match for federal funds for the program. In the years after 2012, the state had been able to use leftover funding to make the match, but now that funding had run out. In addition, North Carolina transportation officials had political obstacles at the state level to continuing support for the program.

In 2011, a supermajority of Republicans had been elected to the North Carolina Statehouse. Two years later, in 2013, they passed a law saying that no stand-alone bike or pedestrian project would be eligible for state funding. "We have not had one single dollar go to bicycle or pedestrian projects in any part of the state" since then, said Terry Lansdell, the executive director of BikeWalk NC.[21]

Prior to 2013, North Carolina had been making progress on bike and pedestrian safety, trying to tie it to other statewide health and welfare programs. Smart Growth America recently named North Carolina the seventh most dangerous state in the country for pedestrians and cyclists, and the loss of funding, said Lansdell, "hurts dramatically."[22]

There was yet another painful effect of the 2012 federal spending bill: in addition to slashing total support, it made investing in biking and walking optional for states—to a big degree. The law (MAP-21) allowed states to transfer up to half of their transportation alternatives funding to other things, like highway projects, and many chose to do so.

In a single quarter in 2017, for example, eight states—Alabama, Connecticut, Iowa, Louisiana, New Hampshire, Nevada, Oregon, and Wisconsin—transferred a total of $29 million out of their transportation alternatives funding and moved it to other programs: namely, roads and highways.[23] Margo Pedroso, deputy director of the Safe Routes to School National Partnership, said that about 20 percent of the $850 million the federal government provides to states for walking and biking projects gets transferred to roads projects. "The largest offender is Texas," she said. "They get so much money and they transfer 50 percent pretty regularly."[24]

Texas does so even though it had 615 pedestrian deaths in 2017, roughly 10 percent of the national total.[25] Each year, Texas "flexes" away about $35 million that could be used to help its embattled pedestrians and cyclists.

The Trump Era

Following the presidential election of Donald Trump, Elaine Chao, a former Bush administration appointee and "distinguished fellow" for the Heritage Foundation, was appointed to head the US Department of Transportation (US DOT). As transportation secretary, Chao's US DOT echoed a right-wing talking point that biking, walking, and transit were local concerns that should be funded by the local government, not the federal government.[26] When the Republican Party wrote its 2016 presidential platform, the transportation policy recommendations were borrowed almost verbatim from the Heritage Foundation. The platform called mass transit "an inherently local affair that serves only a small portion of the population, concentrated in six big cities." Trails and sidewalks, the platform said, "should be funded through other sources."[27]

Congress ignored the platform, however, and proceeded to fund transit and walking and biking at Obama-era levels. Still, Chao was able to weaken federal funding through a smaller pool of $1.5 billion discretionary funding provided to the US DOT. Chao, to a large extent, reoriented a popular $500 million Obama-era program that had funded bike and pedestrian projects toward highway spending.

During the Obama administration, the US DOT called the grant program TIGER (Transportation Investment Generating Economic Recovery) and allocated $142 million for biking and walking in a single grant cycle. In addition, nearly $400 million was awarded to "multimodal projects," mostly road projects that had a biking or walking element.[28] But the same grant program, renamed and run by Chao's DOT, allocated 70 percent of the funding to roads and bridges and none—zero dollars—to walking and biking projects.[29] What had once been a welcome source of safety funding for urban areas was neutralized.

Even so, Pedroso said that she thinks some of the worst partisan fights are in the past. She adds that biking and walking investment has recovered somewhat in recent years thanks to increased local support. "This temporary period where it became very partisan did coincide with death rates rising," she said. "Communities could have taken steps, but they were hamstrung a little bit by federal funds."[30]

Fortunately, as federal biking and walking policy regressed, taxpayers in many urban (and suburban) areas were stepping up to fill the gap. Responding to the recent increased interest in walkability, a number of major metro areas passed big measures to support safer sidewalks and other biking and walking infrastructure.

In 2017, for example, Kansas City, Missouri, voters approved a bond package that included $150 million for sidewalk repairs.[31] Atlanta passed a $150 million infrastructure bond in 2015, with $80 million in spending earmarked for "complete streets"—street safety projects that incorporate bike and pedestrian elements.

Maybe the most promising example is from Hillsborough County, Florida, home to Tampa. The greater Tampa region was ranked the ninth most deadly for pedestrians in 2019.[32] In 2018, voters there elected to raise the sales tax by 1 percent, and the tax will generate $276 million annually, of which 12 percent is reserved for walking and biking and 45 percent is reserved for transit. The remaining funds will be dedicated to road projects. Remarkably, the roads money was specifically earmarked not for projects that increase car capacity and widen streets, but for projects that improve safety and accessibility.

"These kinds of local initiatives are bubbling up from the people saying, 'We've had enough,'" Christina Barker, a volunteer activist who helped lead the effort, said following the measure's passage. "We have some of the most dangerous streets in the country and we have next to no options for people who don't have a car. This funding is really going to transform the city of Tampa and the county around it."[33] There seemed to be strong consensus for change in Tampa, and the measure passed by a ten-point margin.[34]

Unfortunately, even in these cases, partisan acrimony can be an obstacle. That is especially true in the states that need investment the most, many of which are so-called red states. Just under a year after the Hillsborough County measure passed, José Oliva, Republican Speaker of the Florida House of Representatives, asked the Florida Supreme Court to overturn the measure. A Republican county commissioner named Stacy White had challenged the constitutionality of the ballot language. The case was heard by the state supreme court in February 2020, and a decision is forthcoming.[35]

Tyler Hudson, a Tampa lawyer and campaign chair for All for Transportation, the citizen-led campaign that placed the transportation initiative on the ballot by petition and advocated for its passage, said that even when public consensus is clear—like 57 percent support for a ballot measure—state and local Republicans cannot accept it. "State lawmakers gave Floridians the power to tax themselves to fix transportation, and when Tallahassee Republicans disagree with how voters use that power, they fight tooth and nail in court to avenge their political defeats," he said.[36]

Chapter 8

Pedestrian Safety on the Technological Frontier

J UST OUTSIDE DOWNTOWN TEMPE, ARIZONA, along a wide, dusty highway, there is a small memorial to the victim of the most famous pedestrian-vehicle crash in history. Two wooden crosses and some flowers stand alongside Mill Avenue, where the dense brick buildings of downtown Tempe thin out into desert and parking lots. Here is where Elaine Herzberg, a forty-nine-year-old homeless woman, was killed by a computer-piloted Uber car on March 18, 2018. She was the first pedestrian ever killed by a self-driving car.

That night around 10 p.m., Herzberg had been walking her bike across the street in a dark location about 360 feet from a crosswalk. The red Hyper-brand bike she was riding—the kind you can buy for one hundred dollars at Walmart—was loaded with plastic bags containing her belongings, which might help explain why the laser-based sensor system (or LiDAR, for light detection and ranging) in the Volvo SUV did not immediately recognize her as either a bicyclist or a pedestrian.

Normally when a pedestrian is killed, investigators have to resort to unreliable witnesses and guesswork to reconstruct what happened—if anyone even bothers—but this was not an ordinary pedestrian death. The death of Elaine Herzberg was an international media event.

The last moments of her life were recorded by a camera and turned over to police and federal investigators and then viewed by people all over the world. In this, the rarest of cases, everyone could see exactly what happened.

The video footage, shot in black and white from the dashboard camera, shows the SUV proceeding down the dark desert highway. Very shortly before impact, the car's headlights light up Herzberg's lower body. She appears suddenly, emerging from a shadow in the road.

Less than a second before her death, the headlights finally light up her face. It is turned away from traffic, directed at the median ahead. She had almost arrived at that landscaped refuge, and until those final milliseconds, she seemed relatively relaxed. She probably expected the driver to notice her and slow down. Herzberg did not know that the car heading toward her was driven by a computer program undergoing high-stakes beta testing on Arizona residents.

Finally, she turns and looks over her shoulder at the approaching car, her eyes appearing to lock with the camera with an expression that is not fully captured. Then her face is obscured, at close distance, by a motion blur, and the video is clipped, right before impact, for her sake and viewers'.

Will Self-Driving Cars Save Us?

Some people believe that self-driving cars will someday eliminate pedestrian crashes entirely—or nearly so. A system of perfectly calibrated self-driving cars could reduce traffic fatalities 90 percent or more, the *Atlantic*'s Adrienne LaFrance, among others, has said,[1] but that assertion relies on many flawed assumptions—including that 94 percent of crashes can be attributed to so-called human error.

Nevertheless, the companies pursuing the self-driving cars tout safety as a foundational moral imperative for the technology, and on some level, it is a compelling vision. As discussed in earlier chapters, people are just not very reliable drivers. They get sleepy and drunk and very old and distracted. And they contribute to the deaths of more than thirty-five thousand Americans a year in countless ways.

The early experience with self-driving cars in the United States has been far from utopian, however. An investigation by local police and, later, by the National Traffic Safety Board showed that before striking Herzberg, Uber's forty-four-hundred-pound Volvo XC90 SUV did not brake significantly. She was hit at about 40 miles per hour, even though the car's self-driving system detected an object in the road—Herzberg—a full six seconds before the crash. It would later be revealed that Uber's cars did not "include a consideration for jaywalking pedestrians"—an astonishing oversight.

"Even the most junior human driver knows to expect that people sometimes walk outside of crosswalks," Jason Levine, executive director of the Center for Auto Safety told the *Washington Post*. He added that other autonomous vehicle companies could be testing cars with similar limitations, but it is not known because there is really no day-to-day government oversight of the industry.[2]

The Herzberg case is a cautionary tale about how self-driving car technology, in the absence of robust protections, can go very badly for the public—and especially the most vulnerable.

At the time Herzberg was hit and killed, there were no specific regulations at all—from either the federal government or the state of Arizona—to protect the public from self-driving cars. The US DOT has issued a set of voluntary best practices[3] for autonomous vehicle companies but has not yet imposed any specific regulations.

Self-driving cars were a common sight in Maricopa County at the time Herzberg was killed. Arizona's governor, Doug Ducey, had welcomed Uber to test its self-driving cars in 2015, bragging about the state's industry-friendly environment.[4] "While California puts the brakes on innovation and change with more bureaucracy and more regulation, Arizona is paving the way for new technology and new businesses," Ducey boasted the following year.[5]

Uber was considered—correctly, it turns out—to be one of the more freewheeling companies testing self-driving cars. California had recently ousted Uber's Advanced Technologies Group after one of its cars was caught on camera running a red light in San Francisco.[6]

Although Ducey was enthusiastic—boastful, in fact—about the partnership, many ordinary Arizona residents felt differently. A 2018 *New York Times* article highlighted a number of vigilante "attacks" on robot cars by enraged residents armed with sticks and knives. A Chandler, Arizona, man told the *New York Times*, for instance, "I don't want to be their real-world mistake."[7]

Autonomous vehicle testing *does* raise a lot of ethical questions. Arizonans—people like Elaine Herzberg—did not explicitly consent to have a potentially life-threatening technology beta-tested on them and their families. In other fields—pharmaceuticals, for example—companies are forbidden from testing potentially lethal new products on patients without their explicit consent. Self-driving car companies, meanwhile, are expected to police themselves.

Governors like Ducey, for their part, have been relatively enthusiastic about inviting the companies to test on public streets. Autonomous car testing offers government officials an aura of tech and business friendliness—and perhaps some jobs—usually without requiring any upfront public investment.

Twelve US states currently allow companies to test or market vehicles that operate without a driver.[8] Google's self-driving car operation, Waymo, claimed to have driven twenty million miles on public roads as of January 2020.[9] That company already offers driverless taxi service to a small group of screened riders, who sign nondisclosure agreements, in Arizona.

Uber and other autonomous vehicle companies like Arizona in part because environments like Mill Avenue—where Herzberg was struck—are so hostile to pedestrians. On Google Maps' satellite images, the area around the crash appears as a wasteland of highways and parking lots. It is a place designed for machines, not people.

Thanks to environments like Mill Avenue, ubiquitous across Arizona, the state has relatively few pedestrians. That was a selling point for autonomous car companies still trying to work out the bugs in their software. Interacting with pedestrians is one of the more difficult challenges for the artificial intelligence that is beginning to replace drivers. In addition, Arizona's warm weather eliminates the need to deal with the additional complexity of driving on snow and ice.

It would have been impossible for the state of Arizona or the federal government to know—because they were not monitoring Uber's self-driving operation in any formal capacity—but there was plenty of warning that a fatality might occur. Just the week before Herzberg was killed, Robbie Miller, a whistleblower at Uber's Advanced Technology Group, emailed company executives warning about safety problems: "A car was damaged nearly every other day in February," he said. "We shouldn't be hitting things every 15,000 miles." He also noted prophetically, "Several of the drivers appear to not have been properly vetted or trained."[10]

The one thing standing between Herzberg and the front end of the Volvo—in case of a programming failure—was supposed to be a backup driver. But, it turns out, that was completely inadequate.

Following the crash, Uber provided video of the interior of the car as it approaches Herzberg's bike. In that video, a woman named Rafaela Vasquez is seen in the driver's seat, and her face is turned downward, lit up by a screen. An investigation would later reveal that Vasquez was streaming the television show *The Voice* on her smartphone.[11]

Had the disastrous encounter between an Uber car and Herzberg played out more than a year earlier, there would have been a second backup driver in the car. But in late 2017, Uber had changed its policy, moving from two backup drivers to one, presumably to save money.[12]

That was a fateful decision, one that safety experts have criticized. The level of concentration required to monitor a self-driving car for hours and hours is nearly impossible for a single person to maintain. The task is simply too boring for the human brain to remain vigilant for an extended time.

The National Transportation Safety Board (NTSB) refers to this phenomenon as "automation complacency" and said that Vasquez's inattention—she checked her phone twenty-three times in the three minutes before the crash—was a "typical effect." In its report about the event, the NTSB notes that Vasquez's boredom was rational: she had passed the same site of the crash seventy-three times previously without any problems.[13]

What was worse, however, was that the system did not even notify Vasquez that an object had been detected in the road, which might have given her time to take over and brake or swerve. Uber, meanwhile, had disabled the automatic braking feature.

Looking back, it is clear that financial considerations outweighed safety for the company. In his book chronicling Uber's rise, *New York Times* technology writer Mike Isaac noted that Uber executives gave the self-driving car program the code name "$" because it would allow them to cut out the cost of drivers and create billions in profits.[14] Uber wanted to introduce fully driverless taxi service by the end of 2018—a goal that in hindsight looks like wild hubris.

But the financial pressure was intense. Uber had lost a jaw-dropping $577 million in the first quarter of 2018, mainly on its driver-based taxi service.[15] Meanwhile, at the time that Herzberg was struck, the company was looking ahead to a 2019 initial public offering. Execs hoped that it would attract $100 billion in investment[16]—despite it being what *Bloomberg Technology* described as "a serially unprofitable business."[17] Eliminating drivers from its business model was considered one of the few avenues to profitability for Uber ahead of its much-anticipated stock market debut.[18] "A lot of that is the Silicon Valley move-fast-and-break-things attitude," said auto writer Dan Albert. "[But] when you're not talking about just apps . . . the things you break are actual people."[19]

Uber was not only rushing to stem billions in annual losses, but it was also vying with companies like Waymo, Ford, and others to bring self-driving car technology to market. It was a race covered breathlessly by the media in competitive terms.

All that should help explain why the car did not brake when it detected Herzberg in the road. In its preliminary report, the NSTB explained,

> According to Uber, emergency braking maneuvers are not enabled while the vehicle is under computer control, to reduce the potential for erratic vehicle behavior.[20]

Why was Uber so concerned about "erratic vehicle behavior"? The answer, again, goes back to money.

Self-driving cars can be programmed to drive very cautiously, braking every time the LiDAR system detects some unknown object—such as a plastic bag blowing in the breeze—in the roadway. But riding in a car that is constantly braking is uncomfortable; it makes people nauseated.

Uber was trying to introduce a new product—self-driving taxis—that could make money for them later that year, and they wanted the rides to be competitive with its traditional taxi service. So Uber programmed its self-driving cars not to brake.

It is clear now that the company was, without any external supervision and under competitive and financial pressure, acting quite recklessly. Part of that appears to be explained by cultural deficits within the company. According to Isaac, executives at the self-driving car operation that eventually became Uber Advanced Technology Group, prior to its acquisition by Uber, reportedly pasted stickers around the Silicon Valley with their informal motto: "safety third."[21]

Nevertheless, in 2019, local prosecutors determined that the company would not be charged criminally in the case.[22] Vasquez, for her part, may still face charges.

Corinne Kisner, executive director of the National Association of City Transportation Officials, called Uber out for its "negligent safety culture" but emphasized that this case "did not occur in a vacuum." She said in a statement, "The absence of federal leadership, including mandatory safety standards, contributes to an inherently risky and unaccountable [autonomous vehicle] testing environment."[23]

At the time she was killed, Herzberg was reportedly trying to get her life together. A divorced mother of two, she had struggled with drugs and addiction for more than a decade, having spent some time in jail for petty crimes, mostly related to drug possession. At the time of her death, the investigation showed, she had marijuana and methamphetamines in her system.

She was, however, reportedly well liked and generous—Ms. Elle, they called her in Tempe's tight-knit homeless community.[24] At the time of her death, she was living with a group of other homeless people in an encampment in Papago Park, just near the site where she was killed.

Around that time, the city of Tempe was making efforts to clear out the encampment, following complaints from neighbors. But in lieu of just evicting everyone and destroying the little community, social services providers were sent out to the park. Herzberg, according to her friends, had arranged to get an apartment and was trying to kick her drug habit.[25] She never got that chance.

Jake Fisher, senior director of auto testing at *Consumer Reports*, said that there are really no guarantees that self-driving cars will improve safety for pedestrians at all. Many experts, Fisher included, believe that fully autonomous vehicles may still be decades away from the market or more.

Meanwhile, "the testing that is being done absolutely can put pedestrians and cyclists at risk," he said. "I don't think it is necessarily decided that self-driving vehicles are going to be better for pedestrians," said Fisher. "Despite what you read, I don't think it's necessarily going to be a positive outcome for society."[26]

In addition, although safety is often touted as the impetus for self-driving cars, the vision presented by industry leaders is sometimes at odds with pedestrian safety and rights. For example, an unnamed auto industry official told the *New York Times* that perhaps instead of cars simply detecting pedestrians and stopping for them in Manhattan, pedestrian "gates" could be constructed at intersections that would prevent them from crossing against the light.[27] Others have suggested that pedestrians or cyclists be forced to wear special homing devices that would allow them to be detected by autonomous vehicles.[28] But that itself is a scary possibility, setting up a scenario in which people who fail to wear special equipment when they leave the house not only are killed but are blamed for it.

The Future Will be Partially Automated

What is perhaps more promising in the near term for addressing the pedestrian safety crisis are advanced technologies that perform certain functions for drivers. Today, cars coming on the market are increasingly *partly* automated, with potentially enormous impacts for traffic safety.

Lane keeping, forward collision warning, adaptive cruise control, automatic emergency braking, and pedestrian detection features are becoming more and more common in new cars. Already there is some evidence that these features can help reduce crashes and injuries. An Insurance Institute for Highway Safety study, for example, found that Subaru's EyeSight—an advanced technology package that includes forward collision warning, automatic emergency braking, adaptive cruise control, and lane departure warning—reduced the rate of pedestrian-related insurance claims by 35 percent.[29]

Automatic emergency braking (AEB) is one of the most promising of these technologies. This feature, which automatically brakes when an object is detected in front of the front bumper, has been shown to not only reduce crashes, but also to lessen the severity of crashes when they occur. The NHTSA estimates that if AEB were installed in all new cars by 2025, it would prevent twenty-eight thousand crashes, resulting in twelve thousand fewer injuries overall.[30]

Although these new technologies are making their way into new cars, the introduction of them has, in many cases, been limited to luxury models. AEB was standard in only about 30 percent of new cars in model year 2017.

According to experts like Fisher, automakers are moving slowly in part because there has been no move from the federal government to mandate these technologies, despite escalating pedestrian fatalities.[31] Instead, all the major automakers have signed a voluntary agreement to include AEB in all their new vehicles by model year 2022. But consumer advocacy groups say that voluntary agreements are "weak and unenforceable" and that more direct federal action is needed.[32]

In addition, more cars, especially higher-end models, are beginning to come with pedestrian detection systems. In model year 2019, pedestrian detection came standard on 38 percent of vehicles sold, according to *Consumer Reports*,[33] but even though it is a very promising frontier in vehicle safety, at this stage there remain concerns about its overall effectiveness.

In 2019, AAA tested the pedestrian detection systems in four midsized sedans with dummy pedestrians. The systems performed respectably at 20 miles per hour in daylight conditions, stopping about 40 percent of the time. But at 30 miles per hour, they were practically useless. AAA called them "completely ineffective at night," when "none of the systems detected or reacted to the adult pedestrian."[34] That was an extremely disappointing result given that three-fourths of fatal pedestrian collisions occur at night.

Without regulation, said Shaun Kildare, research director at the consumer protection group Advocates for Highway and Auto Safety, these features cannot be expected to perform reliably. "The systems that are out there that call themselves automated pedestrian braking aren't really up to any standard," he said. "There's no actual testing protocol that's universal. The companies can kind of put whatever they want in there and call it what they want."[35]

Today there is wide diversity in how well different brands' pedestrian detection systems perform. The Insurance Institute for Highway Safety has started rating the available systems and will incorporate scores into its influential auto safety ratings, which should motivate automakers to include them and give consumers better information about their effectiveness. In addition, Fisher said, beginning in 2020, cars will not be eligible to be one of *Consumer Reports'* influential "Top Safety Picks" if they do not include the technology. "It's not regulated but we're trying to do what we can," he said. "We do give extra points to vehicles that have automatic pedestrian detection and AEB."[36]

Lack of regulation and limited deployment may help explain why a huge increase in pedestrian deaths is being seen at a time when promising new safety technology is becoming available. There just may not be enough cars with the technology on the roads right now to have a noticeable impact on traffic fatalities, said Fisher. "The fleet turnover is so slow," said Fisher. "The average vehicle's on the road for about 11 years. Just because they're selling them now, it's only a very very tiny fraction of vehicles on the road that can detect and stop for pedestrians."

In addition, some of the automated technologies, like lane keeping, should be considered more convenience technologies than safety technologies, he said. Could lane keeping, for example, prevent a driver from swerving to avoid a pedestrian walking on the shoulder of a highway? Right now, it is alarming to say, the answer is unknown.

"These systems are being marketed in a way that almost makes it seem like they're assisting you in driving or even autonomous," Fisher said. "And we don't know if they're helpful or perhaps put more people at risk."

Safer Cars, More Dangerous Drivers?

Another concern is that as cars begin to come standard with potentially helpful automated features, they might encourage drivers to take more risks, counteracting their benefits.

That kind of behavior has been seen with Tesla's "autopilot" system, which is essentially a package of partially automated features such as automatic parking, lane keeping, lane changing, and adaptive cruise control.

There have been five deaths associated with autopilot: four in the United States and one in China. In many cases, the crashes involved drivers who were wildly inattentive. Tesla driver Joshua Brown, for example, was killed in 2016 after crashing into a fire truck. An NTSB investigation showed that Brown had had his hands off the wheel for almost thirteen minutes prior to the crash.[37] But despite what its name suggests, autopilot is not a fully autonomous system and is only safe to use with intermittent monitoring from a human driver and on limited-access highways. German regulators, for example, have, for safety reasons, barred Tesla from using the "misleading" term *autopilot*.[38] Tesla still maintains that its partially automated features improve safety, but without access to the company's data, it is difficult to evaluate the claim.

In academia, they call this kind of behavior "risk compensation." People adjust their behavior, to some extent, with the introduction of new safety technologies and take on more risk. Risk compensation behavior, however, varies a lot depending on the type of safety feature, said Offer Grembek, codirector of Berkeley's Safe Transportation Research and Education Center. "This phenomenon is much more present when countermeasure or safety improvement is easily perceptible," he said. "Seat belts, helmets—these things are very perceptible."[39]

Safety additions like airbags and antilock brakes—safety technologies that assist only when needed—are less perceptible to drivers and thus are less subject to risk compensation, said Grembek. AEB and pedestrian detection are these kinds of features—not overtly perceptible, only deploying when you need them, which is rarely. "This phase of high-level technological improvement to the vehicle, such as automatic braking and maybe some steering assist, are extremely beneficial and are an important step," Grembek said. "I think of them as a transitional phase to the aspirational full autonomy state that we will likely never get to." In addition, even for the most perceptible safety improvements, like seat belts, behavioral adjustments to risk come far from negating the benefits, he added.[40]

Safety First . . . Later

While we look to an autonomous future to save lives lost in traffic crashes, many very promising technological solutions that already exist go forgotten or are rejected politically. A prime example is speed governors. In the United States, about ten thousand traffic deaths a year are speeding related, according to the US Centers for Disease Control and Prevention.[41] That is about as many annual deaths as drunk driving.

But in the United States, there has not been the political will to make the hard decisions that could save a lot of lives relative to controlling speeding. For example, the technology exists to install speed governors in cars that could automatically cap speeds on or around the legal limit.

In Europe, these governors will soon become required. In 2019, the European Parliament ruled that by 2022, all new cars will come equipped with speed governors that physically limit the cars from exceeding the posted speed limit. The decision is expected to save fifteen thousand lives over fifteen years.[42]

Meanwhile in the United States, many new cars come with the technology to regulate speed, but it is left to consumers whether they choose to use it. Even though there is massive bloodshed related to speeding, there is simply little to no political will for bolder action. In 2019, bipartisan federal legislation was introduced to require speed limiters—a maximum of 65 miles per hour—on freight trucks only. Despite tearful pleas from devestated families, it was opposed by the trucking industry and never made it out of committee.[43]

Vehicle-to-Vehicle Communication

Under a regulation-averse Trump administration, other opportunities to improve vehicle safety have languished, with little outcry. For example, Toyota had been developing the capacity for vehicle-to-vehicle (V2V) and vehicle-to-infrastructure (V2I) communication.

There is incredible potential in these technologies, which use what are called dedicated short-range communications (DSRC) to prevent collisions between vehicles. This kind of technology could, for example, prevent red-light-running crashes by sending a signal to the vehicle and instructing it to brake after the traffic light turns red. The NHTSA has estimated that vehicle-to-vehicle communication alone could save 1,366 lives annually and prevent 615,000 injuries.[44]

V2V and V2I safety systems have a big potential benefit over autonomous vehicles as well: they can be installed retroactively in used cars. A safety improvement based on autonomous vehicles, by contrast, would require waiting perhaps fifteen years for the US vehicle fleet to entirely turn over.

For a time a few years ago, it looked as if this kind of safety tech—V2V, V2I—was inevitable. In late 2016, the Obama administration proposed adding DSRC to all new vehicles. Toyota had planned to begin installing DSRC in cars in 2021 and make it standard by the mid-2020s.[45] Cadillac had also installed it in some of its cars beginning in 2017. But instead of developing the technology, the Trump administration has left V2V and V2I communication for dead.

DSRC required a "dedicated and adequate spectrum" in which automakers can have assurance that they will not have to worry about hacking or other kinds of more innocent interference. But the Trump administration's FCC (Federal Communications Commission) chair, Ajit Pai, announced in late 2019 that he was beginning a rule-making process to open up half of the 5.9 GHz radio frequency that had, for twenty years, been reserved for DSRC to other uses. Tech groups like Facebook as well as right-wing groups like the Koch brothers' political arm, Americans for Prosperity, supported the move.

Even before then, auto companies had been abandoning plans for V2V and V2I as it became clear that the federal government was not going to preserve the spectrum. In 2019, for example, Toyota announced that it had stopped pursuing the technology in the United

States. *Automotive News* wrote, "Toyota said Friday's decision was based on 'a range of factors, including the need for greater automotive industry commitment as well as federal government'—ie the Trump Administration—'support to preserve the 5.9 GHz spectrum band for DSRC.'"[46]

Meanwhile, regular Americans were paying a high price for lack of action on safety technologies. In 2017, red-light-running deaths hit a ten-year high, rising by more than one-fourth since 2012, an AAA study found.[47]

That currently available technology that could save thousands of lives lost to traffic is being rejected should make everyone question the promises of a fatality-free future with self-driving cars. In addition, there is still no real clarity on how autonomous vehicles would affect important traffic safety–related questions, such as whether cars would be required to obey the speed limit.

According to Albert, the obstacles to better traffic safety currently are more political than technological. "Automakers and tech companies do things to earn money, not save lives," he said. "Everything from speed limits to seat belt laws are not a function of physics but of contested ideas about what's right and proper."[48]

Chapter 9

The International Context

Every morning, Cecilia, ten years old, wakes up in a slum in Dar es Salaam, Tanzania. She makes herself a chai tea and heads out alone on the city's chaotic roads on her way to school.

Three-quarters of Dar es Salaam's children walk to school in this fast-growing city of 4.4 million located on the Swahili coast in eastern Africa. The dangers they face on those journeys are extreme.

About 70 percent of the city's population lives in informal settlements, in families earning the equivalent of just a few dollars a day. Cecilia's family will likely never be able to afford a car. Only a small portion of Tanzania's richest people drive. Cecilia's father earns around one hundred dollars a month as a security guard.

In Dar es Salaam, slum dwellers rely almost exclusively on walking. Although car ownership is growing, Tanzania remains primarily a walking country. For every one thousand people in Tanzania, there are only 39 vehicles; in the United States, by comparison, there are 873.[1]

But even with so few cars, lower-income nations like Tanzania have staggering traffic death rates. According to the World Health Organization, people in "developing nations" account for just 1 percent of the world's cars, but 13 percent of the world's 1.3 million annual fatalities.[2]

People in sub-Saharan Africa are particularly vulnerable. In Tanzania, for example, two-and-a-half times more people are killed on a population-adjusted basis than in the United States and about eleven times more than the world's safest country, Norway.[3]

These traffic deaths are, in significant share, pedestrians. In the United States, 16 percent of traffic deaths are pedestrians, but walkers make up 40 percent of the dead in sub-Saharan Africa.

Official transport data from many lower-income countries are unreliable, but Julie Babinard, a senior transport specialist with the World Bank, said that 40 to 60 percent of trips in Africa are made on foot.[4] By contrast, according to the US Census Bureau, only 2.7 percent of US workers commuted by walking in 2017.[5]

Workers crowd into the streets in fast-growing African cities like Dar es Salaam, Lagos in Nigeria, and Abidjan in Côte d'Ivoire every morning when it is still dark, often hauling wares to sell at markets. Many cannot afford the price of urban housing and commute long distances from rural areas. "Often there are no transport services available," said Babinard. "The poor are still needing to walk to work."[6]

In many so-called developing countries, transportation mode is stratified to an extreme degree by class. The World Resources Institute analyzed transportation modes by income in Nairobi, Kenya, for example. Among low-income people, walking was their primary mode for some 62 percent, and only a vanishingly small share—3 percent—traveled by car. For those belonging to the upper class, however, it was different; almost one-third—29 percent—used cars for transportation, a slightly higher proportion than those who walked.[7]

"Sub-Saharan Africa, in particular, has a vast income and mobility divide—a wealthy elite and small middle class while more than 90 percent of people earn less than ten dollars per day," said Kate Turner, a spokesperson for the auto safety foundation Fédération Internationale de l'Automobile (FIA), which supports road safety initiatives around the world.[8]

Until very recently, infrastructure development in much of Africa has catered almost exclusively to drivers. According to a survey by the International Road Assessment Programme, only a small percentage—less than 10 percent—of roads in sub-Saharan Africa with speed limits greater than 40 kilometers per hour (about 25 miles per hour) have footpaths at all.[9] Even when they do have sidewalks, they are often impassible, crowded with vendors or consumed by motorcycle parking.

At times, international development groups have contributed to the problem. One of the worst examples is in Accra, Ghana, a city with a fast-growing population of 2.5 million.[10]

In 2012, the Millennium Challenge Corporation, an international nongovernmental organization, funded the upgrade of National Highway 1, or N1, between the Accra airport and port. One stretch, 14 kilometers (8.7 miles) long, was widened to a six-lane divided highway. The project was designed to "reduce bottlenecks" on the highway, which carried about twenty-five thousand vehicles a day, and aid Ghana's economy.

Completed in 2012 and renamed the George W. Bush Highway, the N1 has been a disaster for pedestrians. Turner calls it "one of the worst international development mistakes . . . with vast numbers of fatalities."[11] Six of the ten most dangerous areas of Accra are on that highway.[12]

An FIA report explained that the highway runs through residential neighborhoods in Kwashieman, Lapaz, and Abeka, where many residents earn as little as two dollars per day. "The N1 highway has been built through the centre of the Kwashieman community dividing it in two," the FIA reported. "Throughout the day, hundreds of people line up to cross the six-lane highway with traffic travelling at speeds of up to 130km/h [approximately 80 miles an hour]. Whole families stand by the road attempting to get across to their places of work, to services and schools."[13]

Experts say that there is an urgent need for better pedestrian infrastructure—namely, sidewalks—in these countries. "In somewhere like Nairobi, the majority of people walk and bicycle," said Turner. "But the only thing that's happening in Nairobi is building more bypasses. . . . All it does is encourage more people to aspire to have vehicles. They end up back in the same situation where they have gridlock."[14]

In addition to inadequate infrastructure, poor nations have other challenges that make streets much more dangerous than wealthy nations. In many less developed countries, for example, there is little to no police enforcement of traffic rules.

"Basic safety rules just are not respected," said Soames Job, Global Road Safety Lead for the World Bank. "In many countries, seat belts are not even a required element to be used. Some states don't even have a license requirement."[15]

In addition, in many lower-income countries, police departments are often rife with corruption. For example officers, who earn low wages, may insist on a bribe to escort a group of people across a dangerous street.

Inadequate vehicles are also a problem. The cars that often arrive in poor nations are almost exclusively those discarded by wealthy nations. Many vehicles are overloaded, old, and unsafe.

These countries are nevertheless seeing huge increases in vehicle ownership. The United Nations reported in 2018 that Kenya and Ethiopia were seeing growth in their vehicle fleet at the rate of 12 and 10 percent a year, respectively. The United Nations reports that 96 percent of vehicles imported into Kenya are used.[16]

Under these conditions, schoolchildren under age fourteen, like Cecilia, are at the greatest risk. Compared to that of the United States, Tanzania's population is very young, with about 45 percent of the population being less than fifteen years old.[17] But a staggering number of youth in Dar es Salaam have their lives shattered just trying to make their way to school.

A survey by the African road safety group Amend of fifteen thousand children in twenty-two schools in Dar es Salaam was used to estimate death rates for children ages five through fourteen. The group estimated that there were about forty-five traffic deaths per

A schoolboy in Dar es Salaam, Tanzania, conducts a protest after a class-mate was struck trying to cross a busy road in front of Mzambarauni Primary School in 2016. The students of the school wanted a speed bump. (Photo: Mohamed Mambo via Amend)

ten thousand children. This result indicates that far more children are killed by cars, trucks, and motorcycles in urban Tanzania than are killed by AIDS, malaria, or diarrheal diseases.[18]

When looking at six schools, with 2,675 students, the survey found that 59 children were injured in traffic crashes in 2014 alone. That was more than 2 percent of the total school population injured in traffic collisions in a single year.[19]

But people in Tanzania have fought for safer streets heroically. Children in Dar es Salaam sometimes stage impromptu protests, including a boy who sat in the middle of Nyerere Road in Dar es Salaam to protest a crash that injured one of his schoolmates at his school in April 2016.

"Unfortunately, this being a regional road, responsible authorities have always discouraged the use of speed humps—speed reduction—due to the 'political and economic sensitivity' of these roads," said Turner. "In the end, speed humps were not put in place, but a police officer was later brought in to assist pupils to cross."[20]

Cecilia's case was held up as a case study in a report by FIA.[21] In early 2016, she was one of the unlucky ones—she was struck by a motorcycle while walking to school on a footpath by the side of a busy road.

She struck her head and was rushed to the hospital by one of her teachers for treatment. (A lack of prompt medical care is another contributing factor to the high traffic fatality rates in poorer countries.) But even though she was released from the hospital later that day, the effects have been long-lasting for both Cecilia and her family. She had to be seen at several follow-up appointments and missed a month of school. When FIA last reported on her case in September 2016, she had still not caught up with her classmates and had ongoing issues with concentration.

Her family suffered long-term financial repercussions as well. Medical treatment for her injuries cost one hundred dollars—a monthly salary for her family. They were forced to borrow the money from family and friends, and more than a year later, they had not been able to repay.

Incidents like these compound the already enormous inequality in countries like Tanzania, say experts. "The poorest are most likely to be injured and to then become even poorer as a result of losing a breadwinner, the cost of treatment, or a family member giving up work to become a carer," said Turner.[22]

In the aggregate, high traffic fatality and injury rates also prevent poorer nations from becoming wealthier and more stable. Traffic crashes exert huge economic costs on the overall economy and hinder economic growth. A 2017 report from the World Bank estimated that Tanzania could increase its gross domestic product 32 percent if it could reduce traffic injuries 50 percent over a twenty-four-year period.[23]

Although many of the trends are concerning—especially increased motorization and the growth of SUVs globally—there are reasons for hope around the world as well.

Mexico City

In Mexico City as recently as 2015, one thousand people were being killed every year in traffic. About half of those killed were pedestrians and cyclists.[24]

The streets in this North American megacity (population 8.8 million) are Darwinian. The Mexican driver's licensing process essentially consists of having a picture taken. Not until 2005 did the government start using Breathalyzer tests to crack down on drunk driving (a move that caused an almost immediate 43 percent decline in fatalities).[25]

Most importantly, pedestrians simply are not respected on Mexico City's congested streets. Only about 15 percent of trips in Mexico City are made in cars.[26] Still, the whole of the city's transport apparatus seems to be geared toward accommodating that privileged minority.

In 2011, Jorge Cáñez, a lifelong Mexico City resident, decided to do something about it. "Nothing really special happened," he said.

"It was just, I was tired of this chaotic city I live in. I was tired of walking like an extreme sport. I was just tired of all this infrastructure for cars."[27]

Together with some friends, Cáñez painted a bright-green sidewalk along the Avenida de los Poetas Bridge, a terrifying stretch of highway that has heavy foot traffic. "We bought paint with our own money," he said. "Then we just started to paint sidewalks and crosswalks and bike lanes all over the city."[28]

Initially, there was pushback from some neighbors, but Cáñez and his group were able to win the ear of the government. Since then, the group—Camina, Haz Ciudad—has completed demonstration projects like the one on the Avenida de los Poetas Bridge all across the city.

With official government support, they have used flexible bollards and paint to narrow the crossing distance at 150 intersections. At those intersections, crashes have dropped 50 percent, said Cáñez.[29]

Despite the population being heavily dependent on walking, in 2011, when Cáñez got started, there were no advocacy groups devoted to pedestrian safety in Mexico City—or anywhere in Mexico, for that matter.

One of Cáñez's great innovations, however, was helping lighten the mood around the discussion. He began dressing in a Lucha Libre–style costume, used by Mexican professional wrestlers, and doing demonstrations in crosswalks.

Wearing a mask and cape, he would direct traffic or hold out his arms while schoolchildren would pass by. He would even, theatrically, push on the front end of cars that were infringing on the crosswalk. The good-natured energy of the demonstrations disarmed drivers, who were often happy to slowly reverse or yield. It also helped generate some visibility for the issue.

Cáñez calls the character Peatónito, from *peatón*, meaning pedestrian, and *ito*, a term of endearment.

"It's been a good way to communicate the message of pedestrian rights," he said. Even though car crashes are the leading cause of death

Jorge Cáñez, Mexico City's "Peatónito," dressed in a Lucha Libre costume, reminds drivers to be respectful of pedestrians. (Photo: Hector Ríos)

for everyone between the ages of five and twenty-three in Mexico (similar to the United States), "it's been a very invisible topic," he said.[30]

The pedestrian advocacy scene in Mexico City and Mexico overall has since flourished. Today, there are more than a dozen groups advocating for pedestrians in the city, and almost two dozen aligned advocacy groups have formed across the country, including one in almost every Mexican state.

The concept has spread throughout Latin America as well. For example, there are now five active groups in Brazil, including Corrida Amiga and SampaPé in São Paulo.

These efforts are starting to have a real impact, perhaps most apparent in Mexico City. Since the city announced its Vision Zero campaign in 2015, traffic deaths have fallen a remarkable 21 percent.[31]

Advocates like Cáñez hope that they are on the verge of a bigger win as well. They hope that Mexico's new president, Andrés Manuel

RED LATINOAMERICANA DE PEATONES

Map showing the locations of the pedestrian advocacy groups across Latin America in 2016, and the network continues to grow. Inspired by efforts in Mexico City, the region has experienced a surge in pedestrian advocacy since 2011. (Credit: La Liga Peatonal)

López Obrador, will pass the National Road Safety Law. This law, a package of sixty-nine different reforms, would strengthen vehicle regulations, toughen penalties for drunk driving, and task different levels of government with setting goals for crash reductions and monitoring progress toward them, among other things. It would also create a nationwide fund for addressing traffic safety and establish a transportation hierarchy with vulnerable users—pedestrians and cyclists—at the top.[32]

Areli Carreón, known as the bicycle mayor of Mexico City, said that after four years of struggle, the thirty-five citizens organizations fighting for the changes are "really enthusiastic of finally achieving it."[33]

But the battle for more walkable streets in Mexico City is also fighting against some strong cultural headwinds. Vehicle ownership is growing fast in Mexico City. The World Resources Institute estimated that Mexico overall sees a 4.2 percent increase in vehicle ownership per year.[34]

"As the economy develops, and people get more money, the first thing they want to buy is a car," said Cáñez. "To have a car is a social status symbol. If you have a car, you are more important in the mindset of the society, especially in a developing country."

But that mindset has begun to shift perceptibly recently, even in Mexico City, Cáñez said. "In a couple of neighborhoods, it's no longer cool to have a car," he said. "It's only like 2 percent of the city," he said, primarily the Condesa and Roma neighborhoods, which lean toward the young and fashionable, but it is still promising. "At least there's somewhere in Mexico City where car culture isn't the norm."[35]

A Growing Divide

A child in a lower- or middle-income country, like Cecilia in Tanzania, might face extreme risks to walk to school, but things are very different in parts of Western Europe.

In 2019, for example, not a single child was killed in traffic in the city of Oslo, the capital of Norway, a city with a population 673,000. That year, only one person was killed in traffic within city limits in total (and he was a driver, not a pedestrian).

The achievement comes as Oslo city leaders have taken bold measures to limit the dominion of cars and trucks in the city. In 2019, it pedestrianized its entire center city. Cars are forbidden or severely restricted within an area of approximately one square mile of the city's core.

City leaders had been taking aggressive measures to prepare for the transition since 2015. In 2017, the city eliminated almost all its on-street parking and converted the space to additional facilities for walkers and cyclists.[36] The few spots that remain are reserved for people with disabilities or for electric vehicle charging. Other drivers can take advantage of a few garages at the outskirts or are routed around the area on a ring road.

As the city successively removed parking and increased pedestrian space, there was some grumbling and political backlash, but pedestrian activity rose. Overall, the increase in public space makes the city more pleasant, leaders say. Oslo is one of the fastest growing cities in Europe, adding about ten thousand residents a year. Limiting the number of cars not only reduces injuries but also improves air quality and makes more room for more people.

"Cities have been built for cars for many decades, and the car has been seen as a status symbol, and I guess it still is for some people," Hanna Marcussen, Oslo's vice mayor of urban development, told *Fast Company* in 2019. "We need to plan our cities better for the future so that the private car is not setting the premise for how we build our cities anymore."[37]

Banning or greatly restricting cars within the central area of historic European cities is becoming more and more common. Madrid, a leader on this front, banned most cars from its center city in 2018. Despite signs of backlash, the decision has proved popular and enduring. When a far-right government won power in the city the following year and called for reversing the ban, tens of thousands of protesters flooded the streets[38] and were successful in winning political support to continue the car-free zone.

In addition, both Paris and London have long-term plans to phase out cars from central areas and streets. Already London has imposed congestion pricing to limit traffic in its central area. In addition, the city imposes steep fees on high-polluting vehicles within its designated Ultra Low Emissions Zone.

None of these policies would be possible without generous support for transit and years of work building bike facilities and other supportive infrastructure. These European cities also benefit from a housing stock that predates the auto era and a built environment that is dense and pedestrian friendly.

Car-free zones, and other measures, have helped produce dramatic reductions in air pollution, which is a leading killer in many of these cities. In addition, they have helped Western Europe, along with Japan, become the world leader on traffic safety. Norway now has just 2.7 traffic fatalities per 100,000 residents—or less than one-fourth of the United States' per capita fatality rate.

As Europe has improved, however, this has caused a growing global divide on this key public health issue. It is especially apparent as poorer nations with inadequate infrastructure and protections for pedestrians, like Tanzania, become increasingly motorized.

Internationally, the United States lies in a strange middle position. It is clearly a wealthy country. But in the United States, people die on the roads at rates not seen in the rest of the wealthy world, and in recent decades, it has fallen further behind.

In 2016, the US Centers for Disease Control and Prevention released a study showing that wealthy nations in Western Europe and Asia (notably Japan) have seen traffic deaths decline on average about twice as fast as in the United States since around 2000. If the United States were to match the traffic death rate of Sweden, approximately twenty-six thousand American lives a year would be saved.[39] As a result, in part, of the lack of progress on traffic safety, researchers who study life expectancy predict that US life expectancy will decline in the next few decades compared to peer nations. (Besides traffic deaths, guns and opioids are the other big factors.)[40]

Canada

Even compared to countries that are culturally and geographically very similar, the United States is a deadly place to travel. On a population-adjusted basis, Canada, for example, loses less than half as many people on the roads every year as the United States.[41]

What explains Canada's superior performance? Its land use is not much different from the United States'. In fact, Canada's densest city, Toronto, has fewer people per square mile than New York City or Chicago. And San Francisco has greater population density than Vancouver.[42]

There are, however, differences in the ways communities are designed in Canada and in the United States. Many experts point out that the United States' suburbs are more sprawling. And Canada, crucially, provides better alternatives to driving than the United States. Canada's transit commuting rate, at 11 percent, is more than double that of the United States (about 5 percent),[43] and transit ridership is closely associated with lower traffic deaths. Not only does transit ridership reduce driving, but it also supports the kind of walkable neighborhood patterns that reduce driving trips altogether—what planners call a virtuous cycle.

Canadian traffic safety expert Neil Arason, author of the book *No Accident*, said that offering alternatives to driving is an important explanation. Thanks to the presence of functional alternatives, Canada can, for example, set stricter rules about drunk driving. People caught drunk driving in Canada have their licenses revoked automatically, unlike in the United States, where drunk drivers may face jail time but not have their driving privileges interrupted. Canada also has better seat belt compliance than the United States, with only about half as many unbelted passengers.[44]

In this way and many others, traffic laws in the United States are outliers among the wealthy world and are much more lenient than all its peer countries—and many poorer nations as well. US seat belt laws are more permissive than those in all of Europe, Canada, Russia, China, Australia, and India and do not conform to the best practices recommended by the World Health Organization. US impaired driving laws are more permissive than those in Canada, Australia, most of Western Europe, China, and Brazil.[45] Speeding laws are another area where the United States is out of alignment with the United

Nations' recommendations, which call for speeds to be limited to less than 51 kilometers per hour on urban roads (about 31 miles per hour) and allow localities to adjust them. In the United States, speed limit laws are generally governed by each state and are difficult for cities to change. In many urban areas, pedestrians contend with speed limits of 35 miles per hour or more.

"The U.S. is a bit obsessed with freedom," Arason said. "There's two kinds of freedom: 'freedom to' and 'freedom from.' There's freedom to drive fast. And there's freedom from death and injury on the roads. I remember when Texas raised its speed limit, people said it's a matter of personal responsibility. (It now allows a maximum speed of 85 miles per hour.) But if someone is speeding and they're coming at you head on, there's not much you can do."[46]

Chapter 10

Families for Safe Streets

OCTOBER 8, 2013—THE DAY that everything changed for Amy Cohen and her family—was a Tuesday, a normal school day in Park Slope, Brooklyn.

That morning, Amy got on her bicycle and began her daily commute into Manhattan. Her twelve-year-old son, Sammy, turned the other way and walked toward his middle school. It would be the last time she saw him alive.

Park Slope, full of stately brownstones, wine shops, and cafés, is considered one of New York's safest neighborhoods, a destination for well-to-do young families. By early October, however, the days had started to get shorter. It was the time of year that is always the most dangerous for pedestrians.

Most of Park Slope's streets are narrow, many of them with just a single one-way lane and parking on both sides. But Prospect Park West, the street that runs along the park, is an exception. It is a two-lane, one-way street. A protected bike lane was added in 2010, narrowing the vehicle lane width. But Prospect Park West then was still one of the few places in the neighborhood where drivers could really build up some speed. The speed limit on the street was 30 miles per hour, but a 2008 study found that 90 percent of drivers were exceeding it.[1]

At some point around 5:15 p.m. that October evening, later testimony would show, Sammy's soccer ball rolled into the street.

The driver who struck him, Luis K. Quizhpi-Tacuri, told a judge that he was late for a 5 p.m. appointment. When Sammy's ball had rolled into the street, another driver had waved him forward. Quizhpi-Tacuri, driving a commercial van for a Queens-based design firm, saw the cars slowing and saw a ball, later testimony showed, but he wanted to beat the light. He hit the gas and moved to pass on the right.

For killing Sammy, he eventually had his license suspended for six months.

The days following Sammy's death, Amy said, were almost unbearable. The grief was so overwhelming, she said, that she had a constant sensation, a difficulty breathing, "like someone was sitting on your chest."[2]

Amy and her husband, Gary Eckstein, a lawyer, tried everything that was available to cope with the pain. They went to individual counseling, couples' counseling, and support groups for parents who had lost children. "Nothing really worked," she said. Soon after Sammy's death, however, Cohen did find something that helped somewhat: activism.

Most people who lose loved ones in traffic collisions suffer in solitude. If they do call for change—like the family of Ignacio Duarte-Rodriguez from Phoenix—their pleas are ignored. In addition, the drivers in these cases, even if they are negligent, often face shockingly light penalties.

But the Cohen case was special in a few ways. Unlike a lot of the other victims and families mentioned in this book, Cohen, being a white professional, had a lot of social privilege. Sammy, at just twelve years old, bright with a promising future, was a very sympathetic victim as well. But perhaps most important is that in 2014, New York City—and in particular, Park Slope—was the epicenter of safe streets advocacy in the United States. A new movement was taking hold there, right at the time of Sammy's death, that sought to make sure other mothers would not have to experience what Cohen did.

During this time, Prospect Park West, where Sammy was killed, had been the scene of a hard-fought political battle that helped redefine how city streets are apportioned in New York City.

In New York City, everyone is always battling for space: for space on the sidewalk, for a seat on a crowded subway, for a spot in line at Starbucks, for a studio apartment near the subway station. But street space, until Janette Sadik-Khan came on the scene in 2007 as New York City's transportation commissioner, was almost completely uncontested. Streets were the unquestioned domain of honking taxis and anyone with a license and set of keys.

It was a decidedly unjust distribution of space. Only about half of New York City households even own a car. But while the rest of the city was fighting for scraps, a huge portion of the city was reserved for cars and cars only.

Sadik-Khan began changing that. The city started carving not just bike lanes, but large pedestrian plazas as well, out of asphalt that formerly carried a honking, fuming, metal tangle of vehicles. Perhaps the most striking example was in 2009 when she overhauled Times Square, the city's most visited tourist location, and turned much of it into a pedestrian plaza. When the streets were redesigned to better reflect the way New Yorkers traveled, traffic deaths dropped, sometimes precipitously.

In 2010, Sadik-Khan decided to test a protected bike lane on Prospect Park West. One travel lane was painted green and turned into a protected bike lane, separated from car traffic by a parking lane. Protected bike lanes were relatively new in New York City at the time, but they had been used successfully in the Netherlands for decades. The project upset some wealthy and influential neighbors, however, who sued the city in 2011 to have the bike lane removed.

The city's data showed that the bike lane reduced speeding dramatically—injury crashes declined 63 percent—but did not impact average vehicle travel times.[3] The lawsuit dragged on for five years before it was finally dropped in 2016 when the opponents conceded, in a major victory for Sadik-Khan's more people-centered approach to street design.[4] Activists seeking to reshape New York City's streets to be more accommodating to the masses of city users were experienced and emboldened.

Practically speaking, the process of installing the improvements was not difficult. New York City used a mix of epoxy and sand to paint the streets green for the bike lanes or beige for pedestrian plazas. Simple concrete planters or plastic bollards helped keep cars and trucks out. The lanes could be installed practically overnight at a low cost. But politically, they were hard-fought.

Since the Prospect Park West bike lane was first installed, the city has added ninety-eight miles of protected bike lanes and seen traffic deaths, and pedestrian deaths in particular, plummet.[5] About 35 percent fewer people were killed while walking or wheeling in traffic in New York City in 2019 than in 2013, the year Sammy was killed.[6]

After Sammy's death, Cohen became obsessed with what was happening on the streets around her house. Just days after her son was killed, she borrowed a radar gun from some activists she knew and started clocking the cars driving down Prospect Park West. "There wasn't a car that was going less than 40 miles per hour," she said.[7]

Shortly before Sammy had been killed, the family had taken a vacation to London. At the time, London was in the midst of a safe streets campaign. In 2013, the speed limit in a one-square-mile zone in London's center city was converted to 20 miles per hour.[8] Amy remembered the signs. A thought kept nagging her after Sammy's death: "If they had done it here, he would still be alive," she said.[9]

The concept of zones limited to 20 miles per hour began sweeping the United Kingdom in 2007, initiated by a man named Rod King from the small British town of Warrington. When visiting the town's sister city, Hilden, Germany, King noticed that a high percentage of trips were made by bicycle: 23 percent,[10] much higher than in his town. There were not very many bike lanes in Hilden, but the town did have a speed limit of 30 kilometers per hour (about 18.5 miles per hour).

"That made me stop to think," King told the Middle Way radio program in 2015. "For every 100 people that they were moving around their town, they had about 25 fewer cars on the road than we did." King figured that the rule probably did not slow anyone's journey's down by any appreciable amount either. "Our journey times are dictated not by how fast we go but how long we're stopped," he explained.[11]

The approach has proved popular. Slower neighborhood streets give children the freedom to roam around the neighborhood and be active, giving parents less to worry about and more freedom of their own. It also reduces noise pollution and gives people the opportunity to walk and bicycle without fear.

After successfully campaigning to convert Warrington's speed limit to 20 miles per hour in 2004, King formed a nonprofit group and took the campaign national. By 2015, about fifteen million people across the United Kingdom lived in cities that had adopted or were considering adopting the policy, according to the nonprofit group.[12] A variety of British studies have also shown that speed limits of 20 miles per hour reduce fatalities 20 percent on neighborhood streets and 40 percent on arterial streets like the one on which Sammy was struck.[13] In addition, the World Health Organization, in a 2017 report, called residential speed limits of 20 miles per hour a global best practice.[14]

The Beginnings of a Movement

Cohen did not know it right away, but it turned out that in 2013, right around the time that Sammy was killed, New York City was considering something similar.

Sammy's death was galvanizing for the community in Park Slope, which included many influential and powerful New Yorkers. The neighborhood had also been primed by the work of Transportation Alternatives and other activist groups to think of traffic deaths as injustices caused by policy failures.

Overnight, a makeshift memorial was created at the spot where Sammy was killed, with a row of teddy bears holding hearts that spelled his name. "Slow down," said one sign, next to a row of dried flowers.

Just days after Sammy's death, a city council transportation committee held a meeting at which speeding in neighborhoods was a subject of discussion. By that time, New York City had begun establishing special zones with speed limits of 20 miles per hour in certain neighborhoods, but at the meeting, residents complained that the process took too long and that not enough was being done to improve safety.

Cohen, her husband, and their daughter each gave tearful testimony in favor of lowering New York's default speed limit, which was 30 miles per hour. "Every 33 hours, someone is dying. The next one could be someone you love," Cohen told them.

Other advocates—professionals with long histories—had been working on transportation reform in New York, but the tearful Cohen-Eckstein family, still raw from Sammy's death, was something new. Their speeches ended with applause, and some city council members cried. "Cohen's courageous speech turned her and her mourning family into the face of a larger campaign to slow down cars," Sasha Goldstein wrote in the *New York Daily News* at the time.[15]

The year that Sammy was killed, 168 pedestrians were killed in traffic in New York.[16]

The family began a personalized lobbying campaign, targeting every city council member. Cohen printed up little photo albums of Sammy, showing him smiling on family vacations. The family stood at the entryway of the meetings and handed an album to each member.

Activism gave Cohen somewhere to put the frenetic energy that Sammy's death had left her with and an activity to fill the sleepless nights. She now had a new purpose: preventing other families from going through what her family had gone through.

Through her advocacy, Cohen started meeting other New York families who had lost children to traffic crashes. Two of those parents were Amy Tam-Liao and Hsi-Pei Liao, whose three-year-old daughter, Allison, was killed by the driver of an SUV in 2013 while she was holding her grandmother's hand in a crosswalk in Flushing, Queens.[17]

"The shock and suddenness of losing a family member or friend through traffic violence is unexplainable until you have experienced it," wrote the Liaos. "Learning that tragedies like ours happen every day and nothing was being done about it fuels an anger that something needs to change."[18]

In January 2014, with the help of Transportation Alternatives, they and a handful of other New Yorkers launched Families for Safe Streets (FSS), a support group and advocacy arm for those who have lost loved ones to traffic violence in New York City. "We were already in the mindset of seeking change, not just financial compensation, which is what the other lawyers offered," the Liaos said. "So when the opportunity to create FSS came along, there was no hesitation of being part of that."[19]

The group was modeled in some ways after Mothers Against Drunk Driving (MADD) and Everytown for Gun Safety. It operates by the principle of "meet people where they are" and offers individualized support to grieving families. It also encourages members to fight back and push for reforms that can prevent traffic deaths.

"You get incredible support knowing that you haven't been singled out by the universe for this horrific tragedy," said Cohen. "There was literally a member of the group that I would say saved my life. She was there in a way for me that we tried to formally replicate."[20]

There are currently more than two hundred active members of Families for Safe Streets in New York City. All are family and friends who have lost people to "traffic violence," as they call it.

Families for Safe Streets' first fight, in January 2014, was lowering New York City's default speed limits from 30 to 25 miles per hour. It would be a tough battle. Lowering the speed limit is a complicated legal process. Speed limits in the state of New York—as in other states—are governed by state law, and in most states, the laws are set up to protect drivers from speed traps, not to protect pedestrians from injuries.

For example, the city council in Austin, Texas, voted in 2016 to lower the city's default speed limit from 30 to 25 miles per hour, but it was mostly a symbolic gesture. Even though Austin has about sixty traffic deaths a year, the city does not have the authority to lower its speed limits without enabling legislation from the state. That is a tough political battle in Texas, but it is often difficult even in progressive states like New York and Massachusetts because suburban and rural constituencies who have little to gain from lower urban speed limits often dominate state legislatures.

Cohen and Families for Safe Streets started traveling to the state-house in Albany. Often a legal change like the one they were requesting can take a year in New York, but the grieving families and their stories proved powerful in moving legislators.

"Our members provide a different perspective, a sense of urgency and a moral authority on the issue," Cohen told the Vision Zero Network in 2015. "It's hard for an elected official to say 'No' to a change that will save lives when speaking to a parent who has paid the highest sacrifice because a driver didn't want to be slightly inconvenienced."[21]

Families for Safe Streets got the speed limit rule they needed in just one legislative session.

Growing Momentum

In January 2014, New York City's new mayor, Bill de Blasio, announced that the city would adopt a Vision Zero approach to ending traffic deaths.[22] By October 2014, a year after Sammy's death, New York's city council had committed to a speed limit of 25 miles per hour. When the law took effect the following month, the speed limit was lowered from 30 to 25 miles per hour on all streets that were not specially signed.[23] Cohen's and the other families' hard work was paying off.

About a year after the speed limits were reduced, another little boy was struck on Prospect Park West. Five-year-old Roark Bennett was hit just feet from where Sammy's memorial stood in 2014. He survived with only minor injuries. In an interview with the *New York Daily News*, his mother, Karina Bennett, credited Cohen and other activists' advocacy with helping save her son, saying that her son "would not have been OK if he had been hit when someone was going 30 [miles per hour]."[24]

For Cohen, who was still overwhelmed with grief, it was a gratifying recognition, but the fight was not over. Next, Families for Safe Streets was to go back to Albany to fight for speed cameras in school zones—another local safety measure that required state authorization.

Amy Cohen (center) holds a picture of her son, Sammy, who was killed by a driver in New York City, at a press conference calling for speed cameras in school zones. (Photo: Ben Fried via Streetsblog)

Around the time that Sammy was killed in 2013, New York State approved a pilot program using twenty speed cameras in school zones. In 2014, the city began issuing tickets for violations in these zones based on camera evidence. City data later showed that the program reduced speeding in school zones 63 percent and reduced injury crashes 17 percent.[25]

In the summer of 2014, advocates went back to Albany with the goal of expanding the program. They helped win support to expand it to 140 school zones—although that is still just a small fraction of the more than two thousand schools in New York City.

The school zone speeding tickets, although they were only fifty dollars, were surprisingly effective at changing drivers' behavior. The *New York Times* reported in 2018 that 1.2 million drivers had been issued one ticket. But that one ticket was a strong deterrent: only 132,000, about 9 percent, received a second ticket.[26]

One of those rare repeat offenders, however, was in a powerful position. Marty Golden, a state senator who represented parts of Brooklyn, had the infamous distinction of receiving fourteen tickets. And it was with Golden that Families for Safe Streets New York would have its most epic struggle.

Although New York City's data showed that the program was saving lives, it almost died in 2018 when Golden and the Senate Republican majority refused to bring its reauthorization up for a vote. Golden and Staten Island Republican Senator Andrew Lanza instead introduced a measure that would have killed the program and replaced the cameras with stop signs.[27] That might have been the end of it if not for some creative advocacy by Families for Safe Streets.

Just days before the cameras were shut off in June, Amy Tam-Liao, Transportation Alternatives, and Families for Safe Streets held a demonstration in front of Governor Andrew Cuomo's office in Midtown Manhattan. On Third Street, the group—mainly parents who had lost children to traffic collisions in the city—held a banner saying, "Children are going to die." Tam-Liao and Paul Steely White,

Amy Tam-Liao and Paul Steely White, former director of Transportation Alternatives, are arrested at a protest for speed cameras in school zones in 2018. Tam-Liao's three-year-old daughter, Allison, was killed by a driver in 2013. (Photo: Ben Fried via Streetsblog)

Transportation Alternatives' director at the time, were arrested for blocking traffic and handcuffed by the New York City Police Department in front of news reporters.[28]

"I was never arrested before and was very nervous," said Tam-Liao. "But I thought that maybe this is what it takes. I just felt like I had to do it."[29]

Cohen, meanwhile, helped with a twenty-four-hour vigil in front of Golden's Brooklyn office. Members of the community were invited to visit all night and post sticky notes on Cohen's car—parked in front—outlining their own experiences with traffic violence in New York City. "It was a real community event," said Cohen. "Ultimately we couldn't change him, but we put enough pressure on him that he lost the election."[30]

Weeks before school resumed, on August 27, Cuomo issued an executive order restoring the program.[31] A smiling Cohen stood next to him, flanked on all sides by other New York City families who had lost loved ones, as he signed the measure. And just a few months later, in November, Golden lost his reelection campaign to safe streets advocate Andrew Gounardes.

In the summer of 2019, the speed camera program was dramatically expanded when de Blasio announced that the city would add thirty cameras per month until the cameras reached 750 school zones.

The Golden speed camera fight was a tipping point, Cohen believes, in the way New York City leadership thought about the issue.[32] In late 2019, Corey Johnson, the city council's Speaker, passed a streets master plan that Cohen called "the largest investment in street redesign that the city has ever undertaken."[33] This plan calls for building 150 miles of dedicated transit lanes and 250 miles of protected bike lanes by 2025. It also clarified that the Department of Transportation's role should not be to emphasize vehicle throughput.

"The passage of the Streets Master Plan sends a clear message that New York City is committed to protecting cyclists, pedestrians and straphangers over cars," said council member Donovan Richards, chair of the Committee on Public Safety, in a press release.[34] "The new bill should be celebrated as a sea change in agency philosophy," Benjamin Kabak wrote on the real estate news site Curbed.[35]

Going National

As Cohen, the Liaos, and a growing number of New York City families were getting organized to demand changes, they were also attracting attention from outside the region. Cohen received inquiries from grieving parents in other states who wanted to start their own chapters, and so the group formed chapters in New Jersey, the Bay

Area, Oregon, Virginia, and Texas. There are now eleven chapters of Families for Safe Streets.

Could Families for Safe Streets someday be like the movement against drunk driving? In his history of drunk driving in the United States, Barron Lerner describes how prior to the arrival of a few grieving mothers with powerful stories the early 1980s, the American public was "uninterested" in drunk driving. That was despite official statistics showing that drunk driving killed an astounding twenty-five thousand Americans a year and was the leading cause of death for people younger than thirty-seven.

That began to change when mothers like Candy Lightner and Cindi Lamb came on the scene in the early 1980s. Their dramatic stories gave a voice to the wider injustice of drunk driving.

Lightner, whose thirteen-year-old daughter was killed by a driver with four prior drunk driving arrests, including one two days before, had not been "a political person," according to Lerner, prior to the event. The thirty-three-year-old real estate agent was not even registered to vote. But she was telegenic, she was angry, and she knew how to tell a powerful story. Lightner "would be the main reason MADD would undergo enormous growth, having more than 300 chapters and 600,000 volunteers," by 1985, Lerner said.[36] By the 1990s, MADD was listed among the country's favorite charities.

Lightner and Lamb were featured in the biggest news outlets in the United States. Lamb's daughter, Laura, who was paralyzed at five months old by another repeat offender, became a symbol of the problem and was featured in a multipart exposé in the *Washington Post* in 1980. "I remember the last time Laura felt a hug," her mother told legislators in Annapolis, Maryland, in 1980, a quote that found its way into the paper. "I remember the last time Laura moved her fingers and hands and feet and legs. Now she doesn't feel any kisses, doesn't feel any hugs, doesn't feel anything."[37]

Through their work, Lightner and Lamb were able to dramatically shift the discussion around drunk driving in the United States.

Under pressure from MADD and associated groups, President Ronald Reagan established a commission on drunk driving and in 1984 compelled states to raise the legal drinking age to twenty-one.

In many ways, the work remains unfinished. MADD never successfully took on the primacy of the automobile in American life and the lack of practical alternatives to driving in much of the United States. That is an intimidating thing for activists to take on, especially outside of New York City.

Kristi Finney, who lost her son in a Portland, Oregon, bicycle crash to a drunk driver, helps oversee the Oregon and Southwest Washington chapter of Families for Safe Streets. Organizing the family members of victims, however, is challenging. She said that people will say, "Why should we bother because nobody cares anyway?" She added, "It's really difficult to speak out under the best of circumstances."[38] She now makes an effort to reach out to the family members when she hears of someone killed in a crash.

Grieving parents cannot fight this battle on their own. Cohen said that what she has done would not have been possible without the support of trained advocacy professionals like the people at Transportation Alternatives who cultivated her leadership and included her in key campaigns. "We did not sign up for this work. Many of us were not naturally inclined activists, but we were overwhelmed with pain," she said. "It's hard to live with this pain . . . but speaking out has given us a productive challenge."

"I had no idea this was a preventable epidemic," she continued. "That [it] wasn't just a freak accident . . . that our family was marked for this tragedy. That it could have been prevented."[39]

The challenge of confronting the problem is made more difficult because there is really no umbrella group that provides a national platform to confront traffic deaths as a leading American killer and supports the local chapters. "We have advocates on gun violence and advocates on opioids," said Cohen. "For a problem of this scale, there is no national movement."[40]

But Cohen and Families for Safe Streets are nevertheless trying to set a national agenda. In late 2019, they set about trying to convince the Democratic presidential candidates to make addressing traffic violence part of their platforms. Cohen and a core group drafted a list of suggestions. They called for a national Vision Zero program, required speed governors for cars, and increased federal spending for transit and safe streets. The letter was signed by the organization's leaders and sent to all the presidential candidates.

No presidential candidate released a plan at the time, but there was some evidence the letter had reached its target. Presidential candidate Elizabeth Warren tweeted to mark World Day of Remembrance, a day that honors people killed in traffic crashes. "Traffic violence kills thousands and injures even more Americans every year," she wrote. "On World Day of Remembrance for Traffic Crash Victims, I'm sending my love to the families and friends of those who have lost loved ones. It's time to #EndTrafficViolence."[41]

It is notable that Warren adopted the language used by Families for Safe Streets almost exactly. Activists prefer the use of the term *traffic violence* over the euphemistic *accident* because it helps desanitize the issue for the public. The term was so unheard of that after Warren tweeted it, Seattle's alternative weekly newspaper, *The Stranger*, wrote a whole article investigating the roots of the word.[42]

Families for Safe Streets' struggle has been difficult in New York City, and Cohen acknowledges that it will only be harder in cities that are much more reliant on driving.

"Change is hard. We are David against Goliath," she said. "We are fighting a huge culture that has been indoctrinated in our society that we must drive everywhere by car and it's an acceptable price to pay to have 100 people die every day."

"No one is talking about it as a preventable crisis," she continued. "We're not going to change that cultural complacency without some activism."[43]

Conclusion

O N A RAINY WINTER'S DAY IN 2020, a group of Nashville's top elected officials gathered at Metro Courthouse and stood solemnly behind a collection of empty shoes. That day, January 18, was Nashville's Day of Remembrance for victims of traffic violence, an event organized by local nonprofit groups. Each pair of shoes—thirty-two in total—represented a pedestrian killed on city streets in 2019. A handful of Metro Council people took the microphone and read the names of the victims, one after another.

The year 2019 had been the most dangerous year for walkers in the city's history. Compared to 2018, ten additional people had lost their lives. The thirty-two dead represented a near tripling of the number killed a decade before, in 2009.[1]

The event did not attract a huge crowd, but it seemed to be effective anyway. On hand was the city's new mayor, John Cooper. At times in his political career, Cooper had resisted addressing the issue. As a city council member in 2017, for example, he had opposed a $30 million sidewalk spending measure. At that time, only 37 percent of the street network in Nashville-Davidson County had sidewalks.[2]

But Cooper spoke at the event, telling attendees that he would commit to Vision Zero. "One of the most substantive ways that the city of Nashville can honor [the victims'] memory is to make a lasting and effective change to our transportation infrastructure, and a change that protects all of our residents," he said.[3] His remarks were not a guarantee of broader changes in any way, but they were a verbal commitment at least, a glimpse of what is needed, a way forward.

The problem of pedestrian deaths in the United States will not be solved without an initial recognition of the problem. Step one is to reframe. "Pedestrian deaths are preventable deaths," Lindsey Ganson with Walk Bike Nashville told the crowd that morning. "We know they're largely preventable when the city invests in infrastructure and enforcement."[4]

In 2010, without groups like Walk Bike Nashville, each of the thirty-two victims being remembered that day—as long as the driver was not drunk and stayed at the scene—would likely have been blamed individually. The deaths would not have been viewed as a distinct issue. If a fatality did rise to a notable level, perhaps local police would spend a few shifts ticketing jaywalkers, which would almost certainly have racially discriminatory effects. In this respect, a shift is under way in Nashville and many other cities, but there is a long way to go.

Bringing families of the victims—like Amy Cohen in New York City—face-to-face with lawmakers at such events can play a key role in shifting dialogue by sharing their stories and presenting the moral basis for change. Walk Bike Nashville had hoped to launch a chapter of Families for Safe Streets, but the group could not find anyone from the thirty-two families who were affected in 2019 who was willing to speak at the event. "There's a lot of work to do for people to feel supported," said Ganson. "There's a lot of stigma about pedestrian deaths. It's very sudden and unexpected. The default is that it's always the pedestrian's fault. I think that's what the families are told too."[5]

It will take a big cultural shift to move from seeking the cause in individual behavior to the wider context in which pedestrian deaths occur. But these types of shifts in public consciousness around other social issues have been seen before. For example, "opioid addiction was first viewed as a moral failing," said Tara Goddard, a professor at Texas A&M whose research has examined media biases in pedestrian deaths. "But now that we have a better understanding of how pharmaceutical companies lobby doctors and flood the market with opioids, we see it as a system issue. When we blame the individual like with obesity or smoking, we aren't going to support system change or government intervention."[6]

So far, there has not been a major consciousness-raising event about pedestrian deaths the way that the Harvey Weinstein allegations dramatized sexual assault and gave birth to the #MeToo movement or the way that little Laura Lamb, in a wheelchair, gave a human face to the problem of drunk driving. Groups like Walk Bike Nashville are trying to promote that reframing, but their reach has been limited, and the work is ongoing.

Step two is to make changes to infrastructure. Drivers and pedestrians are human and prone to misjudgment, but a forgiving infrastructure environment can prevent them from dying when they do make a mistake. Groups like Walk Bike Nashville have campaigned for years to promote the kinds of systemic solutions that are needed to reduce not just pedestrian deaths, but traffic deaths overall. In 2014, for example, the organization released a report highlighting the fifty most dangerous corridors in Davidson County, but four years later, when it updated the report to coincide with the Day of Remembrance, only four locations had seen any real pedestrian safety improvements.[7]

Pedestrians need complete sidewalks to be safe. They need comprehensive street lighting. They need curb ramps so that wheelchair users are not stuck in the street. They need bus stops that are located in safe places, preferably with shelter. They need traffic signals that give them enough time to cross. They need crosswalks at locations where pedestrians really want and need to cross, not just where it is expedient for drivers. And because drivers are so bad about yielding at uncontrolled crosswalks, those crosswalks often need additional treatments such as raised speeding tables and flashing lights.

That is basic safety infrastructure. Without it, a certain number of people will be killed.

"It's not money that is the problem," said Norman Garrick, a recently retired professor of civil engineering at the University of

Connecticut. "It's really how we're thinking: that roads are for cars. Right now, everything is governed by the need to move cars and the fear that if we don't move cars quickly, something bad [will] happen."[8]

More focus is needed on reducing vehicle speeds, especially in urban areas. The design tactics used to make "slow roads," like those common in the Western European countries with the best traffic safety outcomes, should be common in the United States, said Garrick. "A slow road is one where it's not really physically possible to go very fast," he said. "It is elevated at the intersection for example."[9]

In Sweden and other leading cities of Europe, this kind of safety engineering has been perfected, with narrowed intersections and bollards that force turning drivers to slow down, among other interventions. "In America, we are putting up signs that encourage people to go slower, but the road still encourages people to go pretty fast," said Garrick. Essentially all the roads in urban areas, Garrick said, should be slow roads, but so far, even the most forward-thinking places have only made a limited commitment to change, he said. "Even in places like New York and Washington that have decided that we need to accommodate pedestrians and bicyclists, the status quo still favors cars over all other solutions," Garrick said. "If you want to put in a bike lane . . . the first question is, How is it going to affect cars? We're trying to have it both ways."[10]

There is unfinished work to bring about this kind of sea change in the field of traffic engineering. It is inexcusable at this moment when so many pedestrians are dying on streets that the industry often uses its authority to stand in the way of low-cost, life-saving measures, hiding behind formulas, bureaucratic norms, or cost.

In addition, it is crucial that the infrastructure changes are well targeted. To have an impact, infrastructure improvements cannot just happen in wealthy, white neighborhoods where almost everyone has alternatives to walking and taking the bus.

In Nashville, for example, pedestrian deaths are clearly concentrated in poorer areas. In 2019, there were no deaths in West

Nashville—"the historic, wealthy area," Ganson said. "Those more established historic neighborhoods have sidewalks," she added. "They don't have arterial streets running through, and if they do, they're very separated from the rest of the neighborhood." There are "one hundred years of racist planning" to make up for, said Ganson.[11]

When it comes to infrastructure changes, lower-income neighborhoods and neighborhoods of color should receive special attention. As Emiko Atherton, director of the National Complete Streets Coalition, said, "Decades of racist policies—and people in power pushing for those policies—created deeply inequitable cities where white neighborhoods prospered and communities of color suffered. The solutions we need to heal those wounds and build places that are safe for everyone are right in front of us."[12]

Other areas where at-risk groups may be concentrated—for example, in areas with lots of older adults, a large homeless population, or where there is a lot of drinking happening—need special attention as well.

In addition, the role that the auto industry plays in the crisis cannot be ignored. Auto safety innovation has saved hundreds of thousands of lives, but until now, pedestrians and cyclists have not benefited and indeed have suffered a great deal due to recent industry trends.

Even as pedestrian deaths have reached crisis levels, the auto industry has promoted larger and more deadly SUVs and high-horsepower sports cars that data have definitively shown kill people on foot. There is more than enough evidence for federal regulators (namely, the National Highway Traffic Safety Administration) to step in and require automakers to make life-saving changes, as has been done in other nations. In fact, those changes might already be in place were it not for the indifference of the Trump administration's Department of Transportation. An additional problem is lack of grassroots energy around regulatory changes that could save hundreds or thousands of lives.

Automated features that have been shown to improve safety, such as automatic emergency braking and pedestrian detection, are low-hanging fruit and should be required on all cars. Even failing that, they could be required on the vehicles known to be especially dangerous—SUVs, pickup trucks, and small, high-horsepower cars—but achieving those kinds of life-saving regulations will require wider recognition, organized effort, and financial support for those efforts.

In addition, we need further research about the effects of aftermarket vehicle modifications, including bull bars that are affixed to the front of cars and trucks. Many buyers (including, notably, public police departments) may not be aware that by purchasing these kinds of products, not only do they impose safety risks on others, but they increase their own risk of being killed or injured in a crash. Although vehicle regulators have never taken on these kinds of modifications in the United States, the escalating carnage that pedestrians are experiencing on American roads provides an opportunity to reexamine this stance.

In short, there is a lot of work to do, and it will primarily be up to ordinary people to do it. That work often looks like the Day of Remembrance demonstration in Nashville: not especially splashy or earth-shattering, but persistent.

Walk Bike Nashville had been quietly building to that moment for a long time. Before the 2016 election cycle, the group, working with an array of organizations from AARP Tennessee to the local chapter of the Urban League, put together a platform calling for a number of reforms to address the problem. The group asked for a Vision Zero policy and also asked for a public process centering on safety, equity, and public feedback.

In the end, the platform was a very broad, conceptual document.[13] The group asked for local politicians to endorse it and was largely successful. Twenty members of the Nashville Metro Council and the mayor signed on. In every council race in which one of the candidates endorsed the platform, the winning candidate did so.

The group has also been working to demonstrate what additional on-the-ground reforms could look like. In 2017, Walk Bike Nashville and the Tennessee Department of Transportation partnered on a demonstration project at Nolensville Pike and Welshwood Drive, the most dangerous intersection in the city. This intersection is near two bus stops with very high ridership as well as a big shopping center. Seven people were killed at this location between 2010 and 2017, when advocates came forward with some inexpensive materials and a plan to help.

They built two temporary median islands enforced by steel bollards. On top were placed two big yellow signs warning drivers of the state law: to yield to pedestrians in the crosswalk. Pedestrians were also given a button-activated flashing warning light.

As a proof of concept, the demonstration was a success. Since it was installed about two years ago, there have been no additional fatalities there.

There is a lot more to do. But the mayor of Nashville's words at the Day of Remembrance Ceremony, said Ganson, meant that some of the important groundwork could begin and that the city would begin to put together the necessary data to evaluate the problem and then develop next steps. "That's a huge step forward," said Ganson.[14]

A temporary crosswalk installed by Walk Bike Nashville on the city's most dangerous street, Nolensville Pike. (Photo: Walk Bike Nashville)

Acknowledgments

Thank you first and foremost to everyone who shared their stories with me, especially the courageous men and women of Families for Safe Streets, Amy Cohen, Latanya Byrd, Amy Tam-Liao and Hsi-Pei Liao, and Kristi Finney. My empathy for you, especially after having children of my own, was the inspiration for this book.

Thank you to Charles T. Brown, who wrote the foreword to this book and served as an advisor on the project. He knows his stuff, and everyone should listen to him.

Thank you to my wonderful editor at Island Press, Heather Boyer. Thank you to Kathleen Lafferty and to everyone who had a hand in copyediting and layout. The whole organization was a dream to work with.

Thank you to my long-time editor at Streetsblog, Ben Fried; to Gersh Kuntzman; and to publisher Mark Gorton and everyone with whom I worked who supported my work there over nine years, which was the basis for much of this book. Thank you to our readers who supported me and taught me so much there as well.

Thank you to Anne Trubek at Belt Publishing, who served as an unpaid literary agent on this project just because she is awesome. Thank you to Aaron Naparstek, who came up with the title for this book when Heather and I could not think of anything snappy enough.

Thank you to my mother, Sarah Hartley, who proofread all my high school papers—and hated them! She proofread some early chapters of this book only to have me reject all the changes. (Sorry, Mom!) Thank you to my husband, who, as cliché as it sounds, is my biggest supporter and confidant in both my life and career.

Thank you to Neil Arason and Robert Schneider, two of the unsung heroes from the world of traffic safety, who helped me track down answers to some of my research questions throughout this process, and to David Zuby at the Insurance Institute for Highway Safety.

Notes

Introduction: Outline of an Epidemic

1. Matt Rodewald, "Family Demands Change after 77-Year-Old Is Killed in a Pedestrian Crash," Fox 10 Phoenix, March 13, 2018, https://www.fox10phoenix.com/news/family-demands-change-after-77-year-old-is-killed-in-pedestrian-crash.
2. National Highway Traffic Safety Administration, Road Safety Topics, "Pedestrian Safety," accessed February 2, 2020, https://www.nhtsa.gov/road-safety/pedestrian-safety.
3. National Safety Council, "Pedestrian Fatalities 2018 Overview," accessed March 26, 2020, https://injuryfacts.nsc.org/motor-vehicle/road-users/pedestrians/.
4. Author's note: According to the National Highway Traffic Safety Administration, 6,283 pedestrians were killed in 2018 compared to 4,092 in 2009—a 53 percent increase over ten years (the beginning of 2009 through the end of 2018). National Highway Traffic Safety Administration, Traffic Safety Facts, 2018 Data, "Fatal Motor Vehicle Crashes: Overview," October 2019, https://crashstats.nhtsa.dot.gov/Api/Public/ViewPublication/812826; National Highway Traffic Safety Administration, Traffic Safety Facts, 2009 Data, "Pedestrians," accessed April 10, 2020, https://crashstats.nhtsa.dot.gov/Api/Public/ViewPublication/811394.
5. National Highway Traffic Safety Administration, "Fatal Motor Vehicle Crashes."
6. Rodewald, "Family Demands Change."
7. Bree Burkitt, "Man Hit, Killed by Car; Police Seeking Driver," *Arizona Republic*, March 11, 2018, https://www.azcentral.com/story/news/local/phoenix/2018/03/11/man-dies-after-being-hit-car-phoenix-police-searching-driver/414708002/.
8. Wasim Riaz, Sveinung Berg Bentzrød, and Carl Alfred Dahl, "1975: 41 døde i Oslo-trafikken, 2019: Én død i trafikken," January 2020, https://

www.aftenposten.no/osloby/i/dO0rzz/1975-41-doede-i-oslo-trafikken
-2019-en-doed-i-trafikken.

9. European Commission, "Traffic Safety Basic Facts on Pedestrians," Directorate General for Transport, June 2018, https://ec.europa.eu/ transport/road_safety/sites/roadsafety/files/pdf/statistics/dacota/ bfs20xx_pedestrians.pdf.

10. St. Louis Federal Reserve, "Moving 12-Month Total Vehicle Miles Traveled," updated August 15, 2019, https://fred.stlouisfed.org/series/ M12MTVUSM227NFWA.

11. Author's note: In 2009, the total miles driven by Americans was 2,932.4 billion. In 2018, it was 3,224.9 billion, a 9.97 percent increase. Federal Highway Administration, Policy Information, "December 2009 Traffic Volume Trends," accessed April 10, 2020, https://www.fhwa.dot .gov/ohim/tvtw/09dectvt/index.cfm; Federal Highway Administration, Office of Highway Policy Information, "December 2018 Traffic Volume Trends," accessed April 10, 2020, https://www.fhwa.dot.gov/ policyinformation/travel_monitoring/18dectvt/.

12. Tim McMahon, "Inflation Adjusted Gas Prices," InflationData.com, accessed March 20, 2020, https://inflationdata.com/articles/inflation -adjusted-prices/inflation-adjusted-gasoline-prices/.

13. R. J. Cross and Tony Dutzik, "Driving into Debt: The Hidden Cost of Risky Auto Loans to Consumers and Our Community," Frontier Group, February 13, 2019, https://frontiergroup.org/reports/fg/driving -debt.

14. Angie Schmitt, "The Best Tool for Reducing Traffic Deaths? More Transit!," Streetsblog USA, August 29, 2018, https://usa.streetsblog.org/ 2018/08/29/the-best-tool-for-reducing-traffic-deaths-more-transit/.

15. Wen Hu and Jessica B. Cicchino, "An Examination of the Increases in Pedestrian Motor Vehicle Crash Fatalities during 2009–16," *Journal of Safety Research* 67 (September 2018): 37–44.

16. Highway Loss Data Institute, "Vehicle Information Report, 1981–2019 Vehicle Fleet, Facts and Figures," December 2018.

17. Jato Dynamics, "U.S. New Vehicle Sales Saw a Slight Increase in 2018 as SUVs Continue to See Market Share Growth," press release, February 27, 2019, https://www.jato.com/usa/u-s-new-vehicle-sales-saw-a-slight -increase-in-2018-as-suvs-continue-to-see-market-share-growth/.

18. Insurance Institute for Highway Safety, Status Report, "On Foot, At Risk," May 8, 2018.

19. Eric D. Lawrence, Nathan Bomey, and Kristi Tanner, "Death on Foot: America's Love of SUVs Is Killing Pedestrians," *Detroit Free Press*, July 1, 2018, https://www.freep.com/story/money/cars/2018/06/28/suvs-killing-americas-pedestrians/646139002/.

20. National Complete Streets Coalition, Smart Growth America, "Dangerous by Design 2019," January 2019, https://smartgrowthamerica.org/dangerous-by-design/.

21. Governors Highway Safety Association, "Pedestrian Traffic Fatalities by State: 2018 Preliminary Data," February 2019, https://www.ghsa.org/sites/default/files/2019-02/FINAL_Pedestrians19.pdf.

22. Bill Fulton, "Large Sun Belt Metro Areas Continue to Drive Growth," Rice University Kinder Institute for Urban Research, March 23, 2018, https://kinder.rice.edu/2018/03/23/large-sun-belt-metro-areas-continue-drive-growth.

23. United States Census Bureau, "QuickFacts," population, 2018, https://www.census.gov/quickfacts/philadelphiacountypennsylvania; https://www.census.gov/quickfacts/phoenixcityarizona.

24. Will Maher, "Poverty Face Sheet: Suburban Poverty," Institute for Research on Poverty, University of Wisconsin–Madison, no. 14, 2017–2018, https://www.irp.wisc.edu/publications/factsheets/pdfs/FactSheet14-Suburban-Poverty.pdf.

25. Centers for Disease Control and Prevention, "Motor Vehicle Traffic-Related Pedestrian Deaths—United States, 2001–2010," *Morbidity and Mortality Report* 62, no. 15 (April 19, 2013): 277–82, https://www.cdc.gov/mmwr/preview/mmwrhtml/mm6215a1.htm#fig.

26. Centers for Disease Control and Prevention, "Distracted Driving," accessed March 20, 2020, https://www.cdc.gov/motorvehiclesafety/distracted_driving/index.html.

27. National Highway Traffic Safety Administration, Traffic Safety Facts, 2016 Data, "Distracted Driving 2016," April 2018, https://crashstats.nhtsa.dot.gov/Api/Public/ViewPublication/812517.

28. Zendrive Research, "Largest Distracted Driving Behavior Study," April 2017, https://zendrive.com/wp-content/uploads/2019/04/Zendrive_Distracted_Driving_2017.pdf.

29. Zendrive Research, "Largest Distracted Driving Behavior Study."

30. Jonathan O'Callaghan, "Drivers Are More Distracted Than Ever Before—and Taking Your Eyes off the Road for Just 2 Seconds Increases Accident Risk 24 Times," *Daily Mail*, March 18, 2015, https://www.dailymail.co.uk/sciencetech/article-3000917/Drivers-distracted-taking-eyes-road-just-2-seconds-increases-accident-risk-24-times.html.

31. International Transport Forum, Road Safety Data, "Road Safety Annual Report 2019: Canada," October 7, 2019, https://www.itf-oecd.org/sites/default/files/canada-road-safety.pdf.

32. J. L. Nasar and D. Troyer, "Pedestrian Injuries due to Mobile Phone Use in Public Places," *Journal of Accident Analysis and Prevention* 57 (August 2013): 91–95, https://www.ncbi.nlm.nih.gov/pubmed/23644536.

33. Centers for Disease Control and Prevention, "Pedestrian Safety," accessed March 20, 2020, https://www.cdc.gov/motorvehiclesafety/pedestrian_safety/index.html.

34. National Highway Traffic Safety Administration, Traffic Safety Facts, 2017 Data, "Pedestrians," March 2019, https://crashstats.nhtsa.dot.gov/Api/Public/ViewPublication/812681.

35. Mike Maciag, "Pedestrians Dying at Disproportionate Rates in America's Poorer Neighborhoods," Governing, August 2014, https://www.governing.com/gov-data/pedestrian-deaths-poor-neighborhoods-report.html.

36. Author's note: The National Household Travel Survey showed that the percentage of trips walked by Americans declined from 10.5 percent to 10.4 percent of trips between 2009 and 2017 (the latest year for which data are available); the report notes, however, that this change was within the margin of error. Federal Highway Administration, "Summary of Travel Trends, National Household Travel Survey 2017," July 2018, https://nhts.ornl.gov/assets/2017_nhts_summary_travel_trends.pdf.

37. Transportation for America, "Rethinking the Gas Tax: Suddenly It's the Theme of 2013," January 31, 2013, http://t4america.org/2013/01/31/rethinking-the-gas-tax-suddenly-its-the-theme-of-2013/.

38. Griffin Smith Jr., "The Highway Establishment and How It Grew and Grew and Grew," *Texas Monthly*, April 1974, https://www.texasmonthly.com/travel/the-highway-establishment-and-how-it-grew-and-grew-and-grew/.

39. Author's note: Bike and pedestrian programs are contained within a program called Transportation Alternatives, funded at $850 million annually (Federal Highway Administration, "Fixing America's Surface Transportation Act, or 'Fast Act,'" Transportation Alternatives, accessed March 20, 2020, https://www.fhwa.dot.gov/fastact/factsheets/transportationalternativesfs.cfm). The total annual surface transportation budget is about $60 billion (Angie Schmitt, "The 5-Year, $300 Billion 'FAST Act' Will Extend Transpo Policy Status Quo until 2020," Streetsblog USA, December 2, 2015, https://usa.streetsblog.org/2015/12/02/5-year-300-billion-fast-act-will-extend-transpo-policy-status-quo-to-2020/), making the biking and walking share 1.4 percent.

40. Anthony Derrick, "Mayor Durkan Proposes Major Actions to Achieve Vision Zero Goals and Increase Traffic Safety," City of Seattle, Office of the Mayor, December 10, 2019, https://durkan.seattle.gov/2019/12/mayor-durkan-proposes-major-actions-to-achieve-vision-zero-goals-and-increase-traffic-safety/.

Chapter 1. The Geography of Risk

1. Mark Dent, "How Roosevelt Boulevard Became the Most Dangerous Road in Philadelphia," Billy Penn, February 6, 2017, https://billypenn.com/2017/02/06/how-roosevelt-boulevard-became-the-most-dangerous-road-in-philadelphia/.

2. Matthew DeLuca, "Driver Accused of Killing Philly Mother, Boys Had History of Driving Violations," NBC News, July 18, 2013, https://www.nbcnews.com/news/us-news/driver-accused-killing-philly-mother-boys-has-history-driving-violations-flna6C10677250.

3. Latanya Byrd, in-person interview, July 11, 2019.

4. Joseph A. Slobodzian, "Teen Recounts Hit-Run That Killed Her Sister, 3 Nephews," Philadelphia Inquirer, July 10, 2015, http://www.philly.com/philly/news/20150710_Teen_recounts_hit-run_that_killed_her_sister_3_nephews.html.

5. Byrd, in-person interview.

6. Byrd, in-person interview.

7. Tony Hanson, "Trial Ordered for Pair in Roosevelt Blvd. Crash That Killed Mom, 3 Kids," CBS 3 Philadelphia, October 29, 2013, https://philadelphia.cbslocal.com/2013/10/29/trial-ordered-for-pair-in-roosevelt-blvd-crash-that-killed-mom-3-kids/.

8. Chris Palmer, "Appeals Court Reverses Some Counts against Drag Racer Who Killed 4 on Roosevelt Blvd.," *Philadelphia Inquirer*, December 8, 2017, https://www.inquirer.com/philly/news/crime/drag-racing-crash-roosevelt-boulevard-philly-counts-reversed-20171208.html.

9. Dent, "How Roosevelt Boulevard Became Dangerous."

10. Tanya Snyder, "Dangerous by Design: How the U.S. Builds Roads That Kill Pedestrians," Streetsblog USA, May 24, 2011, https://usa.streetsblog.org/2011/05/24/dangerous-by-design-how-the-u-s-builds-roads-that-kill-pedestrians/.

11. David Sachs, "5 Percent of Denver Streets Account for Half of All Traffic Deaths," Streetsblog Denver, July 25, 2017, https://denver.streetsblog.org/2017/07/25/5-percent-of-denver-streets-account-for-half-of-all-traffic-deaths/.

12. Mid-Region Council of Governments, Safety Analysis, "The High Fatal and Injury Network," accessed March 21, 2020, http://www.mrcog-nm.gov/255/Safety-Analysis.

13. Michael Smith and Jennifer Smith, "Safety for Whom?," Strong Towns, August 1, 2018, https://www.strongtowns.org/journal/2018/7/31/safety-for-whom.

14. Emiko Atherton, telephone interview, July 5, 2019.

15. New York City Department of Transportation, "Automated Speed Enforcement Program Report 2014–2017," June 2018, http://www.nyc.gov/html/dot/downloads/pdf/speed-camera-report-june2018.pdf, 11.

16. Jason Laughlin, "Speed Cameras Approved for Roosevelt Boulevard," *Philadelphia Inquirer*, May 16, 2019, https://www.inquirer.com/transportation/speed-camera-roosevelt-boulevard-philadelphia-vision-zero-20190516.html.

17. Michael B. Smith, "Walkable Rockford: Exploratory Research of Pedestrian Collisions on Arterials in Rockford, Illinois," University of Illinois, Fall 2018.

18. Angie Schmitt, "Research Explains Why Pedestrians 'Break the Rules,'" Streetsblog USA, January 7, 2019, https://usa.streetsblog.org/2019/01/07/research-explains-why-pedestrians-break-the-rules/.

19. Schmitt, "Research Explains."

20. Winnie Hu, "No Longer New York City's 'Boulevard of Death,'" *New York Times*, December 3, 2017, https://www.nytimes.com/2017/12/03/nyregion/queens-boulevard-of-death.html.

21. Gersh Kuntzman, "First Death on Queens Boulevard since 2015 Vision Zero Fix," Streetsblog NYC, December 17, 2018, https://nyc.streetsblog.org/2018/12/17/first-death-on-queens-boulevard-since-2015-vision-zero-fix/.

22. Historic census data can be found here: https://www.census.gov/population/www/censusdata/PopulationofStatesandCountiesoftheUnitedStates1790-1990.pdf.

23. Doug Monroe, "Where It All Went Wrong," *Atlanta*, August 1, 2012, https://www.atlantamagazine.com/great-reads/marta-tsplost-transportation/.

24. Sally Flocks, personal interview, July 7, 2019.

25. Karen Pooley, "Segregation's New Geography: The Atlanta Metro Region, Race, and the Declining Prospects for Upward Mobility," *Southern Spaces*, April 15, 2015, https://southernspaces.org/2015/segregations-new-geography-atlanta-metro-region-race-and-declining-prospects-upward-mobility/.

26. Katherine Schaeffer, "In a Rising Number of U.S. Counties, Hispanic and Black Americans Are the Majority," Pew Research Center, November 20, 2019, https://www.pewresearch.org/fact-tank/2019/11/20/in-a-rising-number-of-u-s-counties-hispanic-and-black-americans-are-the-majority/.

27. Data USA, "Clayton County, Georgia," accessed March 13, 2020, https://datausa.io/profile/geo/clayton-county-ga.

28. Flocks, personal interview.

29. Chico Harlan, "A Lonely Road," *Washington Post*, December 28, 2015, https://www.washingtonpost.com/sf/business/2015/12/28/deep-south-4/?utm_term=.cfda8df2f742.

30. Georgia Department of Transportation, "Pedestrian Safety Action Plan, 2018–2022," accessed April 10, 2020, http://www.dot.ga.gov/DriveSmart/Travel/Documents/BikePed/BikePedSAP.pdf, 46.

31. Chelsea Prince, "Clayton County Police Department Works to Reduce Pedestrian Fatalities on Tara Boulevard," *Clayton News Daily*, December 5, 2016, https://www.news-daily.com/news/clayton-county -police-department-works-to-reduce-pedestrian-fatalities-on/article _08fd7525-319c-5d27-9ad5-ff999154ad37.html.

32. Lin Pei-Sung et al., "Application of Demographic Analysis to Pedestrian Safety," Transportation Research Board, April 2017, https://trid.trb.org/ view/1468235.

33. Charles T. Brown, telephone interview, July 1, 2019.

34. Angie Schmitt, "Cities Want to Save Lives with Lower Speed Limits, but States Stand in the Way," Streetsblog USA, December 22, 2016, https://usa.streetsblog.org/2016/12/22/cities-want-to-save-lives -with-lower-speed-limits-but-states-stand-in-the-way/comment -page-5/.

35. American Planning Transit Association, "Cities with Higher Public Transit Use Can Cut Their Road Traffic Death Rate in Half," press briefing, August 28, 2018, http://apta.vzaar.me/16584254.

36. Brian C. Tefft, "Impact Speed and a Pedestrians Risk of Severe Injury or Death," AAA Foundation for Traffic Safety, September 2011, https:// aaafoundation.org/wp-content/uploads/2018/02/2011Pedestrian RiskVsSpeedReport.pdf.

37. Frank C. Palmer, "Physics and Math for Drivers," US Department of Labor Safety Standards, vol. 8, no. 1 (January–February 1959), 6.

38. Neil Arason, *No Accident: Eliminating Death and Injury on Canada's Roads* (Waterloo, ON: Wilfrid Laurier University Press, 2014), 200.

39. Smart Growth America, National Complete Streets Coalition, "Dangerous by Design," 2019, https://smartgrowthamerica.org/app/uploads/ 2019/01/Dangerous-by-Design-2019-FINAL.pdf.

40. Richard Retting, "Pedestrian Traffic Fatalities by State: 2017 Preliminary Data," Governors Highway Safety Association, February 28, 2018, https://www.ghsa.org/sites/default/files/2018-03/pedestrians _18.pdf.

41. Atherton, telephone interview.

42. Geoff Boeing, "Off the Grid . . . and Back Again? The Recent Evolution of American Street Network Planning and Design," paper presented at

the ninety-ninth annual meeting of the Transportation Research Board, Washington, DC, January 12–16, 2020.

43. Boeing, "Off the Grid."

44. Governors Highway Safety Association, "Pedestrian Traffic Fatalities by State: 2018 Preliminary Data," February 2019, https://www.ghsa.org/sites/default/files/2019-02/FINAL_Pedestrians19.pdf.

45. Complete Streets Advisory Board, letter, May 30, 2018, http://usa .streetsblog.org/wp-content/uploads/sites/5/2018/05/CSAB-Letter -of-Resignations-final.pdf, 1.

46. Angie Schmitt, "Phoenix Will Continue to Let People to Die in the Streets," Streetsblog USA, April 24, 2019, https://usa.streetsblog.org/2019/04/24/phoenix-council-votes-to-continue-letting-people-to-die-in-the-streets/.

47. Schmitt, "Phoenix Will Continue."

48. Atherton, telephone interview.

Chapter 2. The Profile of a Victim

1. Portland Bureau of Transportation, "Bicycles in Portland Fact Sheet," updated April 2019, https://www.portlandoregon.gov/transportation/article/407660.

2. Corey Pein, "The Other Portland," *Willamette Week*, October 11, 2011, https://www.wweek.com/portland/article-18071-the-other-portland.html.

3. Portland Bureau of Transportation, "Appendix A: East Portland Demographic Overview," *East Portland in Motion: A Five-Year Implementation Strategy for Active Transportation*, March 2012, https://www .portlandoregon.gov/transportation/article/372607, A7.

4. Meera Powell, "Report: Traffic Deaths Remain Higher in East Portland," Oregon Public Broadcasting, June 11, 2019, https://www.opb.org/news/article/portland-report-reducing-traffic-fatalities/.

5. Pein, "Other Portland."

6. Pein, "Other Portland."

7. Hannah Chinn, "Blindsided: Portland Spends Millions to Stop Cars from Killing People. It's Not Working," *Willamette Week*, accessed March 13, 2020, https://www.wweek.com/blindsided/.

8. Powell, "Report: Traffic Deaths."

9. Centers for Disease Control and Prevention, "Motor Vehicle Traffic-Related Pedestrian Deaths—United States, 2001–2010," *Morbidity and Mortality Report* 62, no. 15 (April 19, 2013): 277–82, https://www.cdc.gov/mmwr/preview/mmwrhtml/mm6215a1.htm#fig.

10. Ben Bradford, "One Way Oakland Is Fighting Racial Inequality? By Fixing Potholes," *Marketplace*, May 15, 2019, https://www.marketplace.org/2019/05/15/one-way-oakland-is-fighting-racial-inequality-by-fixing-potholes/.

11. Xuehao Chu, "An Assessment of Public Transportation Markets Using NHTS Data," National Center for Transit Research at CUTR University of South Florida, Tampa, March 2012, https://www.nctr.usf.edu/wp-content/uploads/2013/01/77920.pdf, 28.

12. Monica Anderson, "Who Relies on Public Transit in the U.S.?," Pew Research Center, April 7, 2016, https://www.pewresearch.org/fact-tank/2016/04/07/who-relies-on-public-transit-in-the-u-s/.

13. Amelie G. Ramirez et al., "The State of Latino Housing, Transportation, and Green Space: A Research Review," Salud America!, May 14, 2019, https://salud-america.org/the-state-of-latino-housing-transportation-greenspace-research/.

14. Federal Highway Administration, "Mobility Challenges for Households in Poverty," National Household Travel Survey Mobility Brief, 2014, https://nhts.ornl.gov/briefs/PovertyBrief.pdf.

15. Robert Schneider, telephone interview, June 10, 2019.

16. Charles T. Brown, telephone interview, July 1, 2019.

17. Eric D. Lawrence, Nathan Bomey, and Kristi Tanner, "Death on Foot: America's Love of SUVs Is Killing Pedestrians," *Detroit Free Press*, July 1, 2018, https://www.freep.com/story/money/cars/2018/06/28/suvs-killing-americas-pedestrians/646139002/.

18. Doug Tribou, "Kaffer: As Detroit's Streetlights Burn Out, Fixing Them Is a Test for the City," *Morning Edition*, Michigan Radio, May 9, 2019, https://www.michiganradio.org/post/kaffer-detroits-streetlights-burn-out-fixing-them-test-city.

19. National Highway Traffic Safety Administration, Traffic Safety Facts, 2017 Data, "Pedestrians," March 2019, https://crashstats.nhtsa.dot.gov/Api/Public/ViewPublication/812681.

20. J. B. Wogan, "How Streetlights Can Bridge Racial Gaps in Cities," *Government Technology*, August 11, 2016, https://www.govtech.com/fs/ How-Streetlights-Can-Bridge-Racial-Gaps-in-Cities.html.

21. Chris Gautz, "$185M Bond Sale Flips Switch on Purchase of 55,000 Streetlights for Detroit," Crain's Detroit, June 26, 2014, https://www .crainsdetroit.com/article/20140626/NEWS/140629890/185m-bond -sale-flips-switch-on-purchase-of-55000-streetlights-for.

22. Todd Scott, "Detroit Public Lighting Improvements Reducing Pedestrian Fatalities," Detroit Greenways Coalition, July 16, 2018, https:// detroitgreenways.org/detroit-public-lighting-improvements-reducing -pedestrian-fatalities/.

23. Scott, "Detroit Public Lighting Improvements."

24. Author's note: According to the Centers for Disease Control and Prevention, the overall pedestrian fatality rate for the United States is 1.58 deaths per 100,000 population. For Native American or Alaskan men, it is 7.73. Centers for Disease Control and Prevention, "Motor Vehicle Traffic-Related Pedestrian Deaths."

25. Kathryn Quick and Guillermo Narváez, "Understanding Roadway Safety in American Indian Reservations: Perceptions and Management of Risk by Community, Tribal Governments, and Other Safety Leaders," University of Minnesota Center for Transportation Studies, October 2018, http://www .cts.umn.edu/Publications/ResearchReports/reportdetail.html?id=2720.

26. Quick and Narváez, "Understanding Roadway Safety."

27. Quick and Narváez, "Understanding Roadway Safety."

28. Wesley Marshall and Nicholas Ferenchek, "Why Cities with High Bicycling Rates Are Safer for All Road Users," *Journal of Transport and Health* 13 (June 2019), https://www.sciencedirect.com/science/article/ pii/S2214140518301488?via%3Dihub.

29. Marshall and Ferenchek, "Why Cities with High Bicycling Rates Are Safer."

30. National Highway Traffic Safety Administration, Traffic Safety Facts, 2016 Data, "Pedestrians," March 2018 (revised), https://crashstats.nhtsa .dot.gov/Api/Public/ViewPublication/812493.

31. Centers for Disease Control and Prevention, "Motor Vehicle Traffic-Related Pedestrian Deaths."

32. Graham Beck, "Streets Safe for Walking," AARP, March 23, 2009, https://www.aarp.org/home-garden/livable-communities/info-03 -2009/streets_safe_for_walking.html.

33. Kay Fitzpatrick et al., "Improving Pedestrian Safety at Unsignalized Crossings,"Transit Cooperative Research Program and National Cooperative Highway Research Program, Transportation Research Board, report 112, 2006.

34. Nuala Sawyer, "Senior Pedestrian Killed at Fell and Baker," *SF Weekly*, October 5, 2017, http://www.sfweekly.com/news/senior-pedestrian -killed-at-fell-and-baker/.

35. J. H. Kell and I. J. Fullerton, *Manual of Traffic Signal Design*, 2nd ed. (Washington, DC: Institute of Transportation Engineers, 1991), https:// trid.trb.org/view/349378.

36. Jordi Jordan Berrett, "Pedestrian Walking Speeds at Signalized Intersections in Utah," Brigham Young University, March 1, 2019, https:// scholarsarchive.byu.edu/cgi/viewcontent.cgi?article=8130&context=etd.

37. Newsroom, US Census Bureau, "Older People Projected to Outnumber Children for First Time in U.S. History," March 13, 2018, https:// www.census.gov/newsroom/press-releases/2018/cb18-41-population -projections.html.

38. Charles Zegeer et al., "Analysis of Elderly Pedestrian Accidents and Recommended Countermeasures," *Transportation Research Record* 1405 (1993): 56–63, http://onlinepubs.trb.org/Onlinepubs/trr/1993/1405/ 1405-009.pdf.

39. Centers for Disease Control and Prevention, "Motor Vehicle Traffic-Related Pedestrian Deaths."

40. National Highway Traffic Safety Administration, Traffic Safety Facts, 2017 Data, "Pedestrians," March 2019, https://crashstats.nhtsa.dot.gov/ Api/Public/ViewPublication/812681.

41. Mike Maciag, "Pedestrians Dying at Disproportionate Rates in America's Poorer Neighborhoods," Governing, August 2014, https://www .governing.com/topics/public-justice-safety/gov-pedestrian-deaths -analysis.html.

42. Caitlin D. Cottrill and Piyushimita (Vonu) Thakuriah, "Evaluating Pedestrian Crashes in Areas with High Low-Income or Minority

Populations," *Accident Analysis and Prevention* 42, no. 6 (November 2010): 1718–28, https://www.sciencedirect.com/science/article/pii/S0001457510001284?via%3Dihub.

43. Kaci L. Hickox et al., "Pedestrian Traffic Deaths among Residents, Visitors, and Homeless Persons—Clark County, Nevada, 2008–2011," weekly report, Centers for Disease Control, June 18, 2014, https://www.cdc.gov/mmwr/preview/mmwrhtml/mm6328a1.htm.

44. Audrey McGlinchy, "Housing Austin's Homeless Will Reduce Road Deaths, but That Will Require a Big Investment," KUT, May 17, 2018, https://www.kut.org/post/housing-austins-homeless-will-reduce-road-deaths-will-require-big-investment.

45. McGlinchy, "Housing Austin's Homeless."

46. McGlinchy, "Housing Austin's Homeless."

47. Centers for Disease Control and Prevention, "Impaired Driving: Get the Facts," accessed March 24, 2020, https://www.cdc.gov/motorvehiclesafety/impaired_driving/impaired-drv_factsheet.html.

48. B. F. Grant et al., "Prevalence of 12-Month Alcohol Use, High-Risk Drinking, and *DSM-IV* Alcohol Use Disorder in the United States, 2001–2002 to 2012–2013: Results from the National Epidemiologic Survey on Alcohol and Related Conditions," *JAMA Psychiatry* 74, no. 9 (2017): 911–23, DOI:10.1001/jamapsychiatry.2017.2161.

Chapter 3. Blaming the Victim

1. Julianne Hing, "Raquel Nelson and the Aggressive Prosecutions of Black Mothers," Colorlines, July 28, 2011, https://www.colorlines.com/articles/raquel-nelson-and-aggressive-prosecutions-black-mothers.

2. Angie Schmitt, "Raquel Nelson Sentenced to Year of Probation, Granted Option of New Trial," Streetsblog USA, July 26, 2011, https://usa.streetsblog.org/2011/07/26/raquel-nelson-granted-option-of-new-trial/.

3. Rebecca Burns, "Report: Metro Atlanta Ranks No. 8 for Pedestrian Danger," *Atlanta*, May 20, 2014, https://www.atlantamagazine.com/news-culture-articles/report-metro-atlanta-ranks-no-8-for-pedestrian-danger/.

4. Angie Schmitt, "Georgia Prosecutor Continues Case against Raquel Nelson," Streetsblog USA, September 11, 2012, https://usa.streetsblog

.org/2012/09/11/georgia-prosecutor-continues-case-against-raquel
-nelson/.

5. Phil Villarreal, "Report: Arizona Is Deadliest State for Pedestrians," ABC 15 Arizona, February 28, 2018, https://www.abc15.com/news/ state/report-arizona-is-deadliest-state-for-pedestrians.

6. Antonia Noori Farzan, "Killer Streets: Phoenix Is a Death Trap for Pedestrians like Kacie Clark," *Phoenix New Times*, June 27, 2018, https:// www.phoenixnewtimes.com/news/south-central-light-rail-survives -phoenix-city-council-vote-10870233.

7. Bree Burkitt and Agnel Philip, "On Phoenix's Most Dangerous Streets, Little Has Been Done to Address the Pedestrian Death Toll," *Arizona Republic*, April 1, 2019, https://www.azcentral.com/in-depth/news/ local/arizona-investigations/2019/04/01/pedestrian-deaths-phoenix -slow-fix-areas-where-walkers-dying/3009674002/.

8. Angie Koehle, "Jaywalking Continues to Be a Deadly Problem in Arizona," ABC 15 Arizona, August 31, 2018, https://www.abc15.com/ news/roads/jaywalking-continues-to-be-a-deadly-problem-in-arizona.

9. City of Phoenix, "Agenda: City Council Policy Session," April 23, 2019, https://www.phoenix.gov/cityclerksite/City%20Council%20Meeting %20Files/4-23-19%20Policy%20Agenda.pdf, 9.

10. Lindsey Blest, "2 School District of Lancaster Elementary Students Hit by Truck on Way to School," Lancaster Online, December 11, 2018, https://lancasteronline.com/news/local/school-district-of-lancaster -elementary-students-hit-by-truck-on/article_1f7b56d2-fd4a-11e8 -814a-271119abfa1a.html.

11. Alex Peterson, "PennDOT: Safety a 'Shared Responsibility' between Drivers, Pedestrians," WHTM Harrisburg, December 12, 2018, https:// www.abc27.com/news/local/penndot-safety-a-shared-responsibility -between-drivers-pedestrians/1654312417.

12. National Highway Traffic Safety Administration, Road Safety Topics, "Pedestrian Safety," accessed May 6, 2019, https://www.nhtsa.gov/road -safety/pedestrian-safety.

13. American Automobile Association, "Exchange: Tips for Pedestrian Safety," accessed May 6, 2019, https://exchange.aaa.com/safety/ pedestrian-safety/tips-pedestrian-safety/#.XNB2RC3MzOQ.

14. Alissa Walker, "Pedestrian-Shaming Campaigns Have Got to Stop," Curbed, October 28, 2016, https://www.curbed.com/2016/10/28/13455962/pedestrian-shaming-streets-safety-campaigns.

15. Doug MacEachern, "You Can't Protect Stupid Pedestrians from Themselves," *AZCentral*, August 13, 2014, https://www.azcentral.com/story/dougmaceachern/2014/08/13/governing-pedestrians-dangerous-phoenix-tucson/14007489/.

16. Kevin Lewis, "7 Pedestrians Killed by Vehicles in Mont. County since June 1, Laziness a Key Factor," WJLA Washington, DC, August 22, 2018, https://wjla.com/news/local/pedestrians-killed-montgomery-county-md.

17. Stephanie Tinoco, "Family of Man Hit and Killed by Charlotte Police Car Wants Answers," WSOC, June 9, 2018, https://www.wsoctv.com/news/local/pedestrian-injured-when-struck-by-police-officer/760515021/.

18. Lavendrick Smith, "80-Year-Old Man Seriously Injured He Ran in Front of Cop Car, CMPD Says," *Charlotte Observer*, June 1, 2018, https://www.charlotteobserver.com/news/local/article212322309.html; Kimberly Johnson, "80-Year-Old Man Hit by Police Car while Crossing Road in the Rain," *Charlotte Patch*, May 31, 2018, https://patch.com/north-carolina/charlotte/pedestrian-hit-cmpd-officer-while-crossing-s-tryon-street; Tinoco, "Family of Man Hit, Killed."

19. Tinoco, "Family of Man Hit, Killed."

20. Tara Goddard et al., "Does News Coverage of Traffic Crashes Affect Perceived Blame and Preferred Solutions? Evidence from an Experiment," *Transportation Research Interdisciplinary Perspectives*, December 2019, https://www.sciencedirect.com/science/article/pii/S2590198219300727.

21. Heather Magusin, "If You Want to Get Away with Murder, Use Your Car: A Discursive Content Analysis of Pedestrian Traffic Fatalities in News Headlines," *Common Earth Journal*, October 2017, https://journals.macewan.ca/earthcommon/article/view/1229/1026.

22. Magusin, "If You Want."

23. Magusin, "If You Want."

24. E. Scheffels, J. Bond, and L. E. Monteagut, "Framing the Bicyclist: A Qualitative Study of Media Discourse about Fatal Bicycle Crashes,"

Transportation Research Record 2673, no. 6 (April 18, 2019): 628–37, https://doi.org/10.1177/0361198119839348.

25. Goddard et al., "Does News Affect Perceived Blame?"
26. Tara Goddard, telephone interview, December 2, 2019.
27. Goddard, telephone interview.
28. Kendall Forward, "East Cleveland Community Speaks Out after Woman Was Killed at Dangerous Intersection," 19 Action News, January 2, 2020, https://www.cleveland19.com/2020/01/03/east-cleveland-community-speaks-out-after-woman-killed-dangerous-intersection/.
29. Kevin Freeman, "Governor Visits Intersection in East Cleveland Where Woman Was Hit and Killed," Fox 8 Cleveland, January 7, 2020, https://fox8.com/2020/01/07/governor-visits-intersection-in-east-cleveland-where-woman-was-hit-and-killed/.
30. Barron Lerner, *One for the Road: Drunk Driving Science since 1900* (Baltimore: Johns Hopkins University Press, 2012), 55.
31. Christopher Robbins, "NYPD Finally Makes Sweeping Changes to Crash Investigations," Gothamist, March 11, 2013, https://gothamist.com/news/nypd-finally-makes-sweeping-changes-to-crash-investigations.
32. Matt Richtel, "It's No Accident: Advocates Want to Speak of Car 'Crashes' Instead," *New York Times*, May 23, 2016, https://www.nytimes.com/2016/05/23/science/its-no-accident-advocates-want-to-speak-of-car-crashes-instead.html.
33. Lauren Easton, "Ready to Lowercase 'Internet' and 'Web,'" Associated Press Blog, April 2, 2016, https://blog.ap.org/products-and-services/ready-to-lowercase-internet-and-web.
34. Kristi Finney, telephone interview, September 20, 2018.
35. Aimee Green, "Teen Driver Was a .16 Three Hours after Crash, Gets Five Years in Prison for Killing Cyclist," *Oregonian*, December 21, 2011, https://www.oregonlive.com/portland/index.ssf/2011/12/teen_driver_was_a_16_three_hou.html.
36. Finney, telephone interview.
37. Finney, telephone interview.
38. Rodney Thrash, "Raquel Nelson's Jaywalking Case Headed Back to Cobb State Court," *Marietta Patch*, April 17, 2013, https://patch.com/

georgia/marietta/raquel-nelson-s-jaywalking-case-headed-back-to
-cobb-state-court.

39. NPR Staff, "Child's Death Casts Light on Pedestrian Traffic Woes,"
All Things Considered, July 30, 2011, https://www.npr.org/2011/07/30/
138855279/convicted-suburban-mom-has-city-planners-nervous.

40. CNN Wire Staff, "Mom Granted New Trial in Death of Son Struck by
Driver," CNN, July 11, 2011.

41. Thrash, "Raquel Nelson's Jaywalking Case."

42. Sami K. Martin, "Mom Who Faced More Prison Time Than Drunk
Driver Has Charges Dropped," *Christian Post*, June 14, 2013, https://
www.christianpost.com/trends/mom-who-faced-more-prison-time
-than-drunk-driver-has-charges-dropped.html.

43. Yolanda Pierce, "Why Persecute the Poor for Being Poor?," *Guardian*, August 19, 2011, https://www.theguardian.com/commentisfree/
cifamerica/2011/aug/19/why-persecute-poor-raquel-nelson.

44. Angie Schmitt, "Raquel Nelson Finally Cleared of Homicide Charges,
Pleads to Jaywalking," Streetsblog USA, June 14, 2013, https://usa
.streetsblog.org/2013/06/14/raquel-nelson-finally-cleared-of-homicide
-charges-pleads-to-jaywalking/.

Chapter 4. The Criminalization of Walking

1. Ben Conarck, "Video Shows Jacksonville Cop Threatening Young Black
Man with Jail after Jaywalking," *Florida Times-Union*, June 26, 2017,
https://www.jacksonville.com/news/public-safety/2017-06-26/video
-shows-jacksonville-cop-threatening-young-black-man-jail-after.

2. Topher Sanders, Kate Rabinowitz, and Benjamin Conarck, "Walking
while Black: Jacksonville's Enforcement of Pedestrian Violations Raises
Concerns That It's Another Example of Racial Profiling," ProPublica/
Florida Times-Union, November 16, 2017, https://features.propublica
.org/walking-while-black/jacksonville-pedestrian-violations-racial
-profiling/.

3. Sanders, Rabinowitz, and Conarck, "Walking while Black."

4. Steve Patterson, "Jacksonville Remains One of Country's Most Dangerous Cities for Pedestrians, Study Says," *Florida Times-Union*, January 10,

2017, https://www.jacksonville.com/news/2017-01-10/jacksonville -remains-one-country-s-most-dangerous-cities-pedestrians-study-says.

5. Sanders, Rabinowitz, and Conarck, "Walking while Black."

6. Sanders, Rabinowitz, and Conarck, "Walking while Black."

7. Sarah Heise, "Sacramento PD: Officer Beat Pedestrian after Confrontation," KCRA, April 11, 2017, https://www.kcra.com/article/sacramento -pd-officer-beat-pedestrian-after-confrontation/9260550.

8. Anita Chabria, Nashelly Chavez, and Phillip Reese, "'Racial Profiling'? Jaywalking Tickets Disproportionately Given to Black People in Sacramento," *Sacramento Bee*, April 14, 2017, https://www.sacbee.com/news/ local/crime/article144743834.html.

9. Gene Balk, "Seattle Police Writing Fewer Jaywalking Tickets, but High Rate Still Issued to Black Pedestrians," *Seattle Times*, July 20, 2017, https://www.seattletimes.com/seattle-news/data/seattle-police-are -writing-fewer-jaywalking-tickets-but-high-rate-still-issued-to-black -pedestrians/.

10. Dyer Oxley, "Seattle Could Be on the Road to Nixing Its Jaywalking Law," My Northwest (blog), July 24, 2017, http://mynorthwest.com/ 700636/seattle-council-and-jaywalking/.

11. Aiden Lewis, "Jaywalking: How the Car Industry Outlawed Crossing the Road," BBC, February 12, 2014, https://www.bbc.com/news/ magazine-26073797.

12. Richard Retting, "Pedestrian Traffic Fatalities by State: 2017 Preliminary Data," Governors Highway Safety Association, February 28, 2018, https://www.ghsa.org/sites/default/files/2018-03/pedestrians_18.pdf.

13. W. H. Hunter, J. C. Stutts, and W. E. Pein, "Pedestrian Crash Types: A 1990's Informational Guide," Federal Highway Administration Publication No. FHWA-RD-96-163, April 1997, https://ntlrepository.blob .core.windows.net/lib/20000/20000/20099/PB98109671.pdf.

14. Peter Norton, *Fighting Traffic: The Dawn of the Motor Age in the American City* (Cambridge, MA: MIT Press, 2008).

15. Kat Eschner, "Henry Bliss, America's First Pedestrian Fatality, Was Hit by an Electric Taxi," *Smithsonian*, September 13, 2017, https:// www.smithsonianmag.com/smart-news/henry-bliss-americas-first -pedestrian-fatality-was-hit-electric-taxi-180964852/.

16. Norton, *Fighting Traffic*, loc. 597 of 4858, Kindle.

17. Norton, *Fighting Traffic*, loc. 357 of 4858, Kindle.

18. Norton, *Fighting Traffic*, loc. 376 of 4858, Kindle.

19. Peter Norton, email correspondence, December 7, 2018.

20. Norton, *Fighting Traffic*, loc. 928 of 4858, Kindle.

21. Rebecca Burns, "Report: Metro Atlanta Ranks No. 8 for Pedestrian Danger," *Atlanta*, May 20, 2014, https://www.atlantamagazine.com/news-culture-articles/report-metro-atlanta-ranks-no-8-for-pedestrian-danger/.

22. Sally Flocks, telephone interview, July 2, 2019.

23. Flocks, telephone interview.

24. Jason A. Leonard and Richard Liotta, "Pedestrian Jaywalking under Facilitating and Nonfacilitating Conditions," *Journal of Applied Behavior Analysis* 15, no. 3 (Fall 1982): 469–73, https://www.ncbi.nlm.nih.gov/pmc/articles/PMC1308291/.

25. Brian Mullen, Carolyn Copper, and James Driskell, "Jaywalking as a Function of Model Behavior," *Personality and Social Psychology Bulletin* 16, no. 2 (June 1, 1990): 320–30, https://journals.sagepub.com/doi/abs/10.1177/0146167290162012.

26. Ann H. Do, Stacy A. Balk, and Jim W. Shurbutt, "Why Did the Pedestrian Cross the Road," *Public Roads* 77, no. 6 (May–June 2014), https://www.fhwa.dot.gov/publications/publicroads/14mayjun/04.cfm.

27. Robert J. Schneider et al., "Exploratory Analysis of Driver Yielding at Low-Speed, Uncontrolled Crosswalks in Milwaukee, Wisconsin," *Transportation Research Record* 2672, no. 35 (December 1, 2018): 21–32, http://dx.doi.org/10.1177/0361198118782251.

28. Jon Hilkevitch, "Many Drivers Ignoring Crosswalk Law: Study," *Chicago Tribune*, September 7, 2014, https://www.chicagotribune.com/ct-crosswalk-survey-getting-around-met-0908-20140907-column.html.

29. Tara Goddard and Kimberly Barsamian Kahn, "Racial Bias in Driver Yielding Behavior at Crosswalks," National Institute for Transportation and Communities, April 2014, https://ppms.trec.pdx.edu/media/project_files/NITC-SS-733_Racial_Bias_in_Driver_Yielding_Behavior_at_Crosswalks.pdf.

30. Nichole Morris, "Evaluation of Sustained Enforcement, Education, and Engineering Measures on Pedestrian Crossings," Minnesota

Department of Transportation, July 2019, http://www.dot.state.mn.us/research/reports/2019/201929.pdf.

31. Angie Schmitt, "To Get Drivers to Yield, St. Paul Uses Psych Trick," Streetsblog USA, October 18, 2018, https://usa.streetsblog.org/2018/10/18/want-drivers-to-yield-to-pedestrians-you-gotta-play-mind-games/.
32. Morris, "Evaluation of Sustained Enforcement."

Chapter 5. Killer Cars

1. "Family Mourns Toddler's Death after Being Hit by Car Outside Deerfield Beach Home," NBC 6 Miami, October 16, 2017, http://www.newslocker.com/en-us/region/hialeah/im-angry-mom-of-toddler-struck-and-killed-by-car-speaks/view/.
2. Linda Trischitta, "Driver Pulled from Car and Beaten after Hitting and Killing Toddler," *South Florida Sun-Sentinel*, October 16, 2016, https://www.sun-sentinel.com/local/broward/deerfield-beach/fl-sb-deerfield-child-struck-folo-20171016-story.html.
3. Erica Rakow, "1-Year-Old Boy Struck by SUV in Deerfield Beach Dies," WPLG Channel 10, October 16, 2017, https://www.local10.com/news/1-year-old-boy-struck-by-suv-in-deerfield-beach-dies.
4. Trischitta, "Driver Pulled from Car."
5. US Energy Information Administration, "Crossover Utility Vehicles Overtake Cars as the Most Popular Light-Duty Vehicle Type," July 19, 2018, https://www.eia.gov/todayinenergy/detail.php?id=36674.
6. Sebastian Blanco, "Hyundai's Alabama Plant Ready to Make More SUVs Whenever Demand Requires It," *Forbes*, September 28, 2018, https://www.forbes.com/sites/sebastianblanco/2018/09/28/hyundais-alabama-plant-ready-to-make-more-suvs-whenever-demand-requires-it/#1d4d2c640c79.
7. Tom McParland, "Why Ford Killed Its Cars," Jalopnik, April 25, 2018, https://jalopnik.com/why-ford-killed-its-cars-1825546289.
8. Janet Nguyen, "Why American Auto Companies No Longer Want to Sell Actual Cars," *Marketplace*, November 26, 2018, https://www.marketplace.org/2018/11/26/why-american-car-companies-are-no-longer-selling-cars/.

9. Blanco, "Hyundai's Alabama Plant."
10. "The Most Expensive Cars to Insure," *US News and World Report*, June 3, 2009, https://cars.usnews.com/cars-trucks/daily-news/090603-the-most-expensive-cars-to-insure.
11. Alexis Madrigal, "Why Crossovers Conquered the American Highway," *Atlantic*, July 10, 2014, https://www.theatlantic.com/technology/archive/2014/07/how-the-crossover-conquered-americas-automobile-market/374061/.
12. National Highway Traffic Safety Administration, "New Car Assessment Program Frontal Barrier Impact Test," Report Number TR-P27001-03-NC, 2007 Hyundai Santa Fe, August 2016.
13. WTHR.com Staff, "13 Investigates Reveals Hidden Dangers in Your Vehicle's 'Blind Zone,'" WTHR 13, April 25, 2019, https://www.wthr.com/article/wthrs-blind-zone-check.
14. KidsandCarsUSA, "PSA: 62 Children behind SUV," YouTube, February 22, 2011, https://www.youtube.com/watch?v=fn0RocUSLmk.
15. KidsandCars.org, "Backovers: Chart, Statistics, Graphics," accessed March 29, 2020, https://www.kidsandcars.org/how-kids-get-hurt/backovers/.
16. Author's note: These kinds of crashes—frontovers and backovers—are often not counted in official pedestrian safety records because they are not considered traffic collisions by the federal agencies because they occur mostly on private property.
17. Angie Kohle, "Frontover Deaths Involving Kids Skyrocketing with Truck and SUV Popularity," ABC 15 Arizona, June 4, 2018, https://www.abc15.com/news/roads/frontover-fatalities-involving-kids-skyrocket-with-popularity-of-big-trucks-and-suvs.
18. Eric D. Lawrence, Nathan Bomey, and Kristi Tanner, "Death on Foot: America's Love of SUVs Is Killing Pedestrians," *Detroit Free Press*, July 1, 2018, https://www.freep.com/story/money/cars/2018/06/28/suvs-killing-americas-pedestrians/646139002/.
19. Nathan Bomey, telephone interview, June 4, 2019.
20. Insurance Institute for Highway Safety, "On Foot, At Risk," status report, vol. 53, no. 3 (May 8, 2018), https://assets.documentcloud.org/documents/4453716/Insurance-Institute-for-Highway-Safety.pdf.

21. Author's note: There is not a single agency that tracks these data, but with a tape measure, I was able to get a rough measure on the height of different vehicles' front ends. The measurements will vary somewhat according to model year and tire pressure.

22. C. K. Simms and D. P. Wood, "Pedestrian Risk from Cars and Sport Utility Vehicles—a Comparative Analytical Study," *Journal of Automobile Engineering* 22, no. 8 (August 1, 2006), https://pdfs.semanticscholar .org/576d/d6cff506d0af4fb44d8a45b6d474d72b115d.pdf.

23. National Highway Traffic Safety Administration, "New Car Assessment Program," request for comments, December 16, 2015, https:// www.federalregister.gov/documents/2015/12/16/2015-31323/new-car -assessment-program.

24. Paul Marks, "SUVs Double Pedestrians' Risk of Death," *New Scientist*, December 12, 2003, https://www.newscientist.com/article/dn4462-suvs -double-pedestrians-risk-of-death/.

25. Hannah Sparling, "Dear Drivers: This Man Would Like You to Stop Hitting Him," *Cincinnati Enquirer*, November 20, 2018, https://www .cincinnati.com/story/news/2018/11/20/dear-drivers-stop-running -into-man/1423666002/.

26. Neil Kelly, telephone interview, February 15, 2019.

27. J. D. Kraemer and C. S. Benton, "Disparities in Road Crash Mortality among Pedestrians Using Wheelchairs in the USA: Results of a Capture–Recapture Analysis," *BMJ Open* 5, no. 11 (2015), DOI:10.1136/ bmjopen-2015-008396.

28. Angie Schmitt, "Meet the Cincinnati Wheelchair User Struck Three Times by Drivers," Streetsblog USA, February 19, 2019, https://usa .streetsblog.org/2019/02/19/meet-the-cincinnati-wheelchair-user -struck-three-times-by-drivers/.

29. Insurance Institute for Traffic Safety, "Vehicles Are Packing More Horsepower, and That Pushes Up Travel Speeds," May 2016, https:// www.iihs.org/news/detail/vehicles-are-packing-more-horsepower-and -that-pushes-up-travel-speeds.

30. A. T. McCartt and W. Hu, "Effects of Vehicle Power," *Traffic Injury Prevention* 18, no. 5 (July 4, 2017): 500–507, https://www.ncbi.nlm.nih .gov/pubmed/27753503.

31. Chuck Squatrigalia, "EPA to Automakers: The Horsepower War Is Over," *Wired*, January 29, 2008, https://www.wired.com/2008/01/epa-to-automake/.

32. United States Environmental Protection Agency, "2019 Automotive Trends Report," EPA-420-S-20-001, accessed March 11, 2020, https://www.epa.gov/automotive-trends/highlights-automotive-trends-report.

33. Eric Lawrence, telephone interview, May 14, 2019.

34. Christopher Duerringer, "Be a Man—Buy a Car! Articulating Masculinity with Consumerism in Man's Last Stand," *Southern Communication Journal* 30, no. 2 (2015): 137–52, https://doi.org/10.1080/1041794X.2015.1017654.

35. United Nations, "Global Technical Regulation No. 9," November 18, 2004, https://www.unece.org/fileadmin/DAM/trans/main/wp29/wp29wgs/wp29gen/wp29registry/ECE-TRANS-180a9apple.pdf.

36. Safety Research and Strategies Inc., "European Pedestrian Crash Standards Will Make Global Changes in Car Design," April 1, 2005, https://www.safetyresearch.net/blog/articles/european-pedestrian-crash-standards-will-make-global-changes-car-design-inevitable.

37. Lloyd Alter, "Teslas Sold in Europe Have an 'Active Hood' to Protect Pedestrians. American Pedestrians? Look Both Ways," Treehugger, April 13, 2017, https://www.treehugger.com/cars/teslas-sold-europe-have-active-hood-protect-pedestrians-american-pedestrians-look-both-ways.html; Green Car Congress, "Buick Introduces Active-Hood Technology in China; Developed with GHBMC," October 1, 2017, https://www.greencarcongress.com/2017/10/20171001-buick.html.

38. Claus Pastor, "Correlation between Pedestrian Injury Severity in Real-Life Crashes and Euro NCAP Pedestrian Test Results," Federal Highway Research Institute, 2005, https://cdn.euroncap.com/media/1375/23esv-000308page1-0-3f5feddf-09ec-4066-ba89-064ea19356c7.pdf.

39. C. DiMaggio, M. Durkin, and L. Richardson, "The Association of Light Trucks and Vans with Pediatric Pedestrian Fatality," *International Journal of Injury Control and Safety Promotion* 13, no. 2 (2006): 95–99.

40. National Highway Traffic Safety Administration, "New Car Assessment Program," 2015.

41. Brian Latouf, "Comment on the National Highway Traffic Safety Administration (NHTSA) Notice: New Car Assessment Program: General Motors LLC—Comment," February 16, 2006, https://www.regulations.gov/document?D=NHTSA-2015-0119-0330.

42. Tom Stricker, "Comment on the National Highway Traffic Safety Administration (NHTSA) Notice: New Car Assessment Program: Comment from Tom Stricker," February 26, 2016, https://www.regulations.gov/document?D=NHTSA-2015-0119-0274.

43. National Highway Traffic Safety Administration, "NHTSA Announces Coming Upgrades to New Car Assessment Program," press release, October 16, 2019, https://www.nhtsa.gov/press-releases/ncap-upgrades-coming.

44. Mary Bellis, "The History of Airbags," ThoughtCo., August 9, 2019, https://www.thoughtco.com/history-of-airbags-1991232; Linda Greenhouse, "High Court Backs Airbags Mandate," *New York Times*, June 25, 1983, https://www.nytimes.com/1983/06/25/us/high-court-backs-airbags-mandate.html.

45. Shaun Kildare, telephone interview, November 13, 2019.

46. Christina Rogers, "European Safety-Styled Cars Due in U.S.," *Automotive News*, April 23, 2012, https://www.autonews.com/article/20120423/OEM03/304239967/european-safety-styled-cars-due-in-u.s.

47. Angie Schmitt, "WRONG! Safety Officials Think Tech Gadgets Will Save Pedestrians from Monster SUVs," Streetsblog USA, May 16, 2019, https://usa.streetsblog.org/2019/05/16/wrong-safety-officials-think-tech-gadgets-will-save-pedestrians-from-monster-suvs/.

48. Russ Rader, Insurance Institute for Highway Safety, email interview, May 16, 2019.

49. Jesse Snyder, "Crossovers and SUVs Fatten Profit Margins," *Automotive News*, July 24, 2017, https://www.autonews.com/article/20170724/RETAIL01/170729911/crossovers-and-suvs-fatten-profit-margins.

50. Snyder, "Crossovers and SUVs."

51. Vera Pardee, "Sexy Ads Created Hot Demand for SUVs. Now Automakers Are Using Those Preferences to Weaken Fuel Efficiency," CNBC, April 5, 2018, https://www.cnbc.com/2018/04/05/sexy-suv-ads-created-demand-now-being-used-to-attack-fuel-standards.html.

52. Jeremy Deaton, "Car Companies Aren't Even Trying to Sell Electric Cars," Huff Post/Nexus News Media, January 14, 2019, https://www .huffpost.com/entry/electric-cars-climate-detroit_b_5c3cb981e4b0bc 885f74afc8.

53. Matt Robinson, "10 Images That Show Just How Fat Cars Have Become," *Car Throttle*, accessed March 29, 2020, https://www.carthrottle .com/post/10-images-that-show-just-how-fat-cars-have-become/.

54. Nathan Bomey, "Cars Get Bigger to Compete with SUVs, Meet Demand for Roomier Interiors," *Detroit Free Press*, January 17, 2018, https://www.freep.com/story/money/cars/detroit-auto-show/2018/01/ 17/car-suv-size-detroit-auto-show/1038125001/.

55. Keith Bradsher, *High and Mighty: SUVs—the World's Most Dangerous Vehicles and How They Got That Way* (Cambridge, MA: Public Affairs, 2002).

56. Bradsher, *High and Mighty*, 96.

57. Bradsher, *High and Mighty*, 96.

58. Matthew Curtin, "BMW Unveils Bulletproof Car," *Wall Street Journal*, September 2, 2014, https://www.wsj.com/articles/bmw-and-daimler -unveil-bulletproof-cars-1409149977.

59. Hannah Elliot, "The Market for Bulletproof Vehicles Is Exploding," *Los Angeles Times*, November 10, 2019, https://www.latimes.com/business/ story/2019-11-10/the-market-for-bulletproof-vehicles-is-exploding.

60. Samuel S. Monfort and Joseph M. Nolan, "Trends in Aggressivity and Driver Risk for Cars, SUVs, and Pickups: Vehicle Incompatibility from 1989–2016," Traffic Injury Prevention (TIP), August 2019, https://www .iihs.org/topics/bibliography/ref/2176.

61. Kelly Pleskot, "Police Forces Are Opting for SUVs Instead of Sedans," *MotorTrend*, January 1, 2017, https://www.motortrend.com/news/police -opting-suvs-instead-sedans-report/.

62. Doug DeMuro, "The Most Popular Police Car Is . . . ," Autotrader, November 2016, https://www.autotrader.com/car-news/most-popular -police-car-258655.

63. Phoebe Wall Howard, "Ford Police Interceptor, an SUV That Hits 150 mph, Is Best-Selling Law Enforcement Vehicle," *Detroit Free Press* via WUSA9, October 4, 2018, https://www.wusa9.com/article/news/

nation-now/ford-police-interceptor-an-suv-that-hits-150-mph-is -best-selling-law-enforcement-vehicle/465-60d1f3b7-2cde-4a21-9ad7 -510d6ea4fb37.

64. Brian A. Reaves, "Police Vehicle Pursuits, 2012–2013," Bureau of Justice Statistics, May 9, 2017, https://www.bjs.gov/index.cfm?ty=pbdetail&iid =5906.

65. Ediriweera B. R. Desapriya et al., "Bull Bars and Vulnerable Road Users," *Traffic Injury Prevention* 13, no. 1 (January 2012): 86–92, https://www .researchgate.net/publication/221742080_Bull_Bars_and_Vulnerable _Road_Users.

66. Bomey, telephone interview.

67. Bomey, telephone interview.

Chapter 6. The Ideology of Flow

1. UPI News Service, "Man Arrested for Painting Crosswalk," January 31, 2008, https://www.realitytvworld.com/news/man-arrested-for-painting -crosswalk-50049879.php.

2. "Vallejo Man Arrested for Painting His Own Crosswalk," CBS Sacramento, May 31, 2013, https://sacramento.cbslocal.com/2013/05/31/ vallejo-man-arrested-for-painting-his-own-crosswalk/.

3. Kate Ryan, "DC Residents Join Forces to Paint Crosswalk after Pedestrian's Death," WTOP, April 29, 2019, https://wtop.com/dc/2019/04/2 -dc-residents-join-forces-to-paint-crosswalk-after-pedestrians-death./.

4. Dan Albert, *Are We There Yet? The American Automobile Past, Present, and Driverless* (New York: Norton, 2019), 269.

5. Christopher Monsere, telephone interview, November 14, 2019.

6. Comments by Peter Furth given at the policy briefing hosted by Boston City Council's Committee on Parks, Recreation, and Transportation, December 6, 2016, Northeastern University, http://www.northeastern .edu/peter.furth/wp-content/uploads/2016/12/Pedestrian-Friendly -Traffic-Signal-Policies-Boston.pdf.

7. National Committee on Uniform Traffic Control Devices Signals Committee, "NCUTCD Proposal for Changes to the Manual on Uniform Traffic Control Devices," June 21, 2018, https://ncutcd.org/wp

-content/uploads/Sponsor%20Comments/2018B/Attach03.18B-GMI
-01.ExitNumbering.pdf.

8. Bill Schultheiss (@schlthss), "Another issue with regards to cost was concern installing pedestrian signals would trigger installation of crosswalks, curb ramps, sidewalks, and in some cases require utility work. This cost could be 5-50 thousand per intersection," Twitter, January 10, 2019, 11:04 a.m., https://twitter.com/schlthss/status/1083394093848375296 ?s=20.

9. Bill Schultheiss (@schlthss), "Of course when we discuss cost of infrastructure we are making policy decisions and value judgments regarding who is important and who's life has value. Our design decisions are *social engineering* the behavior of society," Twitter, January 16, 2019, 11:16 a.m., https://twitter.com/schlthss/status/1083397142134358017 ?s=20.

10. Bill Schultheiss, telephone interview, November 16, 2019.

11. Data USA, "Civil Engineering," accessed February 28, 2020, https://datausa.io/profile/soc/172051.

12. Schultheiss, telephone interview.

13. Veronica Davis, telephone interview, January 21, 2020.

14. Mindy Thompson Fullilove and Rodrick Wallace, "Serial Forced Displacement in American Cities, 1916–2010," *Journal of Urban Health: Bulletin of the New York Academy of Medicine* 88, no. 3 (2011): 381–89, DOI:10.1007/s11524-011-9585-2.

15. Davis, telephone interview.

16. Davis, telephone interview.

17. Bill Schultheiss, "How Many Deaths Does It Take to Question 'Standard Practice'?," *PE Magazine*, November–December 2018, https://www.nspe.org/resources/pe-magazine/november-2018/how-many-deaths-does-it-take-question-standard-practice.

18. National Association of City Transportation Officials, "Member Cities," accessed February 28, 2020, https://nacto.org/member-cities/.

19. Federal Highway Administration, "Questions and Answers about Design Flexibility for Pedestrian and Bicycle Facilities," Bicycle and Pedestrian Program, July 25, 2014, https://www.fhwa.dot.gov/environment/bicycle _pedestrian/guidance/design_flexibility_qa.cfm.

20. Dongho Chang (@dongho_chang), "We are piloting a new approach for greenway crossings. We build the appropriate treatments at arterial crossings and count/evaluate usage afterward. This tells us if the treatments have been successful or if additional revisions are needed for the community," Twitter, January 30, 2019, 3:11 p.m., https://twitter.com/dongho_chang/status/1090704061668544512?s=20.

21. Art Pearce and Lewis Wardrip, "DRAFT Spacing Guidelines for Marked Pedestrian Crossings," Portland Bureau of Transportation, November 1, 2018.

22. John MacFarlane, "In 'Paradigm Change,' Montreal Prioritizes Pedestrians over Cars at Traffic Lights," CBC News, November 18, 2019, https://www.cbc.ca/news/canada/montreal/montreal-puts-pedestrian-safety-first-at-traffic-lights-1.5363500?__vfz=medium%3Dsharebar.

23. Hanna Lindberg and Maria Håkansson, "Vision Zero 20 Years: How Dreams Can Become Reality," AF Consult, April 2017, https://www.afconsult.com/contentassets/8f0c19f4f7d24aa5bdbfd338128391ec/2017057-17_0194-rapport-nollvision-eng_lr.pdf.

24. Nathalie Rothschild, "How Sweden Became the EU's Road Safety Champion," Euro News, last updated February 20, 2018, http://www.euronews.com/2018/02/20/how-sweden-became-the-eu-s-road-safety-champion.

25. Vehicle and Traffic Safety Center at Chalmers, "Record Low Number of Fatalities in Road Traffic 2017," January 11, 2018, https://www.saferresearch.com/news/record-low-number-fatalities-road-traffic-2017.

26. Author's note: Deaths per 100,000 population were, in the United States, 14.86 (2000) and 12.4 (2017); and in Sweden, 6.7 (2000), 2.3 (2017).

27. Zainab Mudallal, "Why Sweden Has the World's Safest Roads," Quartz, December 31, 2014, https://qz.com/319940/why-sweden-has-the-worlds-safest-roads/.

28. National Highway Traffic Safety Administration, Traffic Safety Facts, "Critical Reasons for Crashes Investigated in the National Motor Vehicle Crash Causation Survey," February 2015, https://crashstats.nhtsa.dot.gov/Api/Public/ViewPublication/812115.

29. Center for Active Design, "Vision Zero: Learning from Sweden's Successes," accessed March 29, 2020, https://centerforactivedesign.org/visionzero.

30. Daniel Firth, Skype interview, December 4, 2019.

31. Firth, Skype interview.

32. Lisa Groeger, "Unsafe at Many Speeds," ProPublica, May 25, 2016, https://www.propublica.org/article/unsafe-at-many-speeds.

33. Bo Bjerre et al., "A Swedish Alcohol Ignition Interlock Programme for Drink-Drivers: Effects on Hospital Care Utilization and Sick Leave," *Addiction* 102, no. 4 (March 12, 2007), https://onlinelibrary.wiley.com/doi/abs/10.1111/j.1360-0443.2006.01726.x.

34. Vision Zero Network, "Vision Zero Communities Map," accessed March 29, 2020, https://visionzeronetwork.org/resources/vision-zero-cities/.

35. Emma Fitzsimmons, "Traffic Deaths in New York City Drop to 200, a Record Low," *New York Times*, January 1, 2019, https://www.nytimes.com/2019/01/01/nyregion/traffic-deaths-decrease-nyc.html.

36. Marco Conner, telephone interview, December 6, 2019.

37. New York City Department of Transportation, "Protected Bicycle Lanes in NYC," September 2014, https://www.streetsblog.org/wp-content/uploads/2014/09/2014-09-03-bicycle-path-data-analysis.pdf.

38. New York City, "Vision Zero, Year 5 Report," March 2019, https://www1.nyc.gov/assets/visionzero/downloads/pdf/vision-zero-year-5-report.pdf.

39. Laura Bliss, "The Incredibly Cheap Street Fix That Saves Lives," Citylab, January 26, 2018, https://www.citylab.com/transportation/2018/01/the-incredibly-cheap-street-fix-that-saves-lives/551498/.

40. Karen Hao and Amanda Shendruk, "One Small Change to New York's Intersections Is Saving Pedestrians' Lives," Quartz, September 21, 2018, https://qz.com/1315305/one-small-change-to-new-yorks-intersections-is-saving-pedestrians-lives/.

41. Conner, telephone interview.

42. Conner, telephone interview.

43. Conner, telephone interview.

44. Brock Keeling, "SF Declares State of Emergency for Traffic Deaths. Can It Save Pedestrians?," Curbed San Francisco, November 8, 2019, https://sf.curbed.com/2019/11/8/20952029/san-francisco-pedestrian-safety-deaths-emergency-traffic-cars.

45. Danielle Leigh, "New York City Ends 2019 with Overall Increase in Traffic Deaths," WABC, December 31, 2019, https://abc7ny.com/5802477/.

46. "PBOT Says 2019 Has Been a Particularly Deadly Year on Local Roads; 42 Traffic Deaths So Far," Fox 12 Oregon, November 11, 2019, https://www.kptv.com/news/pbot-says-has-been-a-particularly-deadly-year-on-local/article_0d037d30-0515-11ea-9eeb-4f5686f94601.html.

47. Hannah Chinn, "Blindsided: Portland Spends Millions to Stop Cars from Killing People. It's Not Working," Willamette Week, accessed March 13, 2020, https://www.wweek.com/blindsided/.

48. Chinn, "Blindsided."

49. Chinn, "Blindsided."

50. Jonathan Maus, direct message, November 19, 2019.

51. International Transport Forum/OECD, Road Safety Data, "Road Safety Annual Report 2019: Sweden," October 7, 2019, https://www.itf-oecd.org/sites/default/files/sweden-road-safety.pdf.

52. Xinhua, "Norway Best in World in Traffic Safety: Report," Global Times, June 27, 2018, http://www.globaltimes.cn/content/1108618.shtml.

53. Firth, Skype interview.

54. Laura Nelson, "L.A. Backs Venice Boulevard's Controversial 'Road Diet' as Activists Threaten to Sue," Los Angeles Times, March 8, 2019, https://www.latimes.com/local/lanow/la-me-ln-venice-mar-vista-bike-lane-20190308-story.html.

55. Angie Schmitt, "Are We Starting to See Progress toward Vision Zero?," Streetsblog USA, May 22, 2019, https://usa.streetsblog.org/2019/05/22/are-we-starting-to-see-progress-toward-vision-zero/.

56. Transport for London and Mayor of London, "Vision Zero Action Plan," July 24, 2018, http://content.tfl.gov.uk/vision-zero-action-plan.pdf.

57. Firth, Skype interview.

Chapter 7. A Hard Right Turn

1. Safe Routes to School North Carolina, "Walk to School Day Participation in North Carolina Skyrockets," 2015, https://www.eatsmartmovemorenc

.com/News/Texts/North_Carolina_Walk_to_School_Day_Report
_2015.pdf.

2. Safe Routes to School Guide, "The Decline of Walking and Bicycling," accessed March 30, 2020, http://guide.saferoutesinfo.org/introduction/the_decline_of_walking_and_bicycling.cfm.

3. Safe Routes to School Guide, "History of Safe Routes to School," accessed March 30, 2020, http://guide.saferoutesinfo.org/introduction/history_of_srts.cfm.

4. Angie Schmitt, "NC Cuts Safety Program for Kids while Pouring Billions into Roads," Streetsblog USA, August 24, 2018, https://usa.streetsblog.org/2018/08/24/north-carolina-dot-cuts-road-safety-program-for-kids-while-pouring-billions-into-highways/.

5. Transportation for America, "Top Ten Things to Know about the New Map-21 Transportation Law," July 2012, http://t4america.org/wp-content/uploads/2012/07/Top-10-Need-to-Know-MAP-21.pdf.

6. U.S. Census Bureau Newsroom, "Biking to Work Increases 60 Percent over Last Decade, Census Bureau Reports," May 8, 2014, https://www.census.gov/newsroom/press-releases/2014/cb14-86.html.

7. Alex Williams, "Cyclists Go Glam into the Night," *New York Times*, October 22, 2014, https://www.nytimes.com/2014/10/23/fashion/for-the-bike-to-work-generation-a-move-to-fashionable-high-tech-clothing.html.

8. Tanya Snyder, "Coburn Blocks Quick Senate Vote on Transportation Extension," Streetsblog USA, September 14, 2011, https://usa.streetsblog.org/2011/09/14/coburn-blocks-quick-senate-vote-on-transportation-extension/.

9. Andy Clarke, telephone interview, November 21, 2019.

10. Clarke, telephone interview.

11. Clarke, telephone interview.

12. Clayton Nall, telephone interview, November 23, 2019.

13. Nall, telephone interview.

14. Mary Wisniewski, "Why Americans, Particularly Millennials, Have Fallen Out of Love with Cars," *Chicago Tribune*, November 12, 2018, https://www.chicagotribune.com/business/ct-biz-young-adults-cars-attitudes-20181106-story.html.

15. Wisniewski, "Why Americans."
16. Congressional Research Service, "Membership of the 116th Congress: A Profile," January 14, 2020, https://fas.org/sgp/crs/misc/R45583.pdf.
17. Nall, telephone interview.
18. Angie Schmitt, "Koch-Funded Groups: Cut All Federal Funding for Walking, Biking, Transit," Streetsblog USA, January 29, 2015, https://usa.streetsblog.org/2015/01/29/koch-funded-groups-cut-all-federal-funding-for-walking-biking-transit/.
19. Angie Schmitt, "House Dems: We Won't Support a Transpo Bill That Cuts Bike/Ped Funding," Streetsblog USA, September 15, 2015, https://usa.streetsblog.org/2015/09/15/house-dems-we-wont-support-a-transpo-bill-that-cuts-bikeped-funding/.
20. Lawrence Blincoe et al., "The Economic and Societal Impact of Motor Vehicle Crashes, 2010 (Revised)," National Center for Statistics and Analysis, May 2015 (revised), https://crashstats.nhtsa.dot.gov/Api/Public/ViewPublication/812013.
21. Terry Lansdell, telephone interview, December 10, 2019.
22. Lansdell, telephone interview.
23. Margo Pedroso, "Most States Make Big Moves on TAP; Some Squander TAP Funds," Safe Routes Partnership Blog, October 25, 2017, https://www.saferoutespartnership.org/blog/most-states-make-big-moves-tap-some-squander-tap-funds.
24. Margo Pedroso, telephone interview, November 27, 2019.
25. Texas Department of Transportation, "Texas Motor Vehicle Traffic Crash Facts Calendar Year 2017," May 6, 2019, https://ftp.dot.state.tx.us/pub/txdot-info/trf/crash_statistics/2017/01.pdf.
26. Report of the Secretary of Transportation to the United States Congress, "Annual Report on Funding Recommendations," 2019, https://www.transit.dot.gov/sites/fta.dot.gov/files/docs/funding/grant-programs/capital-investments/69556/fy19-annual-report.pdf, 7; Heritage Foundation, "Transportation and Infrastructure: Don't Spend $2 Trillion; Reduce Federal Intervention," June 13, 2019, https://www.heritage.org/article/transportation-and-infrastructure-dont-spend-2-trillion-reduce-federal-intervention.

27. "2016 Republican Party Platform," July 18, 2016, https://prod-static
-ngop-pbl.s3.amazonaws.com/media/documents/DRAFT_12
_FINAL[1]-ben_1468872234.pdf, 5.

28. Tanya Snyder, "TIGER's Love Affair with Freight—and Bikes," Streetsblog USA, April 26, 2013, https://usa.streetsblog.org/2013/04/26/tigers
-love-affair-with-freight-and-bikes/.

29. Angie Schmitt, "Trump Turns Obama-Era Program into a Road Fund,"
Streetsblog USA, December 12, 2018, https://usa.streetsblog.org/2018/
12/12/tiger-is-a-roads-program-now/.

30. Pedroso, telephone interview.

31. Paul Thompson, "GO Bond-Backed Sidewalk Repair Program Taking
Shape," *Northeast News*, June 19, 2017, http://northeastnews.net/pages/
go-bond-back-sidewalk-repair-program-taking-shape/.

32. Smart Growth America, "Dangerous by Design 2019," January 23, 2019,
https://smartgrowthamerica.org/dangerous-by-design/.

33. Angie Schmitt, "Election 2018: The Koch Brothers Lost Big in Tampa
Last Night," Streetsblog USA, November 7, 2018, https://usa.streetsblog
.org/2018/11/07/election-2018-the-koch-brothers-lost-big-in-tampa
-last-night/.

34. Ellin Delapaz, "Hillsborough Voters Approve Sales Tax for Roads,
Transportation," WUSF, November 6, 2018, https://wusfnews.wusf.usf
.edu/post/hillsborough-voters-approve-sales-tax-roads-transportation.

35. Richard Danielson, "Business Groups Boost All for Transportation in
Florida Supreme Court," *Tampa Bay Times*, October 22, 2019, https://
www.tampabay.com/news/business/2019/10/22/tampa-business
-groups-support-all-for-transportation-in-supreme-court/.

36. Tyler Hudson, email interview, January 30, 2019.

Chapter 8. Pedestrian Safety on the Technological Frontier

1. Adrienne LaFrance, "Self-Driving Cars Could Save 300,000 Lives Per
Decade in America," *Atlantic*, September 9, 2015, https://www.theatlantic
.com/technology/archive/2015/09/self-driving-cars-could-save-300000
-lives-per-decade-in-america/407956/?utm_source=SFTwitter.

2. Hannah Knowles, "Uber's Self-Driving Cars Had a Major Flaw: They Weren't Programmed to Stop for Jaywalkers," *Washington Post*, November 6, 2019, https://www.boston.com/cars/car-news/2019/11/06/ubers -self-driving-cars-had-a-major-flaw-they-werent-programmed-to -stop-for-jaywalkers.

3. US Department of Transportation, "Remarks as Prepared for Delivery by U.S. Secretary of Transportation Elaine L. Chao," AV 3.0 Roll Out, October 4, 2018, https://www.transportation.gov/briefing-room/av-30 -roll-out.

4. Doug Ducey (@dougducey), "California may not want you; but AZ does! @Uber," Twitter, December 21, 2016, 10:05 p.m., https://twitter .com/dougducey/status/811769526362611712?lang=en.

5. Laurie Roberts, "Roberts: Uber Experiment Blows Up in Gov. Doug Ducey's Face," *Arizona Republic*, May 23, 2018, https://www.azcentral .com/story/opinion/op-ed/laurieroberts/2018/05/23/uber-arizona-gov -doug-ducey-experiment-blows-up-his-face/639118002/.

6. Julia Carrie Wong, "California Threatens Legal Action against Uber Unless It Halts Self-Driving Cars," *Guardian*, December 16, 2016, https://www.theguardian.com/technology/2016/dec/16/uber-defies -california-self-driving-cars-san-francisco.

7. Simon Romero, "Wielding Rocks and Knives, Arizonans Attack Self-Driving Cars," *New York Times*, December 31, 2018, https://www .nytimes.com/2018/12/31/us/waymo-self-driving-cars-arizona-attacks .html.

8. Governors Highway Safety Association, "Autonomous Vehicles," accessed February 29, 2020, https://www.ghsa.org/state-laws/issues/ autonomous%20vehicles.

9. Kyle Wiggers, "Waymo's Autonomous Cars Have Driven 20 Million Miles on Public Roads," VentureBeat, January 6, 2020, https:// venturebeat.com/2020/01/06/waymos-autonomous-cars-have-driven -20-million-miles-on-public-roads/.

10. Amri Efrati, "The Uber Whistleblower's Email," The Information, December 10, 2018, https://www.theinformation.com/articles/the-uber -whistleblowers-email.

11. Timothy Lee, "Police: Uber Driver Was Streaming Hulu Just before Fatal Self-Driving Car Crash," Ars Technica, June 22, 2018, https://arstechnica.com/cars/2018/06/police-uber-driver-was-streaming-hulu-just-before-fatal-self-driving-car-crash/.

12. Laura Bliss, "Former Uber Backup Driver: 'We Saw This Coming,'" Citylab, March 27, 2018, https://www.citylab.com/transportation/2018/03/former-uber-backup-driver-we-saw-this-coming/556427/.

13. Pete Bigelow, "NTSB Scrutinizes 'Automation Complacency' after Uber Crash," *Automotive News*, December 11, 2019, https://www.autonews.com/mobility-report/ntsb-scrutinizes-automation-complacency-after-uber-crash.

14. Mike Isaac, *Super Pumped: The Battle for Uber* (New York: Norton, 2019), loc. 405 of 880, iBooks.

15. Paayal Zaveri, "Uber's Revenue and Bookings Growth Slowed Slightly in the Second Quarter of 2018, Company Reports," CNBC, August 15, 2018, https://www.cnbc.com/2018/08/15/uber-q2-2018-revenue-bookings-slow-slightly.html.

16. "Uber IPO," *Financial Times*, accessed April 1, 2020, https://www.ft.com/content/b3e70e9e-5c4d-11e9-9dde-7aedca0a081a.

17. Eric Newcomer, "Uber Revenue Slows as Quarterly Loss Surges to $1.1 Billion," *Bloomberg Technology*, November 14, 2018, https://www.bloomberg.com/news/articles/2018-11-14/uber-revenue-slows-as-quarterly-loss-surges-to-1-1-billion.

18. Graham Rapier, "Uber and Lyft Are Betting on Self-Driving Cars to Become Profitable. But That May Not Happen, New Research from MIT Suggests," *Business Insider*, May 29, 2019, https://www.businessinsider.com/uber-lyft-self-driving-taxis-may-not-help-profitability-mit-2019-5.

19. Dan Albert, telephone interview, October 22, 2019.

20. National Transportation Safety Board, "Preliminary Report Released for Crash Involving Pedestrian, Uber Technologies, Inc., Test Vehicle," press release, May 24, 2018, https://www.ntsb.gov/news/press-releases/Pages/NR20180524.aspx.

21. Isaac, *Super Pumped*, loc. 403, iBooks.

22. Richard Lawler, "Uber Will Not Face Criminal Charges for Last Year's Self-Driving Crash," Engaget, March 5, 2019, https://www.engadget .com/2019/03/05/uber-autonomous-fatal-crash-criminal-charges/.

23. National Association of City Transportation Officials, "NTSB Finds Inadequate Safeguards in Place for Self-Driving Vehicle Testing across U.S.," November 21, 2019, https://nacto.org/2019/11/21/ ntsb-finds-inadequate-safeguards-in-place-for-self-driving-vehicle -testing/.

24. Heather Somerville, "Homeless Arizona Woman Killed by Uber Self-Driving SUV Was 'Like Everyone's Aunt,'" Reuters, March 20, 2018, https://www.reuters.com/article/us-autos-selfdriving-uber-victim/ homeless-arizona-woman-killed-by-uber-self-driving-suv-was-like -everyones-aunt-idUSKBN1GW36P.

25. Somerville, "Homeless Arizona Woman Killed."

26. Jake Fisher, telephone interview, October 3, 2019.

27. Eric Taub, "How Jaywalking Could Jam Up the Era of Self-Driving Cars," *New York Times*, August 1, 2019, https://www.nytimes.com/ 2019/08/01/business/self-driving-cars-jaywalking.html.

28. Angie Schmitt, "Wear a Sensor Everywhere Just to Stay Alive? No Thanks," Streetsblog USA, March 23, 2018, https://usa.streetsblog .org/2018/03/23/wear-a-sensor-everywhere-just-to-stay-alive-no -thanks/.

29. Insurance Institute for Highway Safety, "Subaru Crash Avoidance System Cuts Pedestrian Crashes," status report, vol. 53, no. 3 (May 8, 2018), https://www.iihs.org/api/datastoredocument/status-report/pdf/ 53/3.

30. National Highway Traffic Safety Administration, "Manufacturers Make Progress on Voluntary Commitment to Include Automatic Emergency Braking on All New Vehicles," news release, December 21, 2017, https:// www.nhtsa.gov/press-releases/nhtsa-iihs-announcement-aeb.

31. Fisher, telephone interview.

32. Joan Claybrook and Advocates for Highway and Auto Safety, "NCAP at 40: Time to Return to Excellence," October 17, 2019, https://saferoads .org/wp-content/uploads/2019/10/NCAP-at-40-Time-to-Return-to -Excellence-by-Joan-Claybrook.pdf.

33. Jeff Plungis, "Cars Make Progress in Pedestrian Detection, Crash Tests Show," *Consumer Reports*, October 29, 2019, https://www.consumerreports.org/car-safety/cars-make-progress-in-pedestrian-detection/.

34. Ellen Edmonds, "AAA Warns Pedestrian Detection Systems Don't Work When Needed Most," AAA Newsroom, October 3, 2019, https://newsroom.aaa.com/2019/10/aaa-warns-pedestrian-detection-systems-dont-work-when-needed-most/.

35. Shaun Kildare, telephone interview, November 13, 2019.

36. Fisher, telephone interview.

37. Andrew Hawkins, "Tesla's Autopilot Lulled Driver into a State of 'Inattention' in 2018 Freeway Crash," Verge, September 4, 2019, https://www.theverge.com/2019/9/4/20849499/tesla-autopilot-crash-culver-city-2018-ntsb-report.

38. Dan Albert, *Are We There Yet? The American Automobile Past, Present, and Driverless* (New York: Norton, 2019), 277.

39. Offer Grembek, telephone interview, November 15, 2019.

40. Grembek, telephone interview.

41. Centers for Disease Control and Prevention, "Motor Vehicle Crash Deaths: How Is the US Doing?," Vital Signs, accessed April 1, 2020, https://www.cdc.gov/vitalsigns/motor-vehicle-safety/index.html.

42. Angie Schmitt, "Europe Will Use Vehicle Tech to Prevent Speeding, Save Thousands of Lives," Streetsblog USA, March 5, 2019, https://usa.streetsblog.org/2019/03/05/europe-will-use-vehicle-tech-to-prevent-speeding-save-thousands-of-lives/.

43. David Cullen, "Senate Bill Would Require Truck Speed Limiters Set at 65 MPH on All New Trucks," Trucking Info, Heavy Duty Trucking, June 28, 2019, https://www.truckinginfo.com/335147/senate-bill-would-require-truck-speed-limiters-set-at-65-mph-on-all-new-trucks.

44. National Highway Traffic Safety Administration, "Vehicle-to-Vehicle Communication," accessed January 31, 2019, https://www.nhtsa.gov/technology-innovation/vehicle-vehicle-communication.

45. David Shepardson, "Toyota Halts Plan to Install U.S Connected Vehicle Tech by 2021," *Automotive News*, April 26, 2019, https://www.autonews.com/mobility-report/toyota-halts-plan-install-us-connected-vehicle-tech-2021.

46. Shepardson, "Toyota Halts Plans."
47. Tamra Johnson, "Red Light Running Deaths Hit 10 Year High," AAA Newsroom, August 29, 2019, https://newsroom.aaa.com/2019/08/red -light-running-deaths-hit-10-year-high/.
48. Dan Albert, electronic message, January 31, 2020.

Chapter 9. The International Context

1. World Health Organization, "Global Status Report on Road Safety 2018," June 17, 2018, https://www.who.int/publications-detail/global -status-report-on-road-safety-2018.
2. World Health Organization, "Global Status Report."
3. World Health Organization, "Global Status Report."
4. Soames Job and Julie Babinard, telephone interview, June 14, 2019.
5. Richard Florida, "The Great Divide in How Americans Commute to Work," Citylab, January 22, 2019, https://www.citylab.com/transportation/ 2019/01/commuting-to-work-data-car-public-transit-bike/580507/.
6. Job and Babinard, telephone interview.
7. Clare Cummings and Beatrice Obwocha, "At the Crossroads: The Politics of Road Safety in Nairobi," World Resources Institute Case Study, March 2018.
8. Kate Turner, telephone interview, June 10, 2019.
9. United Nations Sustainable Development Goals Partnership Platforms, "Child Health Initiative: Safe and Healthy Journeys to School to Reduce Emissions and Exposure to Air Pollution, Enable Active Transport, and Ensure Safe Roads," June 1, 2016, https://sustainabledevelopment.un .org/partnership/?p=29838.
10. World Population Review, "Accra Population 2020," accessed April 1, 2020, http://worldpopulationreview.com/world-cities/accra -population/.
11. Turner, telephone interview.
12. Saul Billingsley et al., "Step Change: An Action Agenda on Safe Walking for Africa's Children," Amend, FIA Foundation, https://www .fiafoundation.org/media/402416/step-change-spreads.pdf, 27.
13. Billingsley et al., "Step Change."

14. Turner, telephone interview.

15. Job and Babinard, telephone interview.

16. Ariadne Baskin, "Africa Used Vehicle Report," presentation for United Nations Environment, African Clean Mobility Week, March 13, 2018, https://wedocs.unep.org/bitstream/handle/20.500.11822/25233/AfricaUsedVehicleReport.pdf.

17. World Bank, "Population Ages 0–14 (% of Total Population)," 2017, https://data.worldbank.org/indicator/SP.POP.0014.TO.ZS.

18. Billingsley et al., "Step Change."

19. Billingsley et al., "Step Change."

20. Turner, telephone interview.

21. Billingsley et al., "Step Change."

22. Turner, telephone interview.

23. World Bank, *The High Toll of Traffic Injuries: Unacceptable and Preventable* (Washington, DC: World Bank, 2017), https://openknowledge.worldbank.org/bitstream/handle/10986/29129/HighTollofTrafficInjuries.pdf?sequence=5&isAllowed=y, 11.

24. Carolynn Johnson and Gonzalo Peon Carballo, "Teaching Road Safety in Mexico City," *Transportation Alternatives Vision Zero Cities Journal*, November 18, 2018, https://medium.com/vision-zero-cities-journal/teaching-road-safety-in-mexico-city-e934402018c2.

25. Angelica Mercado, "Alcoholímetro baja 43% los decesos de conductores: Ssa," Milenio, February 26, 2018, http://www.cvnoticias.com/notas/14457/alcoholmetro-baja-43-los-decesos-de-conductores-ssa.

26. Sebastián Varela, "Urban and Suburban Transport in Mexico City: Lessons Learned Implementing BRTs Lines and Suburban Railways for the First Time," International Transport Forum, June 2015, https://www.itf-oecd.org/sites/default/files/docs/varela_0.pdf, 7.

27. Jorge Cáñez, telephone interview, July 6, 2019.

28. Cáñez, telephone interview.

29. Cáñez, telephone interview.

30. Cáñez, telephone interview.

31. Johnson and Carballo, "Teaching Road Safety."

32. Nathaniel Janowitz, "Mexico's Pedestrian Activists Are Waging a Battle for Safer Streets," Citylab, April 16, 2019, https://www.citylab.com/

transportation/2019/04/traffic-deaths-mexico-pedestrian-road-safety -law-el-mimo/586783/.

33. Areli Carreón, email interview, July 27, 2019.

34. Maria Angelica Perez Avendaño and Gustavo Jimenez, "Mexico City's Car Congestion Slows Economic Growth, Costs Businesses," World Resources Institute, April 28, 2015, https://www.wri.org/blog/ 2015/04/mexico-city-s-car-congestion-slows-economic-growth-costs -businesses.

35. Cáñez, telephone interview.

36. Alissa Walker, "Watch Oslo Transform into a Car-Free Utopia," Curbed, April 24, 2017, https://www.curbed.com/2017/4/14/15301558/ transportation-oslo-bike-lanes-cars-streetfilms.

37. Adele Peters, "What Happened When Oslo Decided to Make Its Downtown Basically Car-Free?," *Fast Company*, January 24, 2019, https://www.fastcompany.com/90294948/what-happened-when-oslo -decided-to-make-its-downtown-basically-car-free.

38. Feargus O'Sullivan, "In Madrid, a Car Ban Proves Stronger Than Partisan Politics," Citylab, July 24, 2019, https://www.citylab.com/ transportation/2019/07/madrid-car-ban-street-map-city-politics -mayor-court-decision/594487/.

39. Erin K. Sauber-Schatz et al., "Vital Signs: Motor Vehicle Injury Prevention—United States and 19 Comparison Countries," Centers for Disease Control and Prevention, *Morbidity and Mortality Weekly Report* 65, no. 26 (July 8, 2016), http://dx.doi.org/10.15585/mmwr.mm6526e1.

40. Jessica Y. Ho, "Mortality under Age 50 Accounts for Much of the Fact That US Life Expectancy Lags That of Other High-Income Countries," *Journal of Health Affairs* 32, no. 3 (March 2013), https://doi.org/ 10.1377/hlthaff.2012.0574.

41. World Health Organization, "Global Status Report on Road Safety 2018," June 17, 2018, https://www.who.int/publications-detail/global -status-report-on-road-safety-2018.

42. Josef Filipowicz, "Room to Grow: Comparing Urban Density in Canada and Abroad," Frazier Institute, January 9, 2018, https://www .fraserinstitute.org/studies/room-to-grow-comparing-urban-density-in -canada-and-abroad.

43. Statistics Canada, "Commuting to Work," Census Program, Reference Materials, 2011, Labour, modified July 25, 2018, https://www12.statcan .gc.ca/nhs-enm/2011/as-sa/99-012-x/99-012-x2011003_1-eng.cfm; Florida, "Great Divide in Commute."

44. Author's note: The seat belt compliance rate in the United States is 90 percent; Canada's is 95 percent. International Transport Forum, Road Safety Data, "Road Safety Annual Report 2019: Canada," October 7, 2019, https://www.itf-oecd.org/sites/default/files/canada-road-safety .pdf, 19; International Transport Forum, Road Safety Data, "Road Safety Annual Report 2019: USA," October 7, 2019, https://www.itf -oecd.org/sites/default/files/united-states-road-safety.pdf, 9.

45. World Health Organization, "Global Status Report on Road Safety 2018," June 17, 2018, https://www.who.int/violence_injury_prevention/ road_safety_status/2018/en/.

46. Angie Schmitt, "Here's Why Canada's Traffic Safety Record Is Better Than Ours," Streetsblog USA, August 7, 2018, https://usa.streetsblog .org/2018/08/07/heres-why-canadas-traffic-safety-record-so-much -better-than-ours/.

Chapter 10. Families for Safe Streets

1. Ben Fried, "The Prospect Park Road Diet: A Big Improvement That Only Goes Halfway," Streetsblog NYC, February 28, 2012, https:// nyc.streetsblog.org/2012/02/28/the-prospect-park-road-diet-a-big -improvement-that-only-goes-halfway/.

2. Amy Cohen, telephone interview, August 9, 2018.

3. New York City Department of Transportation, "Prospect Park West Bicycle Path and Traffic Calming," accessed April 1, 2020, http://www .nyc.gov/html/dot/html/bicyclists/prospectparkwest.shtml.

4. Raphael Pope-Sussman, "The Prospect Park West Bike Lane Legal War Is Over," Gothamist, September 21, 2016, http://gothamist.com/2016/ 09/21/ppw_bike_lane_lawsuit.php.

5. Steven Higashide, "The Design Bible That Changed How Americans Bike in Cities," Atlantic, March 1, 2018, https://www.theatlantic.com/ technology/archive/2018/03/a-new-bible-for-bike-lanes/554450/.

6. Emma Fitzsimmons, "New York City's Pedestrian Fatalities Lowest on Record in 2014," *New York Times*, January 1, 2015, https://www.nytimes .com/2015/01/02/nyregion/new-york-pedestrian-deaths-are-lowest-on -record.html.

7. Cohen, telephone interview.

8. Brad Aaron, "The Heart of London Adopts 20 MPH Speed Limit," Streetsblog NYC, September 13, 2013, https://nyc.streetsblog.org/ 2013/09/13/the-heart-of-london-adopts-20-mph-speed-limit/.

9. Cohen, telephone interview.

10. The Middle Way Society, "Rod King on 20's Plenty for Us," podcast 60, April 25, 2015, http://www.middlewaysociety.org/tag/rod-king/.

11. The Middle Way Society, "Rod King on 20's Plenty."

12. Sarah Goodyear, "The Grassroots Campaign to Slow Down Traffic in the U.K.," Citylab, September 22, 2015, https://www.citylab.com/ transportation/2015/09/the-grassroots-campaign-to-slow-down-traffic -in-the-uk/406477/.

13. 20sPlenty, "Reducing Speed Limits from 30mph to 20mph Typically Results in More Than 20% Fewer Casualties," May 23, 2018, http:// www.20splenty.org/20mph_casualty_reduction.

14. World Health Organization, "Managing Speed," 2017, https://www.who .int/violence_injury_prevention/publications/road_traffic/managing -speed/en/.

15. Sasha Goldstein, "Park Slope Mom Amy Cohen Becomes Grieving Face of Push for Lower Speed Limits Less Than a Month after Her Son's Death on Prospect Park West," *New York Daily News*, October 31, 2013, https://www.nydailynews.com/new-york/brooklyn/grieving-park -slope-mom-moves-council-tears-article-1.1502862.

16. Brad Aaron, "NYPD: 16,059 Pedestrians and Cyclists Injured, 178 Killed in Traffic in 2013," Streetsblog NYC, January 31, 2014, https:// nyc.streetsblog.org/2014/01/31/nypd-16059-pedestrians-and-cyclists -injured-178-killed-in-traffic-in-2013/.

17. Brad Aaron, "NYPD and Media Declare 'Accident' as Another Child Killed by NYC Motorist," Streetsblog NYC, October 7, 2013, https:// nyc.streetsblog.org/2013/10/07/nypd-and-media-declare-accident-as -another-child-killed-by-nyc-motorist/.

18. Amy Tam-Liao and Hsi-Pei Liao, email interview, January 30, 2020.

19. Tam-Liao and Liao, email interview.

20. Cohen, telephone interview.

21. Vision Zero Network, "From Grief to Action: Families for Safe Streets Takes the Lead in NYC," August 11, 2015, https://visionzeronetwork.org/from-grief-to-action-families-for-safe-streets-takes-the-lead-in-nyc/.

22. David Goodman and Matt Flegenheimer, "De Blasio Announces Steps to Reduce Traffic Deaths," *New York Times*, January 15, 2014, https://www.nytimes.com/2014/01/16/nyregion/de-blasio-announces-steps-to-reduce-traffic-deaths.html.

23. Patrick McGeehan, "New York City Council Passes Bill Lowering the Speed Limit on Most Streets," *New York Times*, October 7, 2014, https://www.nytimes.com/2014/10/08/nyregion/new-york-city-council-passes-bill-lowering-the-speed-limit-on-most-streets.html.

24. Erin Durkin, Maria Vallaseñor, and Joseph Stepansky, "Boy, 5, Hit by Car at Brooklyn Intersection Where 12-Year-Old Was Killed in 2013, Key to Vision Zero Initiative," *New York Daily News*, June 8, 2015, http://www.nydailynews.com/new-york/brooklyn/boy-5-hit-car-deadly-brooklyn-intersection-article-1.2250233.

25. New York City Department of Transportation, "Automated Speed Enforcement Program Report 2014–2017," June 2018, http://www.nyc.gov/html/dot/downloads/pdf/speed-camera-report-june2018.pdf, 2.

26. Jim Dwyer, "Caught on Speed Camera, a Senator Who'd Like to Shut Them Down," *New York Times*, June 27, 2018, https://www.nytimes.com/2018/06/26/nyregion/marty-golden-school-speed-camera-ticketed-10-times.html.

27. Anna Sanders, "State Senators Propose Stop Signs to Replace Speed-Cameras near Schools," *New York Post*, June 23, 2018, https://nypost.com/2018/06/23/state-senators-propose-stop-signs-to-replace-speed-cameras-near-schools/.

28. Ben Fried, "'We Will Not Take No for an Answer': Families for Safe Streets Demand Cuomo Act on Speed Cameras," Streetsblog NYC, June 22, 2018, https://nyc.streetsblog.org/2018/06/22/we-will-not-take-no-for-an-answer-families-for-safe-streets-demand-cuomo-act-on-speed-cameras/.

29. Tam-Liao and Liao, email interview.

30. Cohen, telephone interview.

31. Kevin McKeever, "Speed Cameras Turned Back on with NYC Schools Back in Session," NYC Dads Group, September 4, 2018, https:// citydadsgroup.com/nyc/2018/09/school-zone-speed-cameras/.

32. Cohen, telephone interview.

33. New York City Council, "Speaker Corey Johnson, City Council Members, and Safe Streets Advocates Rally for Streets Master Plan," October 29, 2019, https://council.nyc.gov/press/2019/10/29/1821/.

34. New York City Council, "Speaker Corey Johnson."

35. Benjamin Kabak, "Corey Johnson's Streets Master Plan Is a Great First Step for a More Livable NYC," Curbed NYC, November 4, 2019, https://ny.curbed.com/2019/11/4/20948035/nyc-street-safety-corey -johnson-master-plan-analysis.

36. Barron Lerner, *One for the Road: Drunk Driving Science since 1900* (Baltimore: Johns Hopkins University Press, 2012), 85.

37. Lerner, *One for the Road*, 82.

38. Kristi Finney, telephone interview, September 20, 2018.

39. Cohen, telephone interview.

40. Cohen, telephone interview.

41. Elizabeth Warren (@ewarren), "Traffic violence kills thousands and injures even more Americans every year. On World Day of Remembrance for Traffic Crash Victims, I'm sending my love to the families and friends of those who have lost loved ones. It's time to #EndTrafficViolence," Twitter, November 17, 2019, 2:33 p.m., https://twitter.com/ewarren/ status/1196149347542618121?s=20.

42. Katie Herzog, "Elizabeth Warren Wants to End 'Traffic Violence,'" *The Stranger*, November 19, 2019, https://www.thestranger.com/slog/2019/ 11/19/42040942/elizabeth-warren-wants-to-end-traffic-violence.

43. Cohen, telephone interview.

Conclusion

1. Alejandro Ramirez, "Nashville Remembers Pedestrians Who Were Killed in 2019," *Nashville Scene*, January 20, 2020, https://www.nashville scene.com/news/pith-in-the-wind/article/21111172/nashville-day-of -remembrance-for-pedestrians.

2. Stephen Elliott, "Nashville Missing 1,900 Miles of Sidewalks, Report Finds," *Nashville Post*, January 9, 2017, https://www.nashvillepost.com/ politics/metro-government/article/20848494/nashville-missing-1900 -miles-of-sidewalks-report-finds.

3. Ramirez, "Nashville Remembers Pedestrians."

4. Seena Sleem, "Day of Remembrance Honors Pedestrians Killed," News Channel 5 Nashville, January 18, 2020, https://www.newschannel5 .com/news/day-of-remembrance-honors-pedestrians-killed.

5. Sleem, "Day of Remembrance."

6. Tara Goddard, telephone interview, December 2, 2019.

7. Walk Bike Nashville, "Impossible Crossings," October 26, 2018, https:// www.walkbikenashville.org/impossible_crossings.

8. Norman Garrick, telephone interview, January 21, 2020.

9. Garrick, telephone interview.

10. Garrick, telephone interview.

11. Lindsey Ganson, telephone interview, January 21, 2020.

12. Emiko Atherton, telephone interview, July 5, 2019.

13. Walk Bike Nashville, "Nashville Community Transportation Platform: Making Nashville a Safer and More Equitable Place to Get Around," accessed April 2, 2020, https://www.nashvilletransportation.org.

14. Ganson, telephone interview.

About the Author

Angie Schmitt is one of the best-known writers in the United States on the topic of sustainable transportation. She was the long-time national editor at Streetsblog, covering the movement for safe, multimodal cities. In addition, her writing has appeared in the *New York Times*, the *Atlantic*, *Bicycling*, *GOOD*, *Landscape Architect Magazine*, and a number of other publications. She is frequently sought out as an expert source on transportation topics by the news media. Schmitt holds a master's degree in urban planning from the Levin College of Urban Affairs at Cleveland State University and an undergraduate degree in journalism. She lives in Cleveland with her husband and two children.

Island Press | Board of Directors